ROUTLEDGE LIBRARY EDITIONS: WW2

Volume 41

THE WAR IN BURMA

THE WAR IN BURMA

ROY MCKELVIE

LONDON AND NEW YORK

This edition first published in 2022
by Routledge
2 Park Square, Milton Park, Abingdon, Oxon OX14 4RN

and by Routledge
605 Third Avenue, New York, NY 10158

Routledge is an imprint of the Taylor & Francis Group, an informa business

First published in 1948 by Methuen & Co. Ltd.

All rights reserved. No part of this book may be reprinted or reproduced or utilised in any form or by any electronic, mechanical, or other means, now known or hereafter invented, including photocopying and recording, or in any information storage or retrieval system, without permission in writing from the publishers.

Trademark notice: Product or corporate names may be trademarks or registered trademarks, and are used only for identification and explanation without intent to infringe.

British Library Cataloguing in Publication Data
A catalogue record for this book is available from the British Library

ISBN: 978-1-03-201217-9 (Set)
ISBN: 978-1-00-319367-8 (Set) (ebk)
ISBN: 978-1-03-207878-6 (Volume 41) (hbk)
ISBN: 978-1-03-207884-7 (Volume 41) (pbk)
ISBN: 978-1-00-321192-1 (Volume 41) (ebk)

DOI: 10.4324/9781003211921

Publisher's Note
The publisher has gone to great lengths to ensure the quality of this reprint but points out that some imperfections in the original copies may be apparent.

Disclaimer
The publisher has made every effort to trace copyright holders and would welcome correspondence from those they have been unable to trace.

THE WAR IN BURMA

by

ROY McKELVIE

With 9 Maps

METHUEN & CO. LTD., LONDON
36 Essex Street, Strand, W.C.2

First published in 1948

CATALOGUE NO. 3918/U

THIS BOOK IS PRODUCED IN
COMPLETE CONFORMITY WITH THE
AUTHORIZED ECONOMY STANDARDS

PRINTED IN GREAT BRITAIN

PREFACE

'*There are always three sides to any question. Your side, my side, and the right side*'—Seni Pramoj, Premier of Siam in an interview with the author in Bangkok, September 1945.

AS I completed this book two others, also dealing with the broader side of the Burma war, made their appearance. One, *Wrath in Burma*, was written by an American. The other, the official *Campaign in Burma*, was written by a Britisher. Oddly the American, Fred Eldridge, the Britisher, Frank Owen, and myself, were engaged on similar jobs in South-East Asia. In one form or another we were propagandists. We were also good friends.

When the war ended each one of us set about a different task. Eldridge, because of his devotion to Stilwell, produced a book in which Stilwell is the central figure, the Cinderella of the Burma war, whereas the British are the ugly sisters. Owen, for whom as a journalist and a man I have considerable admiration, completed the official booklet for the M.O.I. (now the Central Office of Information). Because it was official he had no power of criticism and little of comment. He produced, however, a remarkably vivid story of 'what fine fellows we were in Burma'.

This book is an attempt at an objective account of the Burma war, unadulterated by any personal or political bias. Praise and criticism of British and Americans is given freely and, I hope, with a fair amount of British restraint. It is, perhaps, a compromise between *Wrath in Burma* and the official booklet. It runs a course between the two which, for one reason or another, are essentially partisan in character. I mention this though most of this book was written by the time the other two were published.

There is one point of similarity between this story and that of Owen's. Our sources of information were, in many cases, the same. Our accounts of the movements of divisions and armies in battle must therefore contain some similarity. But these are facts which cannot be altered, only their significance can be changed by comment and interpretation.

I share with Eldridge an admiration for the soldierly qualities of the late General Stilwell. He was one of the great figures of the Burma war. Slim was another, and Mountbatten and Wingate. There were not many.

Being an American, and a very colourful one too, in a British theatre of war, Stilwell assumed an importance in international strategy and politics as well as military affairs. By his own personality and determination and through the agency of his own clever publicists he became an international figure more bound up with the Burma war than any other commander, British or American.

I would hesitate to appraise the values and virtues of Stilwell in comparison with Slim, for the latter out-lasted the American in the Burma campaign, starting as a Corps commander at the retreat and ending as Commander-in-Chief at the Singapore surrender. Slim was concerned with fighting battles. He was a domestic figure immortally associated with the 14th Army. He was not concerned with whether Britain or China was pulling its weight out East or with jerking either into doing more, as Stilwell was. Slim's responsibilities lay between his immediate superior and the men he commanded; Stilwell's were to America, China, and Britain, since he held the portfolios of Commander of the China–Burma–India theatre, Chief of Staff to Generalissimo Chiang Kai-shek, and Deputy Supreme Commander to Mountbatten, all at the same time.

I have not included in this book the battle for publicity, domestic or international, partly because I do not think it has much place in military history and partly because, in a small way, I was bound up with it. But it is of interest if only because of the famous tag 'The Forgotten Army' and the defeat Britain received from America in the international field.

It was the late Stuart Emeny of the *News Chronicle* who created the 'Forgotten Army' legend, in late 1943. And he was quite right. The people at home had little idea of what the British and Indians were up against on the Burma border; many, except close relatives, did not know we had an army there.

The Americans were the same. As far as they were concerned any war on the frontier of Burma was fought by a few Chinese prodded on by Stilwell and, perhaps, Erroll Flynn and his parachutists. Those who accepted the presence of Imperial troops considered them hired Indian mercenaries, to use the description of Mr. William Phillips, personal envoy to the late President Roosevelt.

Mountbatten fully realized this propaganda weakness when he arrived at the end of 1943. His own colourful personality brought the theatre into the limelight and the opportunity was there for the taking.

The prime need was more publicity at home, for it had been proved that the morale of forward troops was directly effected by the amount or lack of publicity they received. At first Air Marshal Sir Philip Joubert, Mountbatten's Information Chief, had no easy task since many of the staff he was given were quite useless from a journalistic viewpoint. Gradually the Air Marshal gathered around him a devoted little band of Military Observers who plugged away enthusiastically at producing material for home consumption. He formed his own Agency in London under Wing-Commander Charles Gardner of the B.B.C. It was within the framework but fairly independent of the M.O.I. Editors and the B.B.C. came to the rescue and the 14th Army was forgotten no more. At the end of the war it was probably second only in fame to the 8th Army.

We were not so successful in the international field. America had already made up its mind that Britain's policy in the East was to do as little as possible. Mountbatten's arrival, though interpreted as a sign of action, was nullified when the Japanese invaded Manipur. Stilwell still carried the picture through the astute publicity of Eldridge and such war correspondents as Preston Grover. Eldridge devotes much space to telling, with considerable delight, how Stilwell and he scored off Mountbatten and Joubert over the transmission of communiqués, news, and publicity scoops.

We made several attempts at reaching America with propaganda. I was personally concerned with one of them for, with the idea of seeing how best to publicize our Burma war, I arrived in Washington just after we had captured Rangoon. I followed Frank Owen by a few weeks.

The first thing I noticed was the suspicion with which the British Army Staff in Washington received anyone of an independent mission who might in some way affect their own rather comfortable perch. So far as I know no one on their publicity staff had any experience of the Burma war—one of their colonels made a hurried trip to S.E.A.C. soon after I arrived in America—nor were any of their P.R.O.s members of the National Press Club of America which, it occurred to me, was an ideal place to start some shrewd propaganda. I was made a member (within twenty-four hours) by a former member of my own paper, the *Star*, and an American journalist.

It was originally Joubert's intention to create an agency in America similar to that in London. The British Army Staff did not wish for such an independent organization and finally had their way. Fortunately the war ended before they began serious publicity operations.

In New York Britain maintained a small and efficient British Information Service which was unfortunately handicapped by a lack of suitable material. Most of the stories written by S.E.A.C. observers were for home consumption and required a great deal of twisting to have any sale in America. They were, however, helpful.

I have made several references to American opinion and criticism in the succeeding pages. Much of that opinion was ill-informed and malevolent but at least it shows people in this country what Americans thought and, perhaps, why they thought it. It is certainly not inspired by any sensitiveness on my part. The more we consider why Americans think certain things about us and then realize our own shortcomings the more easily will we understand them. The same applies to the Americans. To-day the need for such understanding is paramount.

I owe a debt of thanks to Air Marshal Sir Philip Joubert, my chief in S.E.A.C., for putting me in a position to take a wider view of the Burma war than most people. My thanks also go to Mr. David Higham for driving me into writing this book, and to my wife, Alex, for seeing me through it, and to the late Mr. E. A. Montague of the *Manchester Guardian* for reading and correcting it, to the Central Office of Information for the endpaper maps, to Mr. W. H. Bromage of the *News Chronicle* for the maps in the text. I might add my ginger cat, who sat on every page of typescript.

I acknowledge with thanks the information received from the cutting library of the *Star* newspaper (by kind permission of the editor, Mr. A. L. Cranfield); the Forces newspaper, *SEAC*, and its supplements; Mr. Sidney Butterworth; Mr. Bernard Gutteridge; Mr. Ian Stewart and Miss Rosemary Jellis of the B.B.C.

CONTENTS

CHAPTER	PAGE
PREFACE	v
1. THE LAST TRAGEDY	1
2. THE ENEMY	16
3. THE RETREAT FROM BURMA	31
4. CEYLON'S ESCAPE	48
5. ARAKAN DEBACLE	62
6. THE ARRIVAL OF WINGATE	75
7. THE FORMATION OF SOUTH-EAST ASIA COMMAND	89
8. THE JAPANESE INVASION OF ASSAM	105
9. THE SIEGE OF IMPHAL	119
10. THE BATTLE OF KOHIMA	132
11. THE RELIEF OF IMPHAL	146
12. WITH STILWELL IN NORTH BURMA	157
13. ANGLO-AMERICAN RELATIONS	173
14. THE RELIEF OF STILWELL	189
15. THE THIRD ARAKAN CAMPAIGN	205
16. THE CLEARANCE OF NORTH BURMA	220
17. FROM THE CHINDWIN TO THE IRRAWADDY	235
18. THE CAPTURE OF MANDALAY	249
19. THE RECAPTURE OF RANGOON	261
20. SURRENDER AND CONCLUSION	277
21. BURMA IN FOCUS	290
INDEX	300

MAPS

POLITICAL MAP OF BURMA	*Front endpapers*
	PAGE
INVASION OF BURMA BY JAPANESE: SPRING 1942	35
JAPANESE OFFENSIVE IN ARAKAN: JANUARY–APRIL 1944	97
THE SIEGE OF IMPHAL: MARCH 1944	123
OPERATIONS IN NORTH BURMA: FEBRUARY–AUGUST 1944	159
THE LAST ARAKAN CAMPAIGN	211
REINVASION OF BURMA AND ATTACK ON MANDALAY: JANUARY–APRIL 1945	239
THE RETURN TO BURMA: DECEMBER 1944–MAY 1945	265
RELIEF MAP OF BURMA	*Back endpapers*

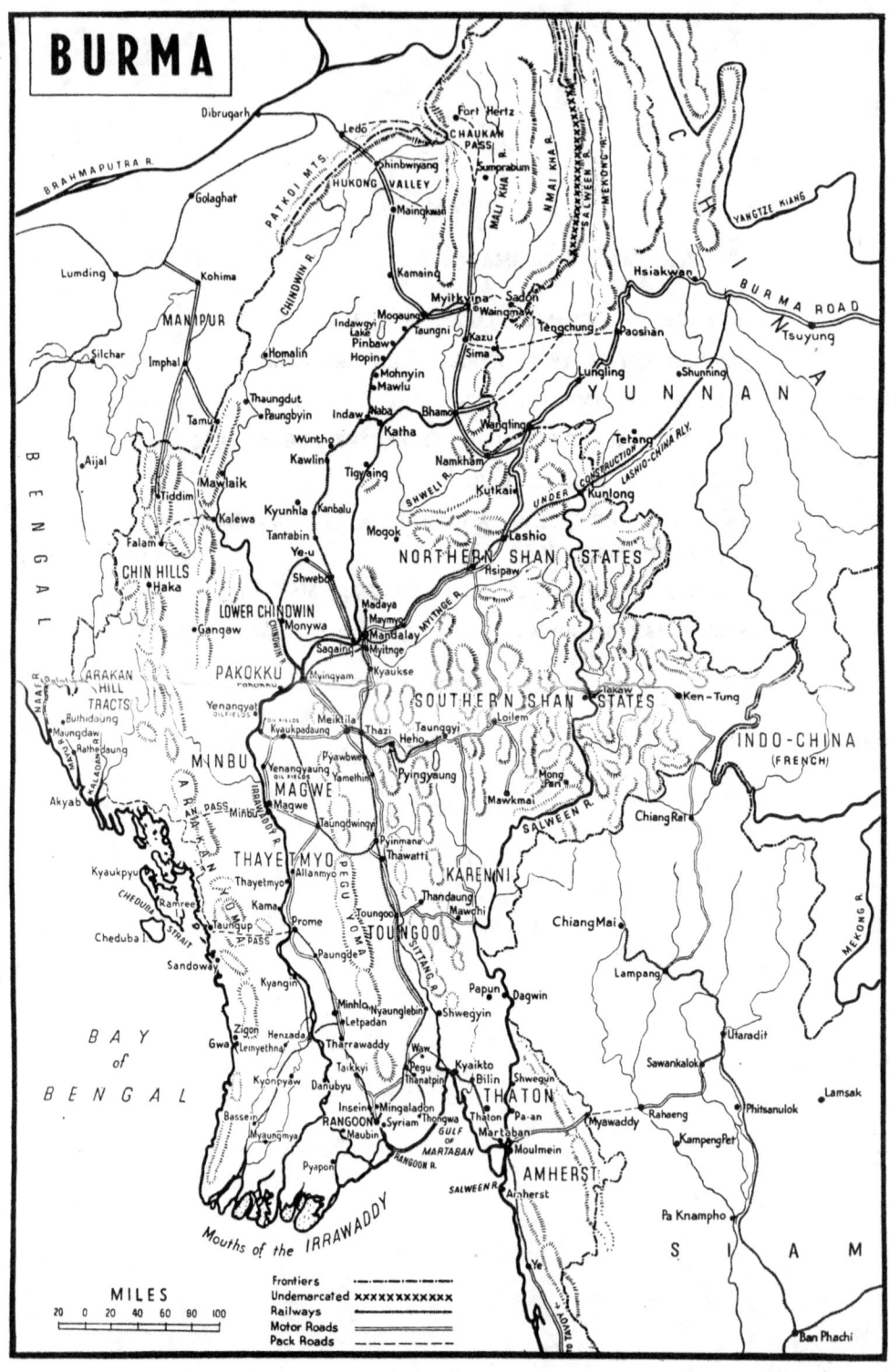

I
THE LAST TRAGEDY

The Hazards of Geography, Climate, and Disease—the Psychology of Jungle Warfare—The Mind of the Soldier

THOUGH it was unknown at the time, the loss of Burma in 1942 was the last great tragedy suffered by the Allies in the unpredictable course of the Far Eastern war. There were further retreats and setbacks as the Japanese sought to increase the size of their new Empire. They threatened Australia, India, and cut farther into Nationalist China, but never again did they wholly conquer any one single country.

Almost immediately the Americans set course for the reconquest of the Philippines and the invasion of Japan itself while the Australians doggedly held back the Japanese advance on Port Moresby in New Guinea. But the British, during the next two years, were destined by circumstances and policy to fight grim battles on the lonely frontier separating India from Burma, and to wait patiently—heartbreakingly patiently at times—before the unexpected opportunity came for the reinvasion of Burma by land and sea.

Burma's place in the scheme of the Far Eastern war was twofold. First, it was the last Allied land link with China through the Burma road which had been completed only in 1939. Secondly, it was considered the eastern land shield of India by virtue of its geographical lay-out. The mountains, the Chin, Naga, and Lushai, which lined the Indo-Burma frontier, were inhabited only by hill tribes and were devoid of any but narrow winding tracks. They were considered sufficient barrier to any modern army that had designs on India.

Even when the fall of Burma had exposed a new flank it was considered by some less likely that the Japanese would invade India by way of Assam than by the capture of Ceylon and the invasion of South India. Since the days when the Mohammedan invasions of India from the north had ceased, India's most vulnerable flank had always been her long uncovered seaboard.

As with India, so with Burma. The attenuated broken coastline of Burma stretching two thousand miles from past Akyab Island to Victoria Point, the mouths of three large rivers, the Irrawaddy at Rangoon, the Sittang at Mokpalin, and the Salween at Moulmein, and the thousands of little coves and bays, all these afforded shelter for ships and stepping-off grounds for troops, making the possibilities of sea invasion far greater than by land from Malaya or Siam.

Burma is so formed that, apart from its seaboard, it is encased in a horseshoe of mountains which only such a lightly equipped army as that of Genghis Khan had previously penetrated. Indeed the Japanese would have found much greater difficulty than they did in overrunning the country had they been forced to rely only on Siam and Malaya as debouching points for their troops. As it was, their acquisition of Singapore gave them command of the Malacca and Sunda Straits and open access, tantamount to command also, of the Bengal Sea and the Indian Ocean. They were able to use Rangoon, after its loss by the British, to place as many troops in Burma as they required or could spare.

Burma and the Federated Shan States, a wild and mountainous bulwark against the land masses of China, Indo-China, and Siam, is a country larger than Germany without any of the man-made geographical advantages found in Western Europe. Over fifty per cent of its 250,000 square miles are covered by forests of a great many varieties of timber, including the most valuable teak.

From north to south the country is twice as long as Great Britain. It is nearly as wide in the centre as France from Strasbourg to Brest. Its figure representation is a diamond, the north-west side of which is shut off from India by the Naga, Chin, and Lushai Hills. The north-east and south-east are separated from Tibet, China, Indo-China, and Siam by a great mass of parallel ridges which run down from the north to form the watersheds of the Salween and Mekong Rivers and eventually divide that long coastal strip of Burma, known as the Tennasserim strip, from Siam.

Also running from north to south is Burma's great system of rivers, of which the Irrawaddy is the largest. Formed in the far north by two large mountain rivers and augmented by the Chindwin below Mandalay, it is navigable by large river steamers for nearly 1,000 miles from its mouth at Rangoon. The Chindwin was once considered navigable for only 350 miles, but early in the Burma war a British officer traversed a further 200 miles north in a variety of river craft.

Rising in Tibet, the Salween runs south almost along Burma's eastern border and enters the sea at Moulmein. For river craft it is useless only a short distance above Moulmein, as its course runs mainly through gorges. Between the two is the Sittang.

These rivers and the network of feeders not only made possible the economical extraction of teak but had an important effect on the whole transport system of the country. So cheap was travel by river that the building of a prodigious system of roads and railways was considered uneconomical and unnecessary for peacetime purposes.

Like the rivers, the main trunk roads and railways run from north to south and lateral systems are few. The Myitkyina-Mandalay-Rangoon railway line, and its attendant road, runs like a spine down Burma and it is along that spine that one finds the most inhabited, wealthy, and civilized parts of the country. But the spine has few vertebrae and the greater part of the country still remains to be opened up, even now after a war in which armies of men and transport have trampled and fought over places where previously no white man had ever been.

The coming of the bulldozer and airplane, which requires landing-strips in the most inaccessible and unlikely spots, has altered, for the moment, the facial expression of Burma. Whether this is a transitory alteration, whether the fast-growing, greedy jungle will reclaim those new-found parts of Burma, as it did those ancient centres of civilization, Pagan and Ava, is a question only history can answer. History and, perhaps, economics. In tropical countries like Burma, Ceylon, Siam, and Malaya, the jungle does not creep slowly upon its victim. It springs up in a night. And man builds only where gold is to be won.

From this it can be seen that the axis of advance or retreat in a war in Burma should, in order to make problems of supply and reinforcement easy, run directly up and down the country, and that the side holding Rangoon, the principal port, would hold Burma. For before this war, when air supply developed on a scale unknown in any other theatre, an army retreating up Burma was forced, theoretically, to back itself eventually against the Himalayan wall of the north, choose the one existing road from Burma to another country—the old Burma road to China—or disintegrate along the hill tracks bordering the Assam-Burma frontier. The possibilities of reinforcing or supplying a northwardly withdrawing army from India except by air—there was so little air in 1942—were hardly considered.

That was just one consideration in the geographically dictated strategy of Burma fighting which everyone, including the Japanese, realized but which, perhaps, Britain did not fully recognize.

There were other considerations. The construction of the country, with its mountain ranges, rivers and valleys all running north–south, would force the Allies, or any army contemplating the land invasion of Burma from India or China, to cut across the grain of the country. Once in Burma, the rivers alone would afford effective barriers against a rapid advance and would entail the bringing up, or building at hand, of suitable craft.

The climate was as great a hindrance to mobility and supply as the physical features. The monsoon, which lasts for five months of the year and gives up to 200 inches of rain in parts of Burma, transformed the countryside into a sea of mud, washed away roads, tracks, and airfields, and bogged down men and vehicles. It is a rain that chills and soaks the soldier, creating a boredom and mental depression only slightly relieved by futile attempts to keep at least something dry.

Once the idea prevailed that fighting stopped during the monsoon, but during the latter part of the Burma war soldiers fought up to their necks in water in the valleys and plains which had become lakes. One of Mountbatten's first directions when he became Supreme Commander in 1943 was that fighting should continue throughout the monsoon.

The 14th Army had to overcome all those things in November 1944 when its chance came to reinvade Burma along the very routes by which it had retreated. By then, fortunately, the tracks of evacuation had become the roads of advance, mechanical equipment was in better supply and the air was full of Allied transport aircraft.

Throughout the Burma war the Japanese, once established in the country, were able to work on internal lines of communication. Even so the four attempts they made at leaving the beaten tracks and cutting away from those lines, either laterally or into the virtually trackless wastes of the north, were unsuccessful. When they attempted to penetrate the region of Fort Hertz or up past Shinbwiyang in the Huwkawng Valley, they were beaten by the country, climate, subterfuge, and force. When twice in 1944 they attempted to invade India they were beaten again by the country and climate, superior force, and their own logistical and tactical miscalculations.

Mistakes in a country like Burma, which rises and falls from 20,000 feet to sea-level, has a diversity of climates from ice-cold to sweating tropical heat, a five-month monsoon, and a heterogeneous population whose temper is so often capricious, can prove very costly. Even when the Allies had built up an army of over a million, supported by tanks and vehicles and squadrons of aircraft, Burma was not a country in which a text-book war could be fought. More often than not it was a case of 'God helps those who help themselves', to use General Sir William Slim's 14th Army motto.

If, on the material side, one factor contributed more than any other to the holding of the Japanese when they invaded India in 1944 and then facilitated the rout and defeat of the Burma armies, it was air supply. Even before the climax in 1944 it permitted a small-scale, experimental offensive in 1943, when the late Brigadier Orde Wingate marched his first Chindit expedition into the 'guts of the enemy', relying on the air for his food, ammunition, mail, and other necessities.

Air supply was the key to jungle warfare or, for that matter, any warfare in countries where roads were rare and difficult to build and the monsoon rains could wash away the labour of months in a few hours. In countries such as Assam, Burma, Malaya, or New Guinea, which are for the most part roadless and are covered by jungle and mountains, air supply was the only answer. Not only did it make possible the supply of isolated garrisons and give formations a freedom of movement they otherwise would not have possessed, but it had a strong psychological effect on the fighting troops of both sides.

The development of the air supply in South-East Asia was a slow process, commensurate at first with the Allies' ability to build and spare aircraft from other and more important theatres of war. Even when the Americans had proved its effectiveness in countering the loss of the Burma road by supplying China by air from India and the British had made due experiment with air supply during 1942 and 1943 to their garrisons along the Burma frontier, the battle for more transport aircraft was a tough one. It was fought hard and successfully by Admiral Lord Louis Mountbatten, whose vision went further than flying Commandos and static garrison supply. He envisaged, and carried out, the transporting of divisions from one part of the 1,000-mile Burma frontier to another. It almost seemed that the traditionally accepted picture of a high commander moving flags on a map had come true.

In the end—during and after the critical period of the Japanese incursion into Manipur in 1944—the fleet of transport aircraft available to the 14th Army and other formations comprising about 100 British and American squadrons was larger than anywhere along the world's battle-fronts and the tonnage of stores flown to the forward troops exceeded, for the 14th Army alone, 2,000 a day. The link-lines and feeder systems for this forward air supply, operated by the Combat Cargo Task Force, not only extended back to Calcutta in India but over thousands of miles to base airfields in the U.S.A.

All this could not have been achieved without air superiority which, directly after the loss of Burma and with the obvious threat to India, became top priority with the R.A.F. and U.S.A.A.F.

Assam, Bengal with its great port of Calcutta, and other parts of Eastern India became very vulnerable to attack by air once the Japanese had completed their conquest of Burma. This became all too clear when Japanese aircraft raided Calcutta, Madras, and Colombo in Ceylon.

The remnants of the Singapore and Rangoon squadrons

joined those which had begun to reach India, and the newly formed Eastern Air Command was given the wide task of covering all phases of air war in South-East Asia, including the winning and holding of air supremacy and the defence of India. It did not take the combined air forces long to reach parity with the Japanese and the evidence of the almost undisturbed supplying of Wingate's 1943 Chindits proved that superiority followed quite soon.

With the Japanese still holding the initiative on land, their weakness and the Allies' strength in the air became most marked as successive Burma campaigns followed. If in 1944 the Japanese had been able to cover their Manipur invasion with combat and supply aircraft and cut off our own considerable garrisons from air supply as they did from land supply, the battle for the Burma frontier and Assam would have become the battle for India which only the fateful dropping of the atomic bombs would have halted. Britain would have been left a legacy in Burma every bit as intricate and conflicting as later faced the Allies in Java and French Indo-China.

Before the last of the retreating British and Chinese armies had reached India or China it was also realized that the future course of any war in this theatre would be influenced by more factors than air supremacy or supply or Japanese strategy. Not only had a hostile geography and climate to be overcome and troops conditioned by experience to living and fighting in jungle country until they acquired full self-confidence but also the dread scourge of disease had to be controlled if not subdued.

Nowhere, except perhaps in New Guinea, did an army suffer worse from disease than in Burma. Malaria, scrub typhus, dysentery, beri-beri, jungle sores which festered and grew, were some of the evils to which the jungle armies were exposed. In ninety per cent of cases it was malaria, which can incapacitate any formation from a platoon to an army.

The retreating armies of 1942 were ravaged by malaria. Unknown thousands of refugees who sought to reach India overland died of malaria. The men who worked selflessly and unsparingly in Assam to evacuate army and refugees suffered from malaria almost to a man. The disease spread through Burma and Assam as a blight might infect an orchard in England, only on a scale unprecedented in modern times. The Japanese suffered no less than British, Indian, Chinese, or Gurkhas, but they, at least, had the advantage of the world's quinine supply.

During the succeeding years the small group of doctors, nurses, and medical staffs who first went up into Assam with the object of alleviating the immediate distress and, if possible, isolating or neutralizing malarial areas by spraying, canalizing swamps, and oiling, swelled to an army of 50,000 with 500 medical units. But not until 1945 when the Allied formations were spreading out fanwise across the length and breath of Burma could one say the battle of disease had been won.

Even in 1944, when the taking of mepacrine tablets had become an accepted commonplace, malaria was responsible for the majority of the half a million hospital casualties. That another half-million men were treated at medical units for one reason or another is sufficient evidence of the burden that fell upon the shoulders of the men and women who tried to keep the Allied armies in the field against the Japanese. Their triumph is apparent since 80 per cent of all hospital admissions, including wounded, were back with their units within three months.

The figures for 1945 up to the Japanese capitulation show that less than one man per thousand per day was going down with sickness—a figure which was better than in any other theatre of war and was an astonishing tribute to the Australian, British, and American scientists and doctors who fought unceasingly to assist the men in the jungles.

As must already be obvious, the fighting of a jungle campaign in a country such as Burma lays stress upon other things besides the commander's ability to supply and maintain an army in the field against the difficulties of geography, disease, and so often during the Burma war, the lack of sufficient equipment. The individual fighting man of this war was not an automaton who, given food, clothing, and ammunition, would plod on unthinkingly in retreat or advance. Whether Indian, African, or British, he reacted to conditions and environment, and jungle warfare had a strange psychology of its own.

In jungle warfare large formations were never massed together or in action simultaneously as in the desert or Western Europe. The fighting was small-scale, sporadic, and often in country where neither side could really see the other, although both might have pin-pointed positions. A whole corps on the advance through jungle was led by only one or two men or a tank. Behind, for hundreds of miles, stretched a vast column. On the two men in front rested the grim responsibility of finding where the enemy was. More often than not they were spotted by the enemy first and killed. Aerial reconnaissance in thick country was useless. All down the lonely tracks of north and eastern Burma one sees the rough wooden crosses marking the graves of leading scouts. And in every move or patrol it was the unenviable task of the junior commanders to appoint the men who led.

In jungly and hilly country men lived, ate, and slept in one- or two-men foxholes, only appearing above ground to move on or patrol. Little groups of foxholes, often full of water, were scattered over the vast wilderness of Burma and its frontier. They were near to each other, and yet far enough apart for a man to be attacked and killed without his neighbour knowing.

Then there was the ever-present fear of the sniper tied to the upper branches of a tree or in a foxhole on a rise in the ground. Just the 'phut' of the bullet, a falling twig or leaf, and another man killed. That alone strained nerves and tempers to the limit. Whole batteries of guns were sometimes put on to a suspected sniper post as much with the idea of restoring men's calm as killing the sniper.

It is small wonder that a war fought by individuals and small units, imposing such stress on the character, make-up, and responsibility of junior commanders and men, should produce a psychosis known as 'jungle happiness'.

It is small wonder too that, until men became very experienced in this type of warfare, the breaking down of one individual so easily led to whole groups of men becoming 'jittery' and loosing off thousands of rounds at shadows or even straight into the air. The Japanese knew this well and had immeasurable success with their 'jitter' tactics. Apart from anything else they were able to locate the positions of complete units.

The lonely, primitive life of the jungle seared its way into the minds of men long exposed to it. Their return to civilization produced a listless, introspective, frightened mood. They were fearful of bright lights and crowds. They appeared awkward with friends and sometimes even wives and sweethearts. There was a strangeness about them of which they themselves knew nothing but which other people could see so clearly. For a time they wanted to get back to their hole in the ground, their comrades in their holes and the constant, nerve-straining atmosphere of waiting for the unknown. Many men refused leave in India not so much because of the lack of leave facilities but because they had become part of the jungle. They felt more at home there than in the cities. They had become used to loneliness and the sense of great remoteness. Their interest was in small, simple things.

'Jungle happiness' as a disease was not necessarily confined to the most forward troops in jungle warfare. Although in larger formations life was more communal and, perhaps, more comfortable, it infected anyone who lived long in jungle country.

The minds and moods of the men who fought in Burma varied according to their race, standard of education, and development of imagination. Indian and Gurkha soldier were so much nearer home than the British and Africans, that this sense of remoteness was not so developed, although it sometimes takes a Gurkha as long to reach his home in Nepal as it does a Britisher to sail to England. The great divide of air and ocean was not there.

Native troops have never stood up to bombing or shelling as well as British. Fortunately after the retreat Japanese aerial activity declined, while they rarely had enough artillery in one place to lay down concentrations such as were known in the desert. Probably the biggest was a concentration of fifty guns on the Kyaukmeyaung bridgehead over the Irrawaddy in 1945. By then, however, all troops were so confident and experienced it had little effect in morale.

During the retreat from Burma in 1942 everyone of whatever race was naturally bewildered and shaken by the confident methods and tactics of the Japanese and the apparent, though exaggerated, hostility of the Burmese. This bewilderment caused the British troops to become bitter and cynical. They felt they had been badly let down. The shakiness of the Indian and Gurkha troops led to a considerable amount of unfair criticism of their quality as fighting troops.

One can forgive troops almost anything during that phase of the war, for few people, if any, really did know what was happening and the whole machinery of the army had virtually broken down. The British troops, being more adaptable, were first to recover, but once the Indians and Gurkhas regained their confidence and got more experience they were magnificent.

While it took some time for the British soldier to lose his sceptical attitude towards the Indian, he always maintained a high regard for the Gurkha who, for most of the succeeding campaign, was probably the best jungle soldier of the lot. The three were mixed in brigades and divisions most of the time. At first the presence of British troops stiffened the others, but towards the end of the war it is fair to say that the Indians and Gurkhas had proved their worth and staying power so well that they out-lasted the British, who had learnt all about repatriation and release to their cost as a fighting force. Towards the end there were whole divisions without a single British battalion in them, and other formations with few British apart from officers. Such a transformation, or Indianization, would not have been considered possible before or immediately after the disastrous start to the Burma war.

There was an undercurrent of cynicism among British troops throughout the Burma war, offset in some measure by the increasing speed of mail and the general comradeship of war. But sad though it is, few really appreciated the reasons for which they were fighting in Burma. Few cared very much what they were. Most would have willingly changed places with their brothers in the desert or Europe, despite the battle casualty rate there being so much higher and the enemy's machine power so much greater.

The pattern of the Burma war was in one respect like so many Britain has fought—continuous defeat or defence, until at last the time, place, and opportunity came for a resurgence and the last battle, or series of battles, was fought and won.

From the day they invaded Burma to the summer of 1944, the Japanese held the initiative on land, although from the end of 1942 they were outnumbered. Their supremacy in the air and at sea lasted only for a few months of 1942.

The Allies were short of equipment during the early part

of the Burma war. They were short of aircraft, tanks, guns, transport, and even automatics. But all these could have been dispensed with, as many were even to the end, if the divisions had been trained and experienced in battle.

Numerical superiority in manpower was one of the first things achieved by the Allies. By early 1943 the number of available divisions exceeded those of the Japanese by at least two to one, not counting any offers of divisions made by Generalissimo Chiang Kai-shek, which the British always considered of doubtful value. But that superiority did not extend to training and it was accepted that ten untrained Indian divisions would probably go down before two battle-hardened Japanese.

During the two years from 1942 to 1944, years during which the British were most criticized for a 'do-nothing' policy, the Allies' attempts at offence were, with one exception, half-hearted or limited in scope. The first attempt at capturing Akyab failed dismally and merely bolstered up the school which believed in caution.

The second attempt, whole-hearted enough in its conception, was General Stilwell's drive into north Burma. Stilwell with first one and then two, increasing eventually to five, Chinese divisions and an American Task Force, was determined to carry out the wishes of the Combined Chiefs of Staff and free north Burma so that a land link might be built between India and China. Stilwell was also determined to fight the Japanese, and the combat area he was given was admittedly the worst in Burma. Stilwell did not like caution. He wanted a full-blooded British-Indian offensive into Burma to assist him. He did not get it. Nor at first did the Chinese back him to their promised extent.

The third attempt was in aid of Stilwell. It was General Wingate's first Chindit expedition in 1943. The idea of long-range penetration on air supply into the heart of enemy-held Burma was bold and spectacular. But its tactics of 'shadow boxing' reduced its military value to the sphere of a nuisance raid.

Britain's policy in the Far East, up to the time of the creation of South-East Asia Command, was to 'go-slow' and fight a cheap war. The defence of India—Britain had always contracted to defend India against invasion—was more important than the reoccupation of Burma. With commitments in Europe and the Middle East, Britain had little to spare in manpower and equipment. The Indian Army was growing up. Britain could not afford to sacrifice lives unnecessarily for the present or the future.

The early failures in Burma demanded the building up of a combat strength and confidence which, when unleashed, would not fail. In doing so there was possibly too much caution and too little vigour.

By the time of the Quebec Conference in 1943 Britain knew, more or less, the extent of her commitments in Europe and could give more attention to the East. The Supreme Commander, Mountbatten, was to be the torchbearer of offensive action. He hoped to carry out a spectacular amphibious operation but was frustrated by the lack of equipment. But there was enough weight on the Burma front for a major land offensive. He found that weight moving ponderously, slowly, and cautiously.

The Japanese interpreted the appointment of Mountbatten as the signal for renewed and revitalized British action. They knew that they had little power to stop an advance into Burma or a landing in south Burma. So they decided to move first; to extend their land frontier of defence and place their feet on Indian soil. They moved fast while the Allies were still crawling along and over the frontier. In doing so they put back the Allied clock at least six months but finally signed their own death warrant.

2
THE ENEMY

*Initial Numerical Advantage—Japanese Training and Equipment—
The Japanese Soldier—His Strength and Weakness*

IN the preceding chapter were considered some of the handicaps, strains, and hazards of the Burma war. These had to be overcome, a force had to be built up, and deficiencies in equipment had to be made good, before the Allies could contemplate the reoccupation of Burma by land or sea and the defeat of the Japanese Burma armies. During the building up process the Allies had to appraise the strength and weakness of the Japanese armies so that they could correctly calculate what superiority in men, materials, and aircraft was required to assure success. The conclusions and figures are interesting.

The Japanese successfully invaded Burma with 60,000 men and held it for three years with never more than 275,000. In the beginning the Allies, outnumbered by two to one, were forced to retreat from Burma. In order to return they eventually amassed the crushing total of over one million troops of all descriptions plus the aircraft necessary to hold the skies and supply such a force. A superiority of five-to-one when calculated against a depleted Japanese army in 1945.

As figures can be misleading, and these certainly seem to an over-estimation of the power of the Japanese Army, some brief explanation is needed. The final numerical superiority of six to one was reached, not so much because the Allies considered it necessary as because the number of Japanese killed reduced the strength of their own armies. Moreover, when analysed it is found that a considerable proportion of the Allies' numerical superiority was dissipated in maintaining the terribly long lines of communication that ran from Assam through Burma. The actual force which struck at the Japanese, chased them from Kohima in Assam through Burma, and then virtually annihilated them, had a superiority in men and fire-power of about three to one.

These superiority proportions correspond almost exactly with those arrived at independently by the Americans in the South-West Pacific. Never did the Americans contemplate any operation unless they were assured of a superiority of at least three to one in men and fire-power and preferably six to one. Gathering together such a force in one place was easier since their armies were supplied from a sea train and did not have the geographical handicaps of the Allies in Burma. They were able to land, say, on an island a force composed almost entirely of combat troops, whereas in Burma for every man who wielded a rifle and bayonet or tommy-gun there were twenty or more maintaining him.

Nevertheless it is obvious from these few facts that the Japanese armies in Burma, as anywhere else, provided formidable opposition and it is worth remembering that of the seven million men Japan had under arms less than half were ever tested. Very few indeed were ever defeated in battle and throughout the war their total land casualties were only 360,000 of which 110,000 were killed in Burma.

If it required a million men to reconquer Burma one can realize the effort Britain would have had to put into the war in South-East Asia to reconquer Malaya, Singapore, the Dutch East Indies, Siam, and parts of French Indo-China, where at least another half-million Japanese were stationed and, as happened, never defeated in battle.

Wherein lay the strength of the Japanese Army and what were its weaknesses?

In Burma most of the ten and a half divisions that were

finally ranged against the Allies were veterans. Some, like the 33rd and 55th, fought through Malaya and then came into the invasion of Burma. The 33rd had had its original blooding in Nanking, China. These two divisions and the 18th had an amazing record of fighting in Burma alone. In fact the 33rd and the 18th became as famous as any Allied divisions. The former, having chased the 17th Indian Division out of Burma in 1942, then forced it to retreat from the China Hills in 1944 and became the only Japanese division to gain a foothold on the Imphal Plain. It had to retreat eventually and was finally seen in action with the same 17th Division on the Sittang in 1945.

The 18th Division held north Burma, including Myitkyina, until finally beaten back by five Chinese divisions, one American Task Force and the Chindits in 1944. It reappeared in the battles around Meiktila in 1945. On the other hand, of the Allied divisions that held the Indo-Burma border when the Japanese invaded in 1944 less than a quarter had ever seen serious action.

Irrespective of whether or not their divisions had previously seen action, the Japanese set about training them for the particular job in hand. Excluding the campaigns the Japanese fought in the early part of the century, most of their pre-war battle experience had come in China, where the terrain is very different from South-East Asia. Therefore they transferred some of the divisions they were to use against the Allies from the China theatre to training-grounds in Hainan and Formosa where the country was similar to Malaya or Burma. The sense in this was well illustrated in the case of Singapore.

In 1937, some years after it had become obvious to some observers that Japan was bent on Empire building, the British held large-scale exercises to test the defences of their eight million pound naval base, Singapore. Troops, ships, and aircraft were brought from as far afield as Iraq and

Hong Kong. The conceptions of defence were founded on land-sea-air operations, modern enough in all conscience. At the close British officers affirmed that Singapore was impregnable against sudden or surprise attacks. Yet on Formosa, only 750 miles from Hong Kong, a Colonel Homma was schooling a Japanese army in jungle warfare for the very job of capturing the base, which General Yamashita did in two months with 30,000 men against nearly 100,000 British, Indian, and Australian troops. If that happened in Malaya, what chance had 35,000 inexperienced British-Indian troops against 60,000 Japanese in Burma?

The Japanese set out to achieve surprise and succeeded. It was nothing new, because surprise is one of the seven accepted principles of war. In South-East Asia and the Pacific this element of surprise won a campaign or series of campaigns for the Japanese, but not the war. It was a transient strength, since specialized jungle warfare ceased to be an asset to the Japanese once the Allies had also learnt and improved the art. That took a year or more.

The Japanese sized and equipped their divisions for a particular operation. In Malaya and Burma they were smaller and more compact than the British or Indian. They numbered about 10,000 men against a normal British establishment of 14,000, which soon increased in Burma to about 18,000 to meet the exigencies of supply and maintenance.

Their divisions were designed for mobility. They possessed less transport and artillery than the British or Indian, for in country where roads were few and the tactics of infiltration were to be exploited, transport and heavy artillery were a hindrance.

The Japanese relied on their infantry armed with a high proportion of short-range automatic weapons, supported by medium machine-guns similar to the British Vickers .303, 4-inch mortars and infantry guns which, like the British mountain gun, were carried in parts. The Japanese infantry battalion was a complete fighting unit in itself. Moreover, all food, ammunition, and guns could be carried by men and mules if necessary.

The needs of the individual Japanese soldier were slender compared with the British. The story of a bag of rice hung round his neck as a week's supply of food is not a gross exaggeration. When the Japanese 15th Army invaded Manipur in 1944 it followed tracks through the Naga and Chin Hills which no transport apart from mules could traverse. It received the order that it would carry everything required for the operation and when all ammunition and food had been expended it would eat off the land and fight with captured British equipment. That, under such circumstances, it remained intact and virile for four months once again proved the tactical soundness of lightly equipped, unencumbered, mobile divisions.

If further proof be needed of the jungle suitability of the Japanese division, it came from the British who, while not cutting down the number of men in each division, trimmed their high establishment of transport to the minimum. Brigades and battalions were made into self-sufficient, independent groups and soldiers were trained to march long distances and carry heavier loads than normal. As an example, one company of the Manchester Regiment man-handled their .303 Vickers machine-guns for over 300 miles through the jungles of north Burma and never failed to be up with the infantry for a battle. Moreover, the British having seen, and felt, the effectiveness of the Japanese mortar, produced one of similar calibre (4-inch) and range and formed whole companies or batteries. The lesson of the short-range automatic as the most effective weapon in the jungle was probably the first lesson the British learnt from the Japanese.

Tactically the Japanese infantry were cunning. They

sited their light automatics and machine-guns on reverse slopes, well hidden and camouflaged. They had the patience to wait until the last moment before firing, which, had their aim not been so poor, should have ensured killing and wounding the maximum number of the enemy. Their bunker systems compared favourably with the better trench systems of the last war and were designed to stand a long siege. They were fast, silent movers when in or near contact. Often the Allies continued to shell and mortar a position from which all Japanese had gone in the night. Their snipers, whom they sprayed out in front in advance or behind in retreat, were suicidally brave and very deadly. Their offensive tactics of infiltration and encirclement were adopted as the pattern for training by the British.

Experience of battle, training, mobility, sound formation, and tactics, were five Japanese assets. They were, however, not lasting, since all could be achieved, and equalled or bettered, by the Allies, given the time. In fact all were. But there were two points of Japanese strength which one might call imponderables and which were distinctly Japanese. They were their high recuperative power and fanatical fighting spirit.

A Japanese division could not be discounted as a fighting force until it was reduced to a mere handful of men. Even then it would carry on fighting. The reason was that every single officer and man, irrespective of his job, was a trained, efficient fighter. There were no specialists who considered fighting the last part of their duties as there were in British or Indian divisions.

On many occasions during the Burma war the Allies found themselves fighting hard against rear echelon men. This policy was proved correct since replacements for their Burma armies never kept pace with their losses after the second half of 1944. Yet the Japanese remained a fighting force with which no one dared to take liberties. When, for instance, the 17th Indian Division fought the 33rd Japanese Division in the Imphal Plain in 1944, the 33rd Division probably did not number more than 3,000. Again, when four Chinese divisions and the American Marauders were poised at Myitkyina in 1944, the 18th divisional garrison of that town was never more than 1,500 men. In comparison, a British or Indian division ceased to become effective once it had lost a third of its strength.

Closely linked with this recuperative power was the fighting spirit of the Japanese soldier. On him and the junior officer the Japanese relied more than anything else for their success in battle. It was this spirit which made the army as a whole such a formidable proposition. It can best be appreciated by describing the individual soldier.

Generals and journalists have described the Japanese soldier as an ant, a beaver, an insect, and in other rather contemptuous terms, but General Sir William Slim said: 'We talk a lot about fighting to the last man and the last round, but the Japanese soldier is the only one who actually does it.'

In dress, on the march, and in battle, the Japanese soldier was astonishingly slovenly. The individual appeared to care little how he looked. In column or file, he loped haphazardly along the roads or paths. He would wear a mixture of any clothes—a Japanese peaked cap or tin helmet, a captured British bush shirt, Japanese breeches, puttees indescribably wound round his legs (or no puttees or gaiters at all) and P.T. shoes or boots that looked much too big.

Officers, in their attempt to ape the Western smartness, but with an Oriental's complete lack of tone or neatness, would parade with coloured sashes round a smart tunic, an arm-band indicating their importance and job, a pair of knee-breeches, no puttees, a pair of coloured socks held up with more coloured suspenders, and gym shoes. Such a rigout can only be described as comically puerile. It amused the British intensely and amazed the Americans who could not figure out how such an apparent rabble had already beaten them in battle.

But the Japanese soldier showed unhesitating obedience to unlimited authority. His training was hard and vividly realistic. He would stick to a position until killed, regardless of the hopelessness of the situation. He was more tenacious than any soldier in any other army. His service life was uncompromising and often cruel. He would tolerate conditions of squalor, lack of food, welfare, and even ammunition which no Allied soldier would tolerate. He did not grouse despite being told his chances of returning to Japan were small. He expected almost nothing and any nostalgia he might have felt was offset by the provision of Korean or Japanese 'comfort girls'. He was in an army which did not pander to any democratic ideas and in which there was no human association between officer and man except in the matter of leadership in battle. He suffered from a rigid N.C.O. caste system which gave a first-class private the right to beat a second-class private to the point of death. He was not afraid to die. He believed it a disgrace to be taken prisoner.

For centuries the Japanese soldier, who came from the peasant class, had been indoctrinated with Emperor worship and the idea that to die in the cause of his Emperor and sacred country (The Land of the Gods) was to ensure a place in heaven among his ancestors. For centuries he had held the belief that this earthly life was only a staging-post between the last world and the next; something very transient and not very valuable. For the last fifty years, since Field-Marshal Yamagata had revised the Conscription Laws, the soldier had received a barrack education with the subjects of Japanese expansion, the evil dominance of the white man over the East and the destiny of Japan as the main themes. And before leaving his country for foreign service the

Japanese soldier worshipped at the shrine of Yashkuni muttering the words, 'I will meet you at the shrine'. How else can one explain the Japanese soldier's willingness to die in battle and his tolerance of the conditions of service life?

If illustrations be needed—they were almost everyday occurrences in the Burma war—there was the case of 'Little Willie' the sniper who, for three weeks, lived in a hole in a tree on the outskirts of Pinwe village in North Burma and, despite frantic efforts by British troops to mortar and shoot him, continued to kill and wound anyone who was foolish enough to show himself, until one night he disappeared with the rest of the Japanese troops in the village. 'Little Willie' was never more than ten yards from the nearest British soldier. Or the officer who, waving his sword, boarded a British tank and slew two of the tank's crew before he himself was killed. Or the innumerable examples of officers armed only with swords who led suicidal charges on to the barrels of the automatics of British and Indian troops. In Allied armies such men would be given the V.C. or Congressional Medal of Honour, but in the Japanese Army it was accepted as the thing to do.

There were cracks even in this armour of bravery which may be counted among the weaknesses in the Japanese Army. The commander who lost a lot of men in battle was hailed as a national hero, but to admit that a battle had been lost was a sign of weakness. In consequence Japanese field commanders never reported the truth to their seniors. The farther one went up the ladder of Army Command the less was known of the actual situation at the front. It is a fact that when the capitulation of Japan came, General Kimura, who was commanding the armies in Burma, admitted that he had not been given the true picture by his subordinates. He had to ask Admiral Mountbatten, the Allied Supreme Commander, the whereabouts of some of his units. Field-Marshal Terauchi, Mountbatten's opposite number in

THE ENEMY 25

South-East Asia, also admitted that he did not know the true state of affairs in Burma.

This was only one of the defects in the Japanese Army Command. There were others in staff work, planning, strategy, and equipment. Some of them became apparent to the Allies early on and were naturally used to advantage.

It came as something of a shock to Allied staff officers whose job it was to take over Japanese Headquarters after the capitulation to discover that, in the Japanese Army, it was considered bad etiquette for a staff officer to know the names of his subordinates, even the name of the officer immediately below him. As the staff is 'the soul of the army' and team work is the essence of good staff work, it is difficult to know how the Japanese ever successfully planned any campaign. In South-East Asia the only successful campaign was the first, the invasion of Malaya, the Dutch East Indies, Burma, and the capture of Singapore. Then they had been able to prepare and plan under conditions of peace, with time on their side.

During the war in Burma the Japanese mounted two offensives under the grandiose title of 'The March on Delhi'. The first was the advance into the Arakan with the object of capturing Chittagong and the second the invasion of Manipur in Assam. Both failed, though the second came very near to success. Both were planned without any regard to the strength of the Allies or any appreciation of what counter-action the Allies might take.

To these two operations the Japanese assigned about 100,000 men, five divisions plus army troops and replacements for casualties lost, against an Allied force which at the start was over half a million. They provided their troops with no air cover and, in the case of the Manipur invasion, paid little or no attention to the problem of supply and maintenance. All General Mutagachi, the 15th Army Commander, gave his troops were the heartening words that the unconquerable Japanese Army must now carry out its destiny and free India from the British. One cannot help coming to the conclusion that the Japanese commanders and staff were not only blind, but conceited and arrogant.

From the top to the bottom the Japanese Army was inflexible and incapable of altering a plan to suit the occasion.

Once an operation was set in motion it was carried out to the last letter or, as happened in the latter part of the Burma campaign, until it failed. The Japanese had time to halt their proposed Manipur invasion and alter their plan once they saw that the Allies had found, in air supply, the answer to being encircled and cut off.

In a different plane a Japanese platoon or company would persist in doing the same thing again and again as, for example, groups of Japanese did in the first Arakan campaign. They had been told to rendezvous in a certain 'chaung' (river-bed). A British sergeant-major and a few men covered it with fire, but for several days small groups of Japanese continued to arrive and stay there until killed despite seeing the bodies of their dead comrades lying around.

The Japanese plan for their retreat from the Arakan through the Pegu Hills, across the Sittang into Siam, in 1945, was an example of all these faults. Though it was made with meticulous care it completely disregarded what the Allies might do; it allowed no room for emergency; it was inflexible, and those who made it were conceited enough to think it might succeed. As a result, in the first ten days of their attempted break-out from the Pegu Yomas, 10,000 Japanese were killed or captured by the two Indian divisions who stood across their path. There was no secrecy about the Allies' dispositions.

Finally there were defects and deficiencies in the equipment and weapons with which the Japanese soldier had to fight. As a generalization, none of it was as well made as the Allies', but some weapons such as their L.M.G.s, mortars, and 'seventy-fives' were more effective than the corresponding Allied weapons in jungle warfare. For example, their L.M.G. which corresponded to the Allies' Bren gun, was not so accurate but had a greater spraying effect ('beaten zone', in military language) which in close country was a good point since targets were never obvious. Their mortars out-ranged those of the Allies and were always skilfully handled. Their 'seventy-fives' were mobile and accurate and had no counter-part except in the Indian mountain gun.

But in heavier types of artillery the Japanese were deficient. Though their 150-mm. and 105-mm. guns out-ranged the British medium and 25-pounder guns by several thousand yards, they did not possess enough, were short of ammunition, and never used them in more than ones and twos. In consequence the troops in Burma rarely had to suffer a barrage and never one comparable with anything in the desert or Europe. Moreover, except for the 'seventy-fives', their artillery was not mobile since it had wooden wheels and had to be dragged by men and mules from position to position.

Most of the motor transport used by the Japanese was captured British or American. Very few Japanese-made trucks were ever found in Burma or anywhere else in South-East Asia. In consequence they neither had the quantity nor the spare parts necessary for a long campaign.

The Japanese began with two brigades of tanks, but they consisted of obsolete or obsolescent types. Though much of Burma was admirable tank country they never, for obvious reasons, challenged the British or American tanks (Lees, Grants, Shermans, and Stuarts) to a battle. Only a few skirmishes were fought and in the first and only recorded instance of Allied tanks 'mixing it' with Japanese was in the Kabaw Valley early in 1944 when five Japanese tanks were blown to pieces by eight General Lees. One Japanese tank was captured more or less intact and later driven round India on exhibition. It was a copy of a 1928 Cardon-Lloyd, resembling a Bren carrier with a lid and armed with a single 37-mm. gun!

The story of the Japanese air forces in South-East Asia is not dissimilar to that in other fields of the Far Eastern war, for their conceptions of aerial warfare were, perhaps, twenty years out of date. It is one of brief numerical superiority and tactical advantage followed rapidly by complete inferiority in men, equipment, organization, supply, and training.

To the end of the war the Japanese maintained two air forces, the Army and Navy. Few, if any, of their senior commanders possessed any special air training, and had no conception of air strategy. General Kinoshita, Commander-in-Chief of the Army Air Force in the Southern Area, which included Burma, confessed he 'had no knowledge of engines or real flying'.

At the time of the Burma invasion the Japanese air theory was that the Navy Air Force would support the advancing armies while the Army Air Force, having lost prestige after its defeat by the Russians in 1939 at Nomoham, on the Manchurian Border, would mop up, garrison, and then take over the defence of the conquered country.

This happened in the case of Burma, and the navy employed their 'Zeke' fighter in support of the army. The 'Zeke' was reckoned as a formidable plane in 1942 because of its high degree of manœuvrability. But as time, and the Allies, went on, the weaknesses of Japanese aircraft in lack of fire-power and armoured protection became apparent. Their losses in pilots mounted.

In the middle of 1942 the Japanese possessed about 150 aircraft in Burma and Siam, with another 220, including naval aircraft, in Malaya, Sumatra, and the Bay of Bengal. But that meant they could never put more than 100 aircraft over Burma or Assam at any one time, while the fact that their bombers were all twin-engined confined the range of their strategic bombing. After 1942 these figures decreased considerably and, apart from a few sporadic raids, not in great force, the only aircraft seen was the reconnaissance 'Dinah', which was fast and flew high but was armed with one free 7.7 machine-gun in the rear!

The Japanese began the war in South-East Asia with all-round superiority. They employed specially trained and mostly veteran troops. They equipped them for the task. They aimed at achieving surprise, and succeeded. With four divisions and 150 aircraft they held Burma for over a year. While they built up their land force to just over ten divisions, they were forced to deplete their air forces and navy to offset losses in the Pacific. For instance, after the battle of the Java Sea their naval forces consisted of at least five battleships, three cruiser divisions, three destroyer flotillas, and an unknown number of aircraft carriers. They were far stronger than the British. The battle of the Midway in the summer of 1942 was undoubtedly the turning-point in Japanese naval strategy. It called off considerable forces from the Indian Ocean.

Therefore the Japanese were forced to hold Burma with some 275,000 men, at the most, and the whole of South-East Asia with another half-million, with virtually no air cover and sea protection. The task was too great. Even the Japanese realized that and, in order to keep the Allies out of Burma, they had to launch an offensive into India. They had no other choice except to wait for the coming invasion. They hoped India would rise to welcome them, but they miscalculated India's temper just as they miscalculated the strength of the Allies.

Anyone who has studied the war in the East cannot fail to come to one very definite conclusion. In attempting the 'greatest land grab in history', the Japanese exceeded their capabilities. In 1941, with time, opportunity, ambition, and the necessary forces on their side, it was not difficult for them to make the grab. But to hold or extend their new Empire was more difficult. Burma was perhaps the most interesting case of any because in the Allies' estimation it was classed as the lowest priority of any war theatre—a point which was frequently stressed by Admiral Mountbatten and others as much with the object of deceiving and deluding the Japanese as with stating no more than the truth.

Burma afforded the Japanese their greatest chance of exploitation and expansion. Yet their final failure and defeat was the greatest they suffered, their losses in Burma more numerous than anywhere else. If the Allies could achieve what they did in Burma with only just sufficient men and equipment—most of the deficiencies were in equipment for combined operations and men for the invasions of Malaya and other lands in South-East Asia—what would have happened to the rest of the Japanese Empire once the flow from West to East began in earnest?

3
THE RETREAT FROM BURMA

The Reasons—The Japanese Build-up and Preparations—The Allied Opposition—Battle of the Sittang Bridge—Arrival of Chinese Assistance—The Route of the British

FIVE months after their eclipse of the American battle fleet at Pearl Harbour the Japanese had completed the conquest of Burma.

Whether the Japanese anticipated or even contemplated such a startling and rapid success is doubtful. It is questionable whether Burma was even included among the countries constituting the first ring of Japanese conquests. One reason for this was that the Japanese, even in their most confident mood, could hardly have anticipated the capitulation of Singapore occurring just two months after they had invaded Malaya. Without Singapore, the Japanese Navy would neither command the Indian Ocean nor be in a position to land troops in Burma.

There were other reasons. Pre-supposing that the Siamese would permit the Japanese armies to land freely in Siam, the difficulties of moving an army westwards across the mountains into Burma against opposition were considerable. Nor was an advance northwards from Malaya, once that country had been overrun, much easier. The army would have to traverse the long, narrow Tennasserim strip and then cross the series of rivers which were natural hazards. Britain's sea and air power would have a direct effect on any move in this latter direction.

That Burma was necessary to Japan, politically as well as strategically, is obvious. Apart from Burma's value as an oil- and rice-producing country—the richest rice-producer in the East—its capture would completely seal off China from the Allies and provide Japan with a troop base, good port facilities and forward airfields for any future move against India or China. Besides this the Burmese, as distinct from the less numerous hill tribes, are a strongly independent-minded people and, for a time anyhow, would prove a good medium for Japanese propaganda against Western colonization and imperialism.

How then did the Japanese achieve such a rapid conquest which took less than four months? They were well on the move into Burma before they had captured Singapore or sunk forty Allied ships in the Java Sea. In fact Rangoon was evacuated only five days after Singapore's surrender and over a month before the Java Sea battle was even fought. Rangoon was the key to Burma.

Some time before Pearl Harbour, Japanese troops had entered French Indo-China; Siam had been more sympathetic than most countries to Japanese business-men and methods. Having helped instigate the Indo-China–Siamese war, the Japanese gratuitiously offered to act as intermediaries. The cause of this miniature and almost bloodless war was Siam's desire to recover Cambodia and other territory lost to France fifty years previously. Japan had thus placed herself in a strong position in South-East Asia even before war had broken out.

On 8 December 1941, Japanese troops landed in force in Siam. For twenty-four hours the Siamese made a show of opposing them and then capitulated. With one exception the Siamese government, under the aged and dictatorial premier, Pibul Songgram, signed, under Japanese influence, a declaration of war on the Allies. That exception was the powerful and popular, Pridi Panomyong, a senior statesman of the country whose title was Luang Pradit.

Marshal Pibul Songgram, fearing disaffection might be

caused by Pradit's refusal, promoted him to the Regency of Siam—the king was too young to rule—an appointment which Pradit accepted.

Under the title of 'Ruth', Luang Pradit became the head and body of a Siamese underground movement which grew finally to fair proportions. When Mountbatten arrived to take over command in South-East Asia contact was made between his staff and Pradit. A force of Free Siamese was raised and, operating with the British Force 136, 'V' Force and the Americans Office of Strategic Services, made regular journeys by parachute into Siam. By the end of the war the Free Siamese movement had attracted some 60,000 fighting men.

After their declaration of war on the Allies the Siamese annexed parts of Malaya and, situated on a flank, became an obvious threat to Burma. The Japanese spread throughout the country.

On 14 December the Japanese, to test any possible reaction from the British Army, occupied Victoria Point, at the southern tip of the Tennasserim strip. None was forthcoming. Even so the Japanese made no further violatory move into Burma until the third week in January. Rather they concentrated on the deployment of their troops, the reinforcement of their Malayan forces and the building up of their air forces in Siam.

Twice during the Christmas of 1941 Japanese Siam-based aircraft raided Rangoon, causing considerable havoc and a panic exodus of over 100,000 people. This 'test' must have assured them that the Burmese people were not disciplined in or likely to appreciate the methods of modern war and would undoubtedly prove a serious embarrassment to the British.

The speed and ease with which their advance down the Malayan Peninsula was progressing and the sinking of the *Prince of Wales* and the *Repulse* off the Malayan coast must have convinced the Japanese that an immediate incursion into Burma was worth attempting even though their initial success might be limited. If they could establish themselves inside Burma, even before more troops were released from Malaya and their shipping had access to the Indian Ocean, the effect on Burmese morale would be considerable. Moreover, it would have the more far-reaching effect of splitting British attention, and any spare troops they possessed, between Singapore and Rangoon.

There remained the two incalculables; the British Army and the Allied air forces. Already the Japanese had met the Burma-based air forces in combat during those Christmas raids, and though it must have been apparent to them that the Allies could not put a great many planes in the air, the striking power of those planes could not be denied. The Japanese had lost over half their Rangoon bombing force of eighty aircraft.

At the time of the opening of the Far Eastern war the British land forces in Burma consisted of two under-strength divisions, the 17th Indian under Maj.-Gen. J. G. Smyth, V.C., and the 1st Burma Division under Maj.-Gen. Bruce Scott. These two divisions totalled some 25,000 combat troops, although it is well known that at the most only a third to half of such a formation are actual fighting troops. The rest are supply and maintenance men. Also in Burma were some 10,000 line-of-communication troops, making a total force of 35,000. The British battalions in these formations included the Royal Inniskilling Fusiliers, Gloucesters, Cameronians, the K.O.Y.L.I., and West Yorks, all of which were regular and had been abroad a long time on their foreign tour. The remainder were Indians, Gurkhas, and local levies.

These troops were neither trained nor equipped for such tactics or methods as the Japanese employed. They had led for the most part the normal peacetime routine of not working

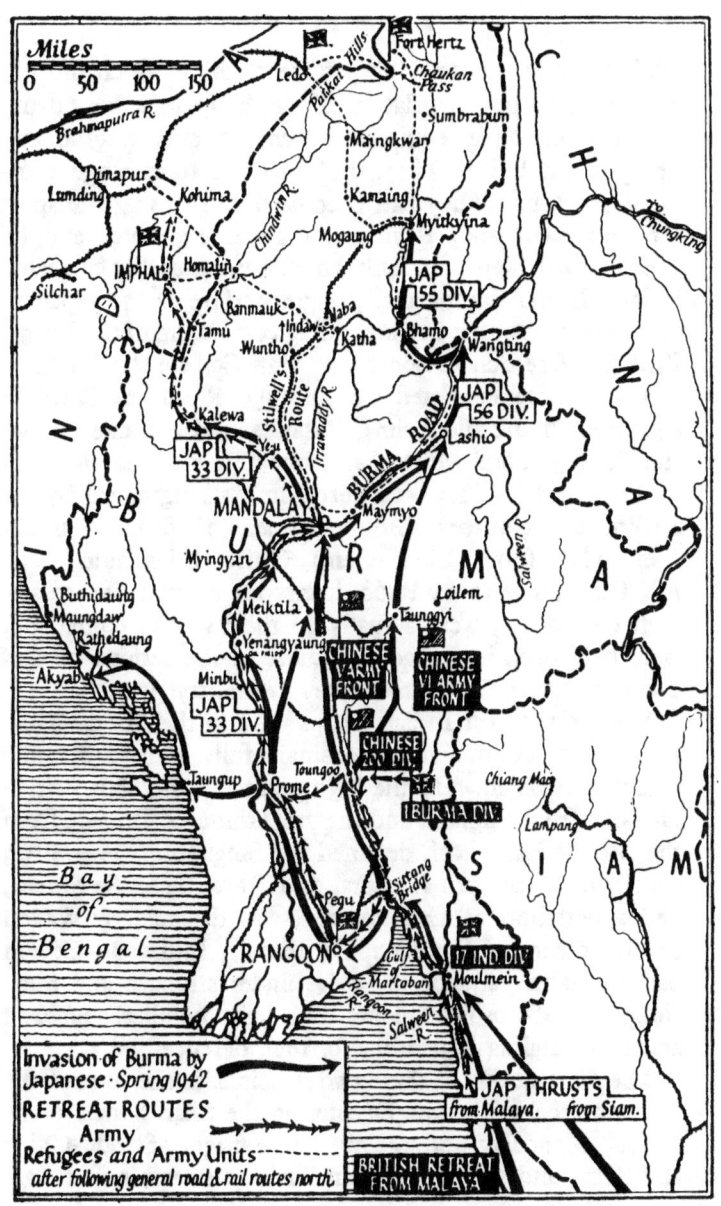

INVASION OF BURMA BY JAPANESE—SPRING 1942

while the sun was up. They wore clothing which did not permit of proper ventilation of the body in a hot, damp climate, and their equipment was too cumbersome and heavy for mobility. There was a lack of short-range automatic weapons. They had become used to using transport for movement and, relying too much on motor supply, became road-bound—a fault which was admirably corrected in later Burma campaigns. Jungle warfare as the Japanese fought it was neither in the training curriculum of the Burma Bush Warfare School nor in any Staff College text-book.

The air forces consisted of a handful of R.A.F. and R.I.A.F. squadrons flying Blenheims, Lysanders, Hurricanes, Brewster Buffaloes, and Mohawks. None of these squadrons was up to strength. They were fortunately strengthened by the American Volunteer Group—airmen of fortune—under Lieut.-Col. (now Lieut.-Gen.) Claire Chennault. The A.V.G., who were paid 500 dollars for every Japanese aircraft shot down, were actually on their way to China, but were held back in Rangoon because of the serious turn of events in South-East Asia. They flew Kittyhawks.

Most of the best Indian troops were in the Middle East. In India there was not one single fully trained or fully complete division. On the high seas were the 18th British Division from England and the 7th Armoured Brigade from the Middle East, both destined for Singapore. The latter, consisting of the 7th Hussars, 2nd Royal Tank Regiment, and a battalion of Cameronians, was directed by Wavell to the defence of Rangoon. In the air, India and Ceylon had six fighter squadrons, some under strength and most composed of obsolete planes, one light bomber squadron and two Catalina Squadrons for their defence.

The dispositions of these two divisions at the start of the war were the 1st Burma Division in the Shan States to the east of Mandalay and facing the frontiers of Indo-China and Siam, and the 17th Indian Division stretching out east

THE RETREAT FROM BURMA

and south of Moulmein down the Tennasserim strip. They were placed to cover all the possible routes of entry from Siam or Malaya. Contrary to general expectations the Japanese chose the south or 17th Division front.

Employing what soon became the characteristic and commonplace methods of movement by infiltration, the Japanese crossed the Kawkereik Pass from Siam in the third week in January. At the same time they advanced up from Victoria Point towards Mergui.

Fearful lest the Japanese should get behind them and cut their line of retreat and supply, the small British outposts withdrew and, evacuating Mergui and Tavoy, deployed around Moulmein along the more defensible Salween River.

The Japanese, only a couple of regiments strong, crossed the Salween some distance above Moulmein and forced the 17th Division to make a hurried evacuation by ferry on 31 January. Knowing what happened later, during the more successful phase of the Burma war, one cannot help thinking 'If only they (the British) had had air supply'. These retreats, enforced by threats to flank and rear, were unnecessary once air supremacy had been achieved and air supply organized.

The next line of defence to the Salween lay along the Bilin River. General Smyth was told to hold out for a week before falling back on the Sittang. He did so, but his troops were fought to a standstill in what proved to be the largest battle in this phase while, during their withdrawal to the Sittang, they were hammered all the way by the Japanese Air Force.

Though Bilin had been a heavy battle there is no question but that the battle for the Sittang Bridge was the most crucial in the whole of the Burma retreat. On General Smyth's success or failure in delaying the Japanese depended not only the length of immunity of Rangoon but also the arrival of reinforcements and the evacuation of civilians and unnecessary mouths. Should the battle of the Sittang be lost quickly and the bridge captured, Rangoon lay straight in front of the Japanese.

The situation at this time was that the 1st Burma Division was still in the Shan States, Rangoon was garrisoned by one weak British battalion, the 7th Armoured Brigade had not yet arrived from India and the 17th Division was withdrawing on to the Sittang. General Hutton, the Army Commander, was fully occupied with the problem of Rangoon and the future of the campaign in Burma.

Although it never materialized, up to the last moment it was expected that an Australian Corps would arrive to help reinforce South Burma.

On 15 February, during General Smyth's withdrawal on to the Sittang, came the news that Singapore had capitulated. Knowing already the weakness of the Royal Navy in the Indian Ocean—much of it was still engaged in the Java Sea—it was realized that it was merely a matter of time before the Japanese Navy appeared in the Indian Ocean and Rangoon ceased to be effective as an Allied port.

Several things remained to be done before south Burma could safely be evacuated. The 7th Armoured Brigade, nearing Rangoon, had to be disembarked; Rangoon had to be evacuated and prepared for demolition; the 1st Burma Division had to be redeployed in a more useful role since by then it was obvious the Japanese were not going to make an entry into Burma through the Shan States; a new defence line north of Rangoon had to be prepared. All these things depended on how long the 17th Division could hold the Sittang Bridge.

As General Smyth moved his division to positions of defence around Sittang Bridge a telegram arrived from General Hutton to say the Japanese were preparing to drop paratroops on the Rangoon side of the river. To meet such a threat Smyth began to move his division across the bridge.

When a third had crossed a lorry capsized and blocked the roadway for two hours—two very vital hours.

A regiment of Japanese, appearing from the northern flank, attacked the two brigades on the east side of the river in an attempt to reach the bridge. The attack was so weighty that it carried them through to Divisional Headquarters, which were partially overrun before the situation was restored. In Rangoon the Armoured Brigade had begun landing to the jeers of the evacuees who were leaving.

During those two hours General Smyth had to make a decision of terrible importance. With two-thirds of his division on the wrong side of the river and a Japanese division boring its way in between, he had to decide whether or not to blow up the bridge. Even if the Armoured Brigade landed in time it could not affect the battle since there were two small bridges on the Rangoon–Sittang road incapable of taking tanks and no bridging material of sufficient strength was available. It was a case of blowing the bridge and sacrificing two-thirds of his troops or opening the way for Japanese advance on to Rangoon. When one of his brigadiers reported he could not hold the bridge for more than another hour General Smyth gave the order to blow; a decision, he says, which took less than four minutes to make.

Oddly enough the Japanese, frustrated in their attempt to gain the bridge intact, sheered off northwards and crossed the Sittang unmolested. And sixty per cent of the two stranded brigades, comprising 150 officers and 3,000 men with half that number of rifles, managed to cross the river and reach their own lines, although most could not swim and many others were drowned. Guns, mortars, and all heavy kit were abandoned.

Though a breathing space had been gained Wavell, the Commander-in-Chief, realized that the fate of Burma was, by then, a matter of time. Early in March he signalled the Chiefs of Staff in London expressing doubts as to his ability to hold Burma. For Wavell the next task was the defence of India and Ceylon. For General Sir Harold Alexander, hero of Dunkirk, who had taken over command of the army in Burma, were the questions, how long could the Japanese be delayed from reaching the Indian frontier and how best could the Allied forces be extricated? Was there any other possible line of defence in Burma? Any attempt at holding Rangoon with all available troops, weakened by the emasculation of the 17th Division, would be useless since the Japanese would cut across the northern lines of retreat and box the Allies between them and the sea.

Since the end of December 1941 negotiations had been going on between Wavell, the Generalissimo Chiang Kai-shek, and certain American generals with a view to sending Chinese troops into Burma first as part of its defence and, when things became serious for the British, in an attempt to hold at least part of the country. The Generalissimo had a direct interest in Burma as it was his last land life-line with the Allies and was the pipe-line for Lease-Lend supplies from America. From a material viewpoint the loss of Burma was more important to the Chinese than the British, whose chief loss would be 'face' in the East and a colonial possession.

The British view had, at first, been that there was neither enough transport available to move the Chinese armies—the Generalissimo had first offered eleven divisions and then two armies of six divisions—nor enough food or equipment in Burma to feed and maintain them. A Chinese army lives off the land in which it is fighting. Those may have been the outward excuses, but behind them was a political antipathy towards the Chinese. The thought of British and Indian troops being saved by Chinese was not entirely to the British liking. The political capital the Generalissimo could make out of it was enough to rock the foundations of Britain's not too strong position in the East at that time. Therefore, at first, the Chinese offer was declined. When, however, the position became virtually impossible and the invading Japanese force had increased from two regiments to three divisions, the British accepted two Chinese armies, the 5th and 6th.

The Chinese marched into Burma down the Burma road from Yunnan. By the time they had reached central Burma, Alexander had ordered the demolition of Rangoon (7 March) and was preparing a new defence line at Prome and Toungoo with the 17th Division at the former and the 1st Burma Division at the latter united as a corps under Lieut.-Gen. W. J. Slim. These two towns lay on the two roads running northwards from Rangoon to Mandalay. He wanted the Chinese to take up the defence of the Toungoo sector.

The question of command of the Chinese troops was most difficult. The Chinese would not submit to British command because they were suspicious of British ability to oppose the Japanese. Also they were unsympathetic to Western Imperialism. The Chinese were therefore under command of Chiang Kai-shek, who could confer with Wavell, who could give orders to Alexander. But Alexander could not give orders to the Chinese.

There had arrived in China some time previously Lieut.-Gen. Joseph Stilwell as head of the American Military Mission. His object was to facilitate Lease-Lend supplies to China and train the Chinese in the use of American equipment. Having successfully acquired Stilwell as his Chief of Staff, with permission of President Roosevelt, the Generalissimo made him commander of the Chinese armies in Burma. Thus he became the fourth foreigner in history to command Chinese armies in the field. Marco Polo, Ward, an American, and the British General Gordon, preceded him. Stilwell was also made commander of the American China–Burma–India theatre.

Stilwell arrived in Lashio on 14 March ostensibly to take over command of the 5th and 6th Armies. But he soon found that the Chinese generals in the field were as unwilling to take orders from him as from the British. Technically he was permitted to move formations within a radius of 100 miles. Anything further had to be referred to the Generalissimo.

By personally showing himself at the front Stilwell managed to get some sort of order into the Chinese at the same time as working with Alexander who was, again technically, his superior officer. The Chinese 5th Army established its H.Q. at Pyawbwe and extended its forward troops down to Toungoo. Here it fought a ten-day action which permitted the 1st Burma Division to cross over the front and join the 17th Division on the Prome axis. Before it had left, the 1st Burma Division had joined Stilwell in a rather grandiosely termed offensive against Rangoon. The Chinese 6th Army was positioned in the Shan States defending the Salween flank against any attack from Siam.

By this time the R.A.F., reduced to three Hurricanes, 10 Blenheims, and 43 Buffaloes, had retired to Magwe. There, reinforced by two fighter squadrons and one light bomber squadron from India, it had been caught and completely shattered by the Japanese Air Force. What was left of the R.A.F. retired to India. The A.V.G., with about 20 Kittyhawks left, retired north to Loiwing.

The Japanese Army, consisting then of the 33rd, 55th, and 56th Divisions and two tank brigades, cut through the country in a series of encircling moves. One arm passed through Rangoon on to the Prome axis, another kept along the Pegu–Toungoo road, and a third moved into the Shan Hills. Their object was to trap the British and Chinese forces.

It was then decided to make a stand with the British at Allanmyo, north of Prome, and the Chinese at Pyinmana, north of Toungoo. Meantime the Yenangyaung oil-fields would be prepared for demolition. For this purpose the 38th Division of a third Chinese army (the 66th) arriving in Burma was split up and one regiment loaned to the British. The Japanese, however, got behind the British, and the Chinese flank was exposed. This necessitated the premature blowing up of the oil-fields by Mr. W. L. Foster while the Gloucesters held the fields and two brigades of the 1st Burma Division fought their way through Japanese road-blocks.

Alexander had one main task left, to extricate as many of the British and Indian troops as possible. The way lay over the Chindwin at Kalewa, up the Kabaw Valley to Tamu and thence over the Naga Hills to Imphal. He had to get what forces he could to India by the time the monsoon broke. After that it would be impossible.

Stilwell hoped to make a stand in north Burma. He still had the 5th and 6th Armies and the 38th Division of the 66th. But the Japanese army that pierced the Shan Hills met the 55th Division of the 6th Army. This Chinese division, not reckoned as first-class by any means, disintegrated into thin air after impact at Loilem. The Japanese crossed the old Burma road from Mandalay to the China border.

The British H.Q. at Maymyu was evacuated and Mandalay was bombed by the Japanese, who killed 2,000 people and set large parts of the town on fire. At the end of April Royal Marines blew the great Ava Bridge over the Irrawaddy and joined their retreating and dishevelled comrades on the road to Kalewa. The fast-moving Japanese nearly beat the British to Kalewa, while other columns advanced north to Lashio, Bhamo, and Myitkyina, arriving at the latter only a few days before Sir Reginald Dorman Smith left by air for India. For Stilwell and a small and motley band of American, British, Chinese, Burmese and hill people there was only one choice—to trek to India. The way they had to take was more difficult than the British route. It lay through Banmauk and across to the Chindwin at Homalin. The Chinese armies had broken up.

During the later stages of this retreat the more extreme Nationalist Burmese elements, inspired by Japanese success, rose up against the Allies in the form of guerrillas. Moreover, dacoits, for which Burma is notorious, saw in the breakdown of the civil power an opportunity to join in the general looting and burning.

It was not easy to appraise the strength of these disaffected Burmese, who were the forerunners of the Burmese Independence Army. General Slim has since computed their strength at five per cent. Certainly in those days it seemed far greater and caused the retreating Allies embarrassment beyond its true value as a fighting force. Even so the high emotional pitch reached by the retreating soldiers accounted for a great deal of over-statement.

The last episode in this act of the Burma tragedy was played out in the little jungled villages of Tamu in the Kabaw Valley and Shinbwiyang, at the northern apex of the deadly Huwkawng Valley. There the hundreds of thousands of refugees of a dozen different races, including European, collected before attempting the final trek through the Naga or Patkai Hills to India.

The scenes at those two places beggar description. Months later when the first British returned to Tamu they found skeletons sitting, lying, or propped up just as they had been before dying. In Tamu Post Office twenty skeletons were around the counter, and one hung round the broken telephone. It is not difficult to imagine the agony and desolation. Disease, which spread through these camps faster than a forest fire, under-nourishment, and weariness had broken down many of these refugees' will to live any more. The prospect of one last drag over the cold, rain-soaked mountains was more than they could stand. Doctors were sent or parachuted in, but the task was too great. Only the strong survived.

Even so nearly 200,000 refugees crossed from Tamu to

Imphal, some to die from the strain, others to die in hospitals so crowded that the staffs were incapable of handling the patients. In one hospital a week elapsed before a doctor could get round to every patient. Over ninety per cent of the army and civilians who tried to cope with this mass trek suffered from malaria as well.

What were the main reasons for the loss of Burma, and could it have been saved? Here are those reasons.

Early in January, when preparations for Burma's defence were being made, it was taken out of India Command and put under the new South-West Pacific theatre of operations known as ABDA (American, British, Dutch, Australian) under the Supreme Command of General Sir Archibald Wavell. Wavell protested about this but was overruled.

This ABDA theatre, stretching from Port Darwin to the borders of India, was so large and the troops, navy, and air forces so thin on the ground, on the sea, and in the air, that no efficient or powerful defence force could be built up in any one place nor could a striking force, especially a Naval striking force, be held ready to move to any trouble spot. It would be too late. Wavell's own headquarters in Java were, for instance, 2,000 miles from Army H.Q. in Burma.

Malaya, Singapore, and Java were obviously the key points in ABDA. When Wavell arrived and ABDA was formed Burma was quiet and remained so until the end of January, by which time Wavell had decided his plan of defence and committed his available forces.

Wavell has admitted that he misappreciated the full Japanese strength and intentions and the move of the Japanese into the Tennasserim strip in late January, though distracting, appeared the least serious of the five Japanese thrusts, the most important of which was down Malaya towards Singapore.

Burma, therefore, was almost a 'forgotten front' from the start of the war. It was out on a limb and not on the top priority list for reinforcements in men and materials though, early in February, Wavell did divert the 7th Armoured Brigade, destined for Singapore and then Java, to Rangoon. This brigade certainly delayed the end though it was incapable by itself of doing more.

There was, of course, a lack of aircraft of all types, bombers, fighters, and supply, but even with limited bomber resources no attempt was made to bomb offensively into Siam where the Japanese had their bases. The Navy had commitments ranging from the northern shores of Australia to Ceylon and with the loss of Singapore it forfeited, temporarily, control of the Bengal Ocean.

The peacetime training of the Army was inadequate and the ideas at the Burma Bush Warfare School were obviously out of date, for there was no proper appreciation of the methods and tactics of the Japanese, which were simple enough in technique once they had been studied. This implies no disparagement of individual units and troops for, under most depressing circumstances, they fought extremely well. But they were really a garrison force and not trained jungle warriors. They just did not know what to expect.

Though requested, the Australian Government refused to permit an Australian Corps to help in the defence of southern Burma, on which the whole defence of the country hinged. Fearful of invasion of their own vast country, the Australian Government were, at the time, probably right. But even an Australian division might have made a difference for, with such resources, General Smyth has reckoned he could have held on to Bilin and Sittang for longer.

The Japanese might have been delayed or unbalanced in their move into Burma had 'Operation Matador', a limited offensive by the Malaya Army from north Malaya into Siam, been put into operation. But for a number of reasons, including the time taken to make decisions, it was not.

Then there was the question of the Chinese divisions offered by the Generalissimo. Admittedly the fighting qualities of Chinese divisions were variable and most of their troops were raw, untrained, and ill-equipped, but their very numbers might have held the Japanese and made available one of the most valuable assets in war—time. The snag would have been command for, as it turned out, liaison between Wavell, Alexander, and Stilwell over the Chinese when they came into Burma was always confused and sometimes as chaotic as the breakdown of the civil power.

Lastly, it was decided to defend and delay everywhere, from Timor to Tennasserim. In itself, such a policy was demoralizing enough, and, in the end, could only lead to the destruction or disintegration of each separate group. The policy of trying everywhere and succeeding nowhere, whether in Dutch or British Imperial territory, may be most honourable and even far-sighted from an Imperial viewpoint but it is obviously not very good warfare. It only proves that Imperial powers cannot defend a scattered empire unless they maintain a very large and uneconomical standing army, and that in future the indigenous peoples themselves must be made responsible for their own defence. It is also the reason, the chief reason, why Burma could not have been saved and why there was no adequate defence.

4
CEYLON'S ESCAPE

The War at Sea—Why the Japanese Fleet Retired—Preparations for the Defence of India—Political Upheaval in India—Plans for Limited Offence

SIMULTANEOUSLY with the last phase of the British and Chinese retreat from Burma in April 1942, the Japanese battle fleet sailed on Ceylon.

It was an obvious move, for the Japanese fleet was, by then, momentarily freed from embarrassments and commitments in the Java Sea, and the westerly exploitation of success had several important advantages.

The acquisition of Ceylon, a jungled, mountainous island, populated by a lazy, quick-tempered race who had suffered hundreds of years of foreign conquest and rule—the Portuguese and Dutch preceded the British—and whose aspirations of independence and home rule were no less strong than those of the Burmese, would place Japan in a very strong position at the cross-roads of the world at war.

Ceylon completed the strategic naval triangle covering the Indian Ocean, with Rangoon as the apex and Singapore and Ceylon as the base points. Moreover, its two harbours at Trincomalee and Colombo provided shelter for a large fleet.

But more important still was the fact that the capture of Ceylon would open the way for Japanese warships to sail into the Arabian Sea as far as Aden and Madagascar and thus blockade India's one remaining port, Bombay. Calcutta was already wellnigh unusable. Chittagong was already blocked.

Lastly, the presence of Japanese troops in Ceylon, only a very short distance from the exposed and sparsely populated mass of southern India would impose an overstrain on India's ability to defend itself.

Although recognizing the threat, Britain and India could do very little about it because of the naval disasters in the Java Sea, the general lack of air protection, and the troop commitments to other theatres of war.

Britain's fleet in Eastern waters at that time had just about reached its nadir. Besides the sinking of the *Prince of Wales* and *Repulse* off the Malayan coast in December 1941 and the closing of Singapore dockyard on 30 January 1942, there were severe losses in the Java Sea. Between 18 January and 4 March, 40 Allied warships were lost, 13 of them British, including *Exeter*, *Electra*, *Encounter*, and *Jupiter*, and one Australian cruiser, *Perth*. The rest were Dutch and American. The dramatic battles on 27 and 28 February, known as the Java Sea battle, accounted for five Allied cruisers including the U.S.S. *Houston* and H.M.A.S. *Perth* (in the Sunda Straits), H.M.S. *Exeter*, and the Dutch cruisers *De Witte* and *Java*, and destroyers.

Admiral Sir James Somerville, commander of the British fleet in the East had very little to match the modern ships and aircraft carriers that sailed across the Indian Ocean to threaten Ceylon. The *Warspite* was his flagship, and the four out-of-date 'R' class battleships (*Royal Sovereign, Renown, Resolution, Revenge*) comprised his heaviest units. They were supported by two cruisers, the *Dorsetshire* and *Cornwall*, of the County class, which have proved almost ineffectual in battle owing to their design, and two aircraft carriers carrying obsolete aircraft. Sir James nicknamed his fleet 'My Old Ladies'.

At the time the forces available for the defence of the whole of India and Ceylon, apart from those allotted to the defence of the N.W. Frontier and internal security, were one British and six Indian divisions. None of these divisions was up to strength. Against Wavell's wishes, the Chiefs of

Staff allotted one brigade of the British 70th Division in India, two Indian brigades, and two Australian brigades to the defence of Ceylon. An East African brigade was *en route*. In the air Ceylon was defended by 50 Hurricanes, delivered in March and formed into three squadrons, one light bomber squadron of Blenheims, and two squadrons of Catalinas comprising 222 Group of the R.A.F.

On Easter Sunday 1942 the Catalinas were performing their normal patrol duties which had become known as the 'bread run'. Two failed to return on time and a third, piloted by Flight-Lieut. Bradshaw and Flying-Officer Charles Gardner, took off.

Flying-Officer Gardner was in the pilot's seat when the Japanese fleet was sighted 400 miles south-east of Ceylon. Having exposed himself for only a few seconds, Gardner came down to 'deck height' and put into operation tactics which, though invented on the spur of the moment, later became standard throughout Coastal Command. He flew just over the curve of the horizon on the course he anticipated the Japanese would take. Once every hour he rose to 150 feet to check on the fleet's position. In doing this he was able to plot and wireless its course back to base. At the same time his personal exposure was so brief that he calculated it would show no more than a tiny transient smudge on any ship's radar.

For hours he followed the Japanese fleet, although he was never able to ascertain its composition exactly. But he did report five battleships and a number of aircraft carriers.

Japanese intentions were to do a 'Pearl Harbour' on the British fleet in Trincomalee and Colombo. Fortunately, though the Japanese did not know it, Admiral Somerville had already put to sea despite the fact that his cruisers the *Dorsetshire* and *Cornwall* and the aircraft carrier *Hermes* had had to remain behind to complete refitting and refuelling. They were given orders to follow out as soon as ready.

Forewarned, the R.A.F. were ready when the Japanese arrived over Ceylon's two almost empty harbours and not only defeated the raiders but replied by sending a force of Blenheims to deliver an heroic but suicidal attack on the Japanese fleet. Since he was outnumbered, Admiral Somerville carefully avoided direct action with the Japanese fleet, and, though he escaped, his two cruisers and the *Hermes* were sunk by aircraft while sailing to join him.

By some freak of fortune the Japanese fleet sheered off and sailed northwards up the coast of India, where it fell upon an unprotected merchant convoy lying off Madras and Vizagapatam and sank 100,000 tons of shipping. This massacre was watched by a Wapiti aircraft whose wireless set had broken down. Ironically that convoy had been ordered out of Madras harbour for fear of air raids.

Why did the Japanese turn away? By doing so they failed to test or appraise the strength of the British fleet which, from then onwards, remained a mystery to them, never to be solved. They also lost control of the southern parts of the Indian Ocean and, oddly enough, made no future attempt to regain it.

No doubt the Japanese were surprised to find the British fleet had sailed. But it is more likely that their loss of 30 planes to the R.A.F. convinced them that the British had greater strength in Ceylon than actually existed.

But, perhaps, there was a deeper reason, founded on the surprising fact of an antagonistic relationship between the Japanese Army and Navy. Even now it is rather astonishing to think over the Japanese successes knowing that there existed a contempt and disdain between the Army and Navy, one for another, unequalled anywhere. Officers of the two services would neither speak nor mix, let alone co-operate, unless ordered to do so from the highest levels. Even their personal rancour came into it. And in 1942 General Tojo, a soldier, was military dictator of Japan.

Thus it is possible the Army, its hands full with conquests in South-East Asia, was not immediately prepared to back the Navy in any new ventures, considering them nothing more than glamour-gathering escapades. And the Navy, not burdened with the necessity of landing troops in Ceylon, preferred to sink merchant ships rather than come to any trial of strength with that unknown quantity, the British fleet. Thus they committed a grave error which, as much as anything else, helped to stem the Japanese onslaught into South-East Asia and give the Allies the breathing space a boxer takes when he stays down for the count of eight.

Within a month of this the Japanese had halted in Burma. The remnants of the British force, some 12,000 of the original 25,000 combat troops, had reached Imphal in Assam over the tea-planters' road from Tamu, just as the monsoon rains broke in May. Stilwell and his little band arrived about the same time as did some 6,000 troops of the Chinese 38th Division. Other Chinese, mostly of the 22nd Division of the 5th Army, reached Ledo in north Assam. Others had returned to China. For the next five months the tracks across the mountain mass of the Indo-Burma frontier were impassable.

For their part the Japanese had run the limit. They were exhausted by their own speed and the stretching of their supply lines. Although they could live off Burma for food and had acquired considerable quantities of British and American equipment, including transport, their legs and planning had given out. They settled down to digest their latest and last conquest in South-East Asia.

Though the Japanese outwardly controlled the whole of Burma they soon found the guerrilla activities of some of the hill tribes a source of considerable worry. These tribesmen's hatred of the new invader was only equalled by their loyalty to the British.

Far up in the north-east corner of Burma, on a plateau

among the mountains, stood the old British frontier outpost, Fort Hertz. There the loyal Kachins rallied to the Union Jack, which still flew since the Japanese had advanced no farther than Myitkyina (pronounced Mitchinar).

To Fort Hertz, Colonel O'Neill Ford, who had spent many years in Burma, had withdrawn with a small group of Kachin levies. There were no land links between the fort and India and the little garrison had to rely solely on air supply.

Colonel Ford's Kachins increased to 700 and a few British officers. More Kachins formed 'Home Guard' units in their own villages. Sixteen British officers, including doctors, were flown or parachuted into the plateau, where rough airstrips were built, capable of landing light planes such as Lysanders.

The Kachins were armed with modern rifles, shot-guns, and flintlocks dating back to 1777, and special ammunition had to be dropped by the R.A.F. until the weather became so bad that nothing—officers, food, or ammunition—could reach them. Then they had to rely on the country.

The Kachins' tactics were to raid, harass, and deceive the Japanese. With their intimate knowledge of the wild country they had such success that the Japanese sent a punitive expedition towards Fort Hertz to subdue the Kachins once and for all. On that occasion they were defeated by a well-conceived deception plan which led the Japanese to believe a large British army, based on the fort, was advancing southwards. That was about the only ray of sunshine in the dark monsoon months of May to November 1942.

As early as April the Chiefs of Staff in London had recognized that the two most likely ways for a Japanese attack on India were by Ceylon and through Assam, the northeast frontier region. They accepted that land forces for the defence of India were deficient by at least an armoured division and four infantry divisions and promised to send out the 2nd and 5th British Divisions.

In defence of north-east India was the Eastern Army under Lieut.-Gen. Sir C. Broad. Its line ran from Bengal along the 800-mile Indo-Burma border, embracing Bengal, the Arakan, and Assam. Its area was larger than the British Isles.

The Eastern Army consisted of three formations. The 70th British Division, less one brigade, the only available reserve for Bengal and Assam, was based at Ranchi. For the immediate defence of Bengal and the Arakan was 15th Corps under Lieut.-Gen. Sir Noel Beresford Pierce. The corps comprised two incompletely trained and equipped divisions, the 14th and 26th Indian.

Lieut.-Gen. N. M. S. Irwin commanded 4th Corps, which was responsible for the defence of Assam. His troops consisted of the remnants of the Burma Army, the 1st Indian Infantry Brigade, and one battalion of the 49th Indian Infantry Brigade.

With this limited force General Irwin had to guard some 500 miles of frontier and cover an area much larger and more mountainous than Wales. It included the 50-square-mile Imphal Plain, the strategically important village of Kohima on the only road leading from Imphal to Dimapur, main railhead for the area, and the great masses of the Chin and Naga hills. His immediate tasks included rebuilding the road from Dimapur to Imphal and creating a new one from Imphal south to Tiddim in the Chin Hills, a distance of 163 miles.

With the exception of those troops who had fought in Burma none had ever seen action and their knowledge of jungle conditions and fighting was virtually negligible. Their learning was to be painful, and many of the troops remained in the combat zone for the next two and a half years.

Resources in the air were just as scanty. Calcutta was

defended by one squadron of eight Mohawks and a light bomber squadron that existed only on paper. There was a squadron of Hurricanes at Akyab and a squadron of Audax aircraft, converted to fighters, at Dinjan in north Assam. There were not enough airfields for the promised reinforcements and construction was begun on the building of 200 new ones.

In India, in the summer and autumn of 1942, the scene was no brighter than on the battlefront. The Commander-in-Chief, General Sir Archibald Wavell, inherited a legacy hardly sufficient to meet his liabilities. It is as well to reflect upon the gigantic task he was given and its attendant difficulties, for that alone may help to dispel the amount of adverse criticism which from time to time had been levelled at India Command.

In peacetime the Indian Army numbered some 200,000 men, only slightly larger than the British. Whereas it takes at the most a year or two to make an American or Britisher into a soldier, it takes at least seven in normal times to produce a sound, efficient sepoy.

Most of India's best troops had been lost in Burma or Malaya or were fighting in the Middle East. Unfortunately those fine divisions such as the 4th, 5th, and 17th Indian had gone into battle at full strength, and few of their senior Viceroy's Commissioned Officers—men with up to 20 years' service—had been left behind to train recruits.

Therefore the vigorous recruiting drive and increased intake, rising to 60,000 men a month, brought with it all the difficulties of housing, equipping, instructing, training, and, by no means least, officering. India is not a place where things can be done as rapidly as in the West although the Americans, by paying exorbitant wages, managed to produce an element of speed and urgency.

The problem of transportation was vital. India relied on two main ports, Bombay and Calcutta, of which one was unusable. There were subsidiary ports at Karachi and Madras but neither could accept the tonnage hoped for. Karachi, moreover, was handed to the Americans as the intake port for Lease-Lend materials.

India's road and rail system was capable of handling a peacetime traffic and, as there was no indigenous skilled labour to expand its internal system, peace traffic had to give way to military. There was a shortage of rolling stock and engines.

Communications complicated the defence of north-east India by their poverty. Assam is cut off from the rest of India by the Brahmaputra river across which there was not, nor is, a bridge. It changes its course annually. The rail system east of the Brahmaputra was single track with limited resources in rolling stock and engines. As there was no all-weather road from India to the Brahmaputra's two ferry stations, all vehicles had to go by rail and be ferried across the river before they became of any value. Even then the road from Gauhati to the body of Assam was second-class. There was a shortage of river steamers as many had previously been sent to Iraq.

On the Bengal side and in the Arakan communications were no better because of the maze of unbridged waterways and the few single-track lines running into the Arakan to Chittagong.

The improvement of the transportation systems was begun early in 1942 but held up by an exceptionally heavy monsoon and a high incidence of malaria among the workers. The improvement of Dimapur (Manipur road) from a wayside halt to a railhead capable of eventually accepting 2,000 tons a day was undertaken. Ledo, in north Assam, had to be made into a new railhead and base. A new ferry was laid out across the Brahmaputra, north of Jorhat. Road, rail, and telegraph systems was generally expanded and improved, slowly at first but faster later when the Americans took a hand. All these works and more got under way during 1942.

Within India were the problems of constant political upheaval and the Japanese fifth column. An intransigent Congress Party not only categorically rejected the Cripps Plan for self-government in India after the war, but initiated a campaign of active resistance against the British. The Congress Party could have found no more suitable moment to sabotage the war effort, and they knew it. Fortunately the great mass of the Indian people remained firmly loyal to the British cause and recruiting went on unabated.

How far the Congress Party was inspired by Japanese fifth column activity is difficult to say. There is no question a fifth column existed and had done so for some time. A fair amount of sabotage, murder, and general hooliganism among the more irresponsible town elements could be ascribed to Japanese influence, but probably Congress was more concerned with getting rid of the British than with welcoming the Japanese.

All these things and, no doubt, many more provided the background to war in India in 1942 and made the burdens of General Wavell, the Viceroy, and the Indian Government no lighter. In fact when measuring the few mentioned against what happened in the next few years it is a tribute to India that these difficulties were overcome and the Japanese were ultimately defeated in Burma.

In the summer of 1942 the military situation had altered little. The 2nd Division British had begun to arrive, although some of its transport had been sunk *en route*. Two brigades of the 5th Division had been diverted to Madagascar, as had the East African Brigade promised for Ceylon. For political reasons the two Australian brigades loaned to Ceylon had withdrawn. When finally the 5th Division did arrive it stayed on a month or two and then, with the 7th Armoured Brigade, left for Iraq.

In India there were command reorganizations. Three armies were formed and called the North-Western, the Southern, and the Eastern. For training purposes there was a Central Command under Lieut.-Gen. H. B. D. Wilcox. Irwin took over the Eastern Army and Sir Beresford Pierce the Southern.

Lieut.-Gen. Scoones and a Corps H.Q. Staff, from Iraq, arrived to take over 4th Corps in Imphal. There the 23rd Indian Division was being formed round the 1st Brigade. Along the rugged frontier a 'phantom' group known as 'V' Force was operating. It consisted of some 2,500 British officers and hill tribesmen. The British were equipped with long-range wireless sets. They were not a fighting force but track watchers and intelligence groups. They were the 'eyes of the army', as the 'Phantoms' were in Europe.

The 2nd Division, commanded by Maj.-Gen. J. M. L. Grover, had suffered severely during the retreat from France and was 'regular' only in name. It was the only completely equipped force in India. It had left Britain in April, with the blessings of the King and Mr. Winston Churchill, with a full first and second line complement of men and vehicles.

The division was maintained as an imperial force and did not come directly under India Command. Its roles were threefold and necessitated its being based near Bombay. First, it was held in readiness to go to the Western Desert; second an overland reconnaissance was carried out from India to Iraq in case of a German breakthrough in the Caucasus; and third, it was to be used in the Burma frontier if the Japanese invaded Assam.

Many lessons had already been learned about jungle warfare and the new masters of it, the Japanese. The question was how to put these lessons into practice? Those troops in the Arakan and around Imphal had a chance of gaining experience first hand through patrolling and skirmishing with the Japanese.

In the training-ground of India, jungle warfare teams were sent out among divisions and corps to spread the new gospel of encirclement, envelopment, and filleting, as the various moves and counter-moves were named.

The leaders of this new movement were two young officers of the Argyll and Sutherland Highlanders, Lieut-Col. Angus Rose and Major David Wilson, who had been forcibly removed from Singapore where their battalion earned immortal fame.

Unfortunately they were not in a position to envisage the change in the whole theory of jungle warfare produced by air supply, for that was a dream not yet realized. They concentrated in explaining the methods the Japanese had adopted against the army in Malaya. In the explanation was the answer, for when reduced to its lowest common denominator jungle warfare in theory was little more than being able to disencircle oneself. In practice, however, jungle acclimatization, psychology, and lore came into it, and the jungle fighter had to be a man strong and fit enough to march for miles in any climate and carry his all, including food and bedding.

In the many places in which jungle exists in India, Rose and Wilson took their student formations, showed them how to 'fillet' their way down a single road with a road-block in front and behind. They gave them confidence by demonstrating how easy it was for them to encircle and envelop the Japanese just as the Japanese had done to the British, and showed that, in fact, there was nothing mysterious or superhuman about it. It was plain rule of thumb providing the battle drill was known by all ranks. They made them live in the jungle, even during the monsoon, and fend for themselves. No tents and beds were allowed. Officers and men had to build their own cover, dig their own foxholes, cook their own food, and learn the art of making themselves as comfortable as possible. To the Gurkha all this came easily; to the town-bred Britisher the road through the jungle was rough.

Throughout the rain, the heat, and the humidity, troops marched without sun helmets or spine pads. To counteract heat stroke they took salt. They aimed at 25 miles in eight hours and 50 miles in twenty-four, often marching in a temperature of over 100 and a humidity of over 90. There was no softness in India in 1942, no sleeping while the sun was up.

There was only one thing that no one could teach them. Despite the realistic battle school produced by the 2nd Division, where men were fired at and went through all the noisy effects of battle, no one could teach them what it was really like to meet the Japanese in battle on the frontiers of India and Burma.

Early in June Wavell had conceived a plan for the partial reconquest of Burma by land, having discarded the idea of a seaborne expedition against lower Burma, at Moulmein, as being unfeasible because of a shortage of landing-craft and trained men, and the hazards of geography and climate.

His plan envisaged a series of columns operating against the Chindwin and two advances from Ledo and Fort Hertz, where the Kachin levies were based. His ultimate objective was the line Myitkyina–Katha–Kalewa, with a push towards the central Burma plain if it was successful. This, and other plans, were scotched by the commanders in the field, who maintained they would not be ready before 1943. The training of their troops, or lack of it, and the poverty of communications were, they said, the strangling factors.

In September the Chinese who had reached India from Burma were lodged at Ramgarh, which was transformed into a large training centre for Chinese troops to be run by the Americans. The Chinese were to be fed and paid by the British, trained and, for the most part, equipped by the Americans. Stilwell was responsible. He too had a plan for the reconquest of Burma, a plan endorsed and supported by the Generalissimo, who had agreed to increase the Ramgarh Chinese to a corps strength of 30,000. Stilwell's plan was the outcome of the directives issued by the Combined Chiefs of Staff at the Cairo Conference that all possible help must be given to China. Interpreted in India, this meant that a way must be found for running supplies to China, preferably overland.

Stilwell proposed that the British-Indian forces on the central front should attack across the Chindwin while he, with his Chinese corps, would drive down north Burma along the route that was later built into the Ledo road. The The Generalissimo had added that a large Chinese force would advance into Burma from Yunnan and suggested that the British should make a seaborne landing in south Burma.

General Irwin had already convinced Wavell that it was not possible to make any major advance into Burma before March 1943. Though agreeing substantially with Stilwell's plan, Wavell claimed the timing could not be fixed. This led to a series of violent criticisms of the British and India Command by the Americans who maintained that the British were making too many difficulties and were trying to avoid fighting.

To assist Stilwell in his drive through north Burma—by the end of the year the Americans had been given the task of building the Ledo road to China—Wavell had permitted Brigadier Orde Wingate to train a small Long-range Penetration Group, consisting of about a brigade of British troops, for a heavy raid into north-central Burma. This group was the first Chindit expedition. At the same time Wavell had initiated an advance into the Arakan with the object of capturing Akyab. Thus, by the end of 1942, there were plans for offence though, from the British side, limited ones. They were too limited to satisfy Stilwell.

5
ARAKAN DEBACLE

Advance down Mayu Peninsula—Defeat at Donbaik—The Retreat from the Arakan—A Brigadier's Reasons—The Ledo Road Project —Expansion of Air Forces

FOR the winter of 1942–3 Wavell instructed his commanders to develop and improve communications within Assam-Bengal and, if possible, bring the Japanese to battle in order to use up their land and air strength. The Japanese still had only four divisions in Burma.

Although his future intentions were to capture Akyab Island, strengthen the Allies' position in the Chin Hills, and occupy the Chindwin line from Kalewa to Sittaung, he was undecided whether to make his major advance in lower or upper Burma. Therefore he desired administrative preparations for both.

Wavell hoped to make a seaborne landing on Akyab Island early in December but, because of a shortage of landing-craft and trained amphibious troops, was unable to carry it out. For similar reasons he was unable to accept as an immediate course Stilwell's plan for a drive into north Burma, supported from Yunnan by the Generalissimo's Chinese divisions, and a British-Indian seaborne landing in south Burma.

Wavell recognized the need for the reopening of a land route to China. Indeed this had been one of the directives of the Chiefs of Staff, but he saw too many administrative difficulties in the way of its immediate application. He did, however, agree with Stilwell that preparations should continue for an advance in north Burma from Ledo and Yunnan and into central Burma from Imphal. By that time the Americans had undertaken the construction of the Ledo road and the supplying China with Lease-Lend materials via the air route over the Himalayan 'Hump'.

Wavell's immediate plan was still to concentrate on Akyab and he was forced to choose the alternative of an advance down the Mayu peninsula and a final hop over the short stretch of sea to the island. Meanwhile, Stilwell trained his two Chinese divisions at Ramgarh and inaugurated a similar system of training at Kunming in Yunnan for a very much larger number of Chinese divisions. Wingate was, at the same time, training his Chindit group which would synchronize its operations with a Stilwell drive into north Burma (aimed at Myitkyina) and a 4th Corps push across the Chindwin. The Chindits would operate inside Burma.

There is no doubt that American pressure had an effect on future strategy in the Burma war. To the Americans priority one was supplies to China; flown, lorried by road, or both. Therefore they wanted plans for offence to be designed round north Burma. There is also no doubt that the British were sceptical of the possibilities of an advance in north Burma or of ever compensating the loss of the Burma road by building a new one. American pressure at the Chiefs-of-Staff table won and, although alternative plans for Burma's reconquest were produced from time to time, none was ever accepted.

For whatever plans were to be put into operation the air took on considerable importance. The air defence of eastern India and Assam and the building up of the air run to China were the major tasks. As has already been said, there were in India early in the war only about 40 airfields. The requirements were estimated at 200. By the autumn of 1942 150 of these were complete, a great many of them being in Bengal and Assam.

The expansion of the air forces was hardly less rapid. In the operational zone were the R.A.F. 224 and 221 Groups, the latter being formed around those squadrons which had got out of Burma and Malaya. The 10th U.S.A.A.F. was also gradually increasing in size. By the end of the year there were some 30 operational squadrons, another 20 forming, and two transport squadrons. The Indian Air Force was being increased to 10 squadrons.

Although the Japanese air forces in Burma and Siam were well placed to menace Calcutta and other important communication centres in Bengal, they concentrated on the chain of airfields which were being built in the Arakan and the Brahmaputra Valley. Only once did they raid Calcutta, during Christmas 1942, when they caused a panic exodus of 100,000 Indians but did very little damage.

On the Burma front there were still only two divisions, the 17th and 23rd, with 4th Corps in Imphal and one, the 14th, in the Arakan, though reserve divisions and brigades were being built up behind. By the beginning of the New Year the Japanese force in Burma was being increased to six divisions, one of which was on the way to augment the division already in the Arakan.

The plan for the recapture of Akyab was completed in November. It called for an advance down the Mayu peninsula to its limit to Foul Point by the 14th Division (Maj.-Gen. W. L. Lloyd) which consisted of the 46th, 55th, 88th, and 123rd Indian Infantry Brigades. The 6th Brigade of the 2nd British Division, partly trained in combined operations, would then land off Akyab which was known to have only a small Japanese garrison.

The Mayu peninsula is a long and desolate stretch of land, much crenellated by creeks and waterways, in the southern Arakan. It is split by the 1,500-foot Mayu range of hills which run down it like a spine.

The Japanese outposts retired as the 14th Division moved

down the peninsula until they reached Donbaik, ten miles from Foul Point. There the British-Indian forces met for the first time a well-planned foxhole and bunker system of defence which the Japanese had had plenty of time to prepare.

The cost of the many subsequent and unsuccessful frontal attacks made on this system was counted not only in lives but morale as well. Still conscious of the 'superhuman' qualities of the Japanese and lacking combat experience, the British-Indian troops of the 14th Division suffered from nervous strain, which was accentuated by such Japanese jitter tactics as rattling tins at night, imitating hyena noises or the shouting of phrases like, 'Come out and fight, Tommy!' When they saw tanks, sent to assist them, bogged in mud or shot up at short range by well-concealed anti-tank guns, it is not surprising they faltered.

General Irwin, commanding the Eastern Army, did not call off the operation but reinforced the 14th Division with the 4th, 23rd, and 36th Indian Brigades. They fared no better against numerically inferior but militarily superior Japanese troops. Finally Irwin committed the 6th British and 71st Indian Brigades. The British brigade consisted of the Royal Scots, the Royal Welch Fusiliers, the Royal Berkshires, and Durham Light Infantry.

To give some indication of the strange things that happened in the Burma war, the 6th Brigade reported after their first night in the line that a neighbouring unit (they were on the retiring 14th Division's flank) had fired off 20,000 rounds during the night at shadows—and had collected all the empty cartridge cases. Later when an officer from the brigade went across to the unit on a liaison visit he got through unchallenged. He asked the Indian sentry why he was not challenged. Nodding his head sideways, the sentry replied, 'Sahib, when all ammunition finished we go to sleep'.

The 6th Brigade carried on where the 14th Division and other brigades had left off without any more success but with some 500 battle casualties. If one episode stood out more than any other in that grim and bloody battle it was the Royal Welch Fusiliers' attacks on two Japanese bunkers known as 'Sugar 4' and 'Sugar 5'. These two bunkers, resembling lumps of sugar on a plate empty except for a few crumbs, were, apparently, impregnable. For hundreds of yards around them the country was barren, blasted by artillery fire. Though shells landed directly on the bunkers, they made no impression. Several times the Welshmen charged the 'Sugars', immolating themselves at the very entrances. The bodies of dead and wounded lay strewn around but no one could get near to carry them away. It is not surprising that the hardest among them broke down, for if ever there was a modern Charge of the Light Brigade in miniature it was the attack on the Sugars.

It then became obvious that the operation would have to be called off for want of better trained men, more air support, and different methods. But as the withdrawal of the 14th Division, covered by the 6th Brigade, continued the Japanese counter-moved. A Japanese regiment under Colonel Tanabashi, a soldier who gained more notoriety later in the Burma campaign, had almost completed its outflanking movement before it was spotted. Moving down the Kaladan Valley to the north-east, it threatened to split the British force in two.

Tanabashi's intention was to cut off and annihilate the 14th Division. On a surprise move he routed the British flank guards and advanced on the village of Rathedaung. If the 2/1 Punjabis had not held six Japanese attacks near the village and then successfully counter-attacked with the bayonet, the 55th Brigade would have been trapped. As it was, the 47th Brigade was forced to escape another trap by splitting up into small groups. The 6th Brigade, which was trying to cover the retreat, did not escape Tanabashi's claws, for a raid overran their headquarters and Brigadier Cavendish and several other officers were captured and murdered. Thus one Japanese regiment precipitated what was tantamount to the rout of nearly one and a half British-Indian divisions.

The 14th Division was replaced by the 26th Indian Division under Maj.-Gen. C. E. N. Lomax, and became a training unit in India. The 6th Brigade, which had been out East less than a year, suffered nearly 2,000 malaria casualties as well as 500 in battle. They returned to the 2nd Division, which was jungle training near Bombay.

Although a heavy censorship allowed little of what had happened to reach the public, especially the Indian public, there was much criticism of the higher conduct of the whole operation from the senior officers taking part. General Wavell took the weight of the blame when he said, 'I set a small part of the army a task beyond their training and capacity'.

One brigadier who had begun the operation commanding a battalion made the following report:

1. His brigade had been ordered to make seven frontal attacks at Donbaik when one, in sufficient strength, might have succeeded.
2. The Higher Command employed stereotyped and open warfare methods.
3. While the Japanese 33rd Division were famed veterans, the British-Indian troops were, for the most part, tired, insufficiently trained and inexperienced.
4. There was a general lack of knowledge and appreciation of Japanese characteristics and methods on the part of all Commands and their staffs.
5. The Indian troops were shaky, untrained, and incapable of offensive patrolling.

6. There was too high a standard of comfort in officers' messes.
7. Commands and staffs had no knowledge of, or made any attempt to discover, the character of the country over which the campaign was fought. They had planned the operation as if it was a normal training exercise.
8. Units were kept too long in contact and were reinforced, while still in contact, with poor quality troops.
9. There was a general lack of either ground-air or artillery-infantry co-operation.

Although this brigadier had good reason for a certain amount of bitterness—he had lost so many of his best officers and men—there was undoubtedly a great deal of truth in his criticisms. New and less stereotyped methods were needed as much as more experienced troops.

No further attempt at recapturing Akyab was made for two years, but when it did occur the methods employed were the right ones. Instead of persisting in frontal attacks from the Mayu peninsula, the main advance was assisted by a series of small seaborne raids hitting at the Japanese southern flank and rear while a West African division advanced down the Kaladan Valley on their north-eastern flank just as Tanabashi had cut down on the 14th Division. Under such pressure the Japanese had no choice but to retire.

The Ledo road was timed to begin as the 14th Division advanced down the Mayu peninsula. Here again there was disappointment, for the Generalissimo refused to permit the Chinese 38th Division, trained by Stilwell and ready at Ledo, to take part in the advance. Even so, on Christmas Day 1942 the lead bulldozer and three American engineer battalions cut the first trace at Milestone Zero just outside Ledo. They aimed at reaching Shinbwiyang, 103 miles away at the head of the Huwkawng Valley, in a year.

For this first part of their journey it was unlikely that they would receive much, if any, interference from the Japanese although the enemy knew what was happening. It was said the Japanese, who had built some sort of road through the Huwkawng Valley, claimed they would use the Ledo road, when the Americans had built it, to invade India.

There were, however, two main screens out in north Burma which could assist in drawing off the Japanese. The first was the British Kachin Levy Group and the other a similar organization under the Americans, the Kachin Rangers. Wingate's Chindits, who moved into Burma in March, were also designed to create as much diversion as possible.

The Ledo road was an ambitious project, so much so that it is reasonable to suggest that only the Americans were capable of accomplishing it. It aimed at cutting a highway from Ledo, railway terminal in north Assam for the Sadiya oil-fields, through the Patkai Hills in north Burma, down the Huwkawng Valley to Myitkyina, across the Irrawaddy to Bhamo, where it would join up with the old British road from Bhamo to Namkam. It would then go on to the little village of Mong Yu where it would meet the old Burma road. From Ledo to Myitkyina was 263 miles; Bhamo another 100 miles. The overall distance to the Chinese border was 478 miles. The eventual destination of the convoys, starting from Ledo, was Chungking, nearly 2,000 miles away.

Many times such an idea had been scotched for economic as well as geo-political reasons. As far back as 1860 the Indian Government had considered, but discarded, the idea of a road linking India and China across Burma. The cost would be vast, the income doubtful, and the possibility of large-scale immigration from China to north Burma and even India was something the Indian Government did not desire.

For centuries the three countries had been linked by

caravan and smugglers' trails—at least five of them known and used during the war—but from a military and commercial standpoint they were useless. Even the old Burma road, completed in 1939 after years of labour by the British and Chinese, was of suspect value since the average monthly tonnage carried over it rarely exceeded 12,000—a figure comparing unfavourably with the load later flown over the 'hump' by the Americans.

It was therefore with some timidity that the British considered building a new road to China. But General Wavell, undoubtedly inspired by the Combined Chiefs of Staff in London and Washington and the urgent needs of China, ordered survey treks to be made by British and American engineers in the early summer of 1942.

The projected British route ran from Ledo across to Fort Hertz and thence into northern Yunnan. The Americans chose a route that ran southwards through the Huwkawng and Mogaung Valleys to Myitkyina. The British survey cut through the range of mountains to the east of Fort Hertz, which formed the watersheds of the Salween and Mekong rivers. These would have to be bridged. It was considered a most difficult way but not impossible. The British verdict on the American route was that it was impossible because of the geography, climate, and disease which would be met along the Ledo–Myitkyina trace.

Nevertheless, the building of the road was assigned to the Americans and their proposed trace accepted. Besides possessing the necessary manpower, materials, and engineering experience on a large scale, America had a political and military interest in China greater than Britain. Stilwell was made responsible for the road. Brig.-Gen. Raymond Wheeler, Chief of C.B.I. supply services, drew up the plans.

The country through which the road was to be cut was amongst the most formidable and seemingly inviolate in Asia. The hazards were not only geographical and climatic,

ARAKAN DEBACLE

but included malaria, blackwater fever, dysentery, and scrub typhus. Stilwell called that corner of north Burma the 'rat hole', and throughout the length and breadth of that country no worse terrain was found. That the Americans finally overcame those handicaps added greatly to the credit of the men who laboured and those who drove them on. The building of the road was a typical American effort—full-blooded, urgent, courageous, and without consideration of cost.

As the American engineering battalions—they were mostly negroes with a cadre of white operatives—pushed forward, so the stream of men and materials behind them increased until it became a river. From far-away airfields in America, by ship to Karachi and Bombay, and across India by train, came more bulldozers, graders, sifters, caterpillars, medical units, hospital units, supply units, and transport. From India and the hills thousands of coolie labourers were enrolled. From Ledo the road rose steadily, sharply, suddenly, twisting this way and that past Hellgate, into the clouds and out again, through the 3,400-foot Pangsau Pass, over Thursday river (so named by the negroes) and the Patkai Hills.

Squads of men fought disease by oiling, disinfecting, and spraying the countryside, but even so the sickness rate was high.

By the end of March 1943 the road had reached Milestone 42. Then came the monsoon, a factor controlling the progress of the road even more than the threat of a Japanese advance northwards to meet the new invader.

Rains up to fifteen inches a day, flash floods, earthslides, fallen trees, cloudbursts and walls of soaked earth all added their weight in the battle for the road. Four times behemoth blocks of earth, nearly five and a half million cubic feet in size, blocked the path of the bulldozers. Mules and vehicles became bogged. Men, wet all the time, slept in waterlogged tents or jungle hammocks. The soggy jungles became infested with long purplish leeches. Bulldozers were lost over steep banks which collapsed or became stalled in seemingly bottomless pits of mud. Often the Americans were thrown back and even lost miles of their road but, working round the clock by paraffin flares, they held nature in check. They could do no more. Progress came to a standstill.

October 1943 found the road no farther than Milestone 42 when Brigadier General Pick, a famous American engineer, arrived. Seventy-five per cent of the men working were in hospital with malaria. General Pick said, 'The Ledo road is going to be built. Mud, rain, and malaria be damned.'

General Stilwell asked to see Pick's charts and received the answer that there were none. He said that he wanted at least a track built to Shinbwiyang by the end of the year, even if it would only take jeeps. General Pick replied that he would build a highway of 54 miles in 60 days. By sheer pluck and drive he did it, and two days after Christmas 1943 the leading American bulldozer cut the tapes at Shinbwiyang.

During the monsoon months when there was little likelihood of interference from the Japanese north of the Huwkawng Valley, the Chinese 38th Division left its Ledo base and was deployed in front of the engineer group. The 22nd Division arrived by the end of the year, while a third Division, the 30th, was not completely trained and equipped until early 1944.

At the Trident Conference in May, attended by both Stilwell and Wavell, the Combined Chiefs of Staff urged the importance of operations in north Burma and directed that an offensive designed to facilitate the building of the road should begin before the end of the year. They also directed that the tonnage of supplies flown to China should be, at a minimum, 10,000 a month. Later in the year at the Quebec Conference the target set was 20,000 tons a month over the 'hump' and, when the Ledo road was complete, a further 65,000 tons by road and over 50,000 tons of petrol via the pipe-line which followed the road.

The pioneers of the air route over the Himalayan 'hump' to China from India were Colonels William Old and Tate. After Colonel Old had made the first surveying flight Colonel Tate proved it was usable by transporting 13,000 Chinese troops to General Stilwell in India during the 1942 monsoon, a most noteworthy achievement.

Flying between 16,000 and 22,000 feet with oxygen, the Americans stepped up the monthly average during 1943 to 20,000 tons, a total only once carried over the old Burma road. They flew through all weathers and when their accident rate became high Chinese pickets were organized all along the route to rescue pilots who baled out. These pickets were paid so much for every pilot saved from that inhospitable country.

The expansion or building of the great depot airfields in Assam, such as Dinjan, Jorhat, and Chabua, by the Americans with local labour out of swampy paddy fields or jungle, was accomplished with surprising rapidity. 300,000 tons of concrete were required for one strip including parkways and ground staff accommodation, and every ton had to be brought from India. To build the temporary fields, which the R.A.F. often used pending the laying down of concrete ones, 600 transport aircraft loads of metal stripping were needed.

The airfield construction engineers, British or Americans, faced many difficulties besides the terrain. During the monsoon, strips which were neither concrete nor metal became seas of mud while in the dry weather they disintegrated into fine dust. Even so, during 1943 the Americans opened enough fields to operate a bus service to China of over 300 aircraft, one taking off every twenty minutes of the day.

The combat air forces increased, early in 1943, by some

250 per cent and were formed into the Eastern Air Command under an American, Maj.-Gen. George E. Stratermeyer, with a British second-in-command, Air Vice-Marshal W. A. Coryton, the King's flying instructor. The order given to General Stratermeyer were to cover all phases of the air war in this theatre, defend India, and win and hold air supremacy over the Japanese.

At his disposal General Stratermeyer had the two R.A.F. Groups, 221 and 224; the Allied Strategic Air Force; the Combat Cargo Task Force composed of British and American piloted transport planes; the 10th U.S.A.A.F., and units of the Royal Indian Air Force.

The Japanese air forces showed a marked liveliness early in 1943 and concentrated on trying to knock out the Allies' forward fighter strips before raiding the bigger rearward ones. Moreover their fighter, the Army 97, proved itself more than the equal of the British Hurricane. By adopting the tactics of shadowing the Japanese bombers back to their more forward bases in Burma, the Eastern Air Command was able to keep Japanese activity down to a minimum and, as time went on, made it extremely unhealthy for any Japanese aircraft to be seen at all in the forward areas. The Japanese moved their air forces back to bases in eastern Burma and Siam, and when required for raids they would shuttle their way across, never remaining on one airfield for very long. The fact that by the middle of 1943 hardly any Japanese planes were seen over Assam and the Indo-Burma frontier proved how effective these shadowing tactics were.

6

THE ARRIVAL OF WINGATE

Wingate's First Expedition—Triumph or Failure

NOT until June 1943, some months after the event, was the news of the Arakan failure allowed past the censorship imposed by G.H.Q. India. Then the release of the news was so timed as to coincide with the release of the tale of Brigadier Orde Wingate's first Chindit expedition into Burma.

By doing this it was naturally hoped to counterbalance bad news with good. But the colourful, heroic tale of two months' sabotage, fighting, and apparent dislocation of the enemy by a small force of British, Burmese, and Gurkha troops made little impression on the Indian press. For the most part they ignored Wingate and lambasted India Command and the Indian Government for the failure in the Arakan, which lay on the doorstep of Bengal.

Britain and America, tired of Allied failures in the war and often sceptical of Britain's war policy in the East, accepted Wingate with acclamation. Here seemed to be a leader who, not for the first time in his life, showed a rebirth of the spirit of Gordon, Clive, and T. E. Lawrence. Here, too, was the first story of a British success against the Japanese. That, at any rate, was how it appeared at the time.

Wingate went East at the request of Wavell. His successes in Abyssinia had marked him out as a first-class guerrilla fighter and commander. He arrived in time to witness a series of disasters including the retreat from Burma and the loss of the Dutch East Indies where Wavell was, at the time, Supreme Commander of the short-lived ABDA

(American, British Dutch, Australian) theatre. While awaiting Wavell's arrival back in Delhi, Wingate made a series of reconnaissance flights over Burma, during which he conceived the idea of a long-range penetration into the country to disrupt the enemy lines of communication.

As has already been said, Wavell's plans for an offensive into Burma included a move from Imphal down to the Chindwin as far as Kalewa and raids across in the Shwebo Plain. He was also instructed to permit Stilwell and his Chinese divisions to advance into north Burma while the Ledo road was being built behind them. The Generalissimo had also suggested an advance from Yunnan. While these operations were complementary, one to assist the other, Wavell considered that a further operation against the Japanese in the north-central area was necessary. The idea for it was provided by Wingate.

Wingate planned to build up a small force of British, Burmese, and Gurkha troops to operate in the interior of Burma for a set period without any kind of land-line communication. Initially his men should carry everything they needed on their back or by mule, elephant, or oxen. They should be replenished by air drop or live off the land. With no ground link, his force would be free to move when and where it wished or was required, providing its wireless link with its supply base was secure.

Wingate also wished to prove that the ordinary British soldier, given a certain amount of specialized training, could survive the hardships of jungle and hill country just as well as, if not better than, the Japanese; or, conversely, that the Japanese were not jungle supermen but ordinary soldiers who could be beaten at the form of warfare they seemed to have invented.

In the summer of 1942 a force was collected together and taken to a jungle training ground in central India, where officers and men lived and trained for the next six months.

THE ARRIVAL OF WINGATE 77

With the exception of 142 Commando Company none of the men and only a few officers were commando trained. Most were just ordinary soldiers and, in fact, many were town-bred men. The King's (Liverpool) Regiment, the 3/2 Gurkha Rifles, the 2nd Battalion of the Burma Rifles and a number of men from some twenty other units, including the R.A.F., made up the complete force, which averaged in age between 28 and 35. Hardly, one might imagine, suitable material for the rigorous and daring exploit planned.

The training proved more than a good many could accept, but finally some 3,000 officers and men, carrying 72-lb. loads on their backs and with a complete train of pack animals, crossed India to Dimapur, the railhead in Assam, for Imphal, and marched the 130 miles through the Kohima Hills to base in Imphal.

The force, named the Chindits after the dragon-like animal the Chinthe, which adorns the entrances to most Burmese 'poongyi chaungs' (Buddhist temples), was expected to be across the border for three months, during which time it would be supplied by air with everything, including mail. Nothing could, however, be sent out and every man knew that should he be wounded he would have to be left to his fate. It was a grim prospect, for even a flesh wound in the leg might prohibit a man from marching on with his column.

The Chindits' rations consisted of biscuits, raisins, cheese, dates, tea, sugar, and milk; not a very sustaining diet for the amount of marching to be done. Besides carrying five days' supply, weighing 15 lb. in his pack, each man was equipped with a rifle and bayonet, dah or kukri, jack knife, toggle rope, water bottle, four spare pairs of socks, rubber shoes, life jacket, canvas water chagul, groundsheet, spare shirt, housewife, ammunition, and three hand grenades. The total load was more than half the weight of some men.

Air transport commitments already included the supply of

Stilwell's Chinese and Americans building the Ledo road and the Kachin columns in north Burma. On the small number of transport squadrons the Chindits were an added weight. It would therefore take three days to supply the whole brigade by air drop.

In preparation for the move into Burma, Scoones's 4th Corps, holding the Imphal front, laid on a fake attack on Kalewa, well south of where the Chindits would cross the Chindwin. Decoy forces were also sent into the hills and valleys along the frontier and across the river.

The whole scheme was nearly ruined even before the Chindits began to move into Burma. Wavell could see no possibility of a British-Indian offensive into central Burma before the autumn of 1943. The Generalissimo refused to permit the Chinese 38th Division to cover the Ledo road engineers into north Burma. The Yunnan Chinese failed to make any move into north-east Burma.

The sudden cancellation of these complementary operations threatened to postpone Wingate's expedition. It was generally conceded that it would be of little value. Wingate, however, was determined. He had the sympathy of Stilwell who, though not agreeing with the tactical method, was willing to back a man who wanted to fight the Japanese. Most important of all, Wingate had the backing of Wavell, upon whom rested the final decision, and he prevailed upon Wavell to let him begin. Thus main operations in Burma during spring and summer of 1943 were Stilwell's move into north Burma and Wingate's expedition in north-central Burma. Neither was on a large enough military scale seriously to effect the Japanese, who were increasing their divisional strength in Burma to eight, and planning operations for the winter months.

In February 1943 Wavell, breaking tradition, saluted the Chindit columns drawn up on the Imphal Plain. As they marched across the hills to Tamu and down to the Chindwin,

THE ARRIVAL OF WINGATE 79

Wingate, promoted brigadier, accompanied them on a charger.

The Chindit Brigade was broken down into three groups and Brigade H.Q. was under Wingate himself. Lieut.-Col. Alexander commanded what was known as the Gurkha Group consisting of four columns under Majors G. Dunlop, A. Emmett, J. M. ('Mad Mike') Calvert, and R. S. G. Bromhead. No. 2 Group, under Lieut.-Col. S. A. Cooke, was mostly composed of men from the King's Regiment. Capt. D. Hasting and Majors B. E. Fergusson, K. D. Gilkes, and W. P. Scott were the column commanders. The third group was picked men from the 2nd Battalion Burma Rifles comprising Burmese, Kachins, and Karens, under Lieut.-Col. L. G. Wheeler, who had spent twenty years in the army in Burma and whose fame and kindliness was known throughout the Kachin country. This 'Burrif' group was the van or scouting element of the expedition.

Realizing he could not keep news of the expedition from reaching the Japanese for long, Wingate decided to secure the main crossing by feinting in other directions. Lieut.-Col. Alexander and two columns crossed the Chindwin at Auktaung, some distance south of the real crossing at Tonhe, while a small party went even farther south. These two parties moved openly. The Japanese reacted as expected, their outposts and outlying garrisons following the trail of information they received.

The general line of the Chindits' advance was from Tonhe on the Chindwin across Burma towards Banmauk and Indaw, junction of the Mandalay-Myitkyina railway and quite close to the Irrawaddy. The expedition's first objective was the railway, a single-line track over which Japanese forces in north Burma were supplied.

During that phase Fergusson's and Calvert's columns were ordered to destroy parts of the railway and the Bonchaung gorge and bridge. They were therefore dispatched independently and were instructed to concentrate across the Irrawaddy in the area of Mogok where they would meet the rest of the brigade.

Unfortunately only a few days after crossing the Chindwin the whole security of the expedition broke down when the troops' mail was dropped on to a Japanese outpost.

Within three days the Japanese knew the complete composition and strength of the Chindits, a knowledge which aided them considerably from then on, for they realized that this was no army invasion and thus never deployed or diverted more of their own forces than necessary. Had this not happened the Japanese might have had to divert some of the force they were building up for their incursion into India early in 1944.

Also, at the beginning of March, one of the columns was forced to disperse after an engagement with the Japanese and, having been separated from the rest of the expedition, had no choice but to return to India.

On 6 March—his thirtieth birthday—Calvert blew up portions of the Mandalay-Myitkyina railway line while Fergusson's column blew the Bonchaung gorge and bridge. Lower down Group 1 blew up more railway line. Though both line and bridge were repairable these were probably the most material achievements, apart from the killing of several hundred Japanese, throughout the brief campaign.

It is no part of this story to trace the various moves and counter-moves of all the groups and columns. They wove an intricate pattern through north Burma and eventually merged in the triangle formed by the Irrawaddy and Shweli rivers, having crossed the former. Such a concentration area could be nothing but a death-trap. To reach the Mandalay-Lashio railway necessitated a march south-east in the direction of Mong Mit and Mogok. One group did in fact execute part of this march. The return to India would require a re-crossing of the Irrawaddy and, perhaps, the Shweli. The

Japanese would be well-informed of the brigade's approximate position, and be able to take counter-measures by bringing up troops from the Shewbo and Mandalay areas.

By 20 March the troops were becoming exhausted. The amount of marching on meagre rations proved an excessive hardship. With so few transport aircraft there were the added difficulties of supplying dispersed columns from the air. This sometimes necessitated columns going for nearly three weeks on five days' rations and what they could obtain from the country.

Originally Wingate had intended to remain inside Burma during the monsoon and, despite receiving the order to return to India, would have done so had he felt it justified. But he realized the fatigue of the troops, even after five weeks in Burma, and decided that what had already been achieved was enough even if it amounted to little more than experience for the future.

Unfortunately the decision to turn back had spread among the troops and their natural reaction was, as Brigadier Fergusson has so aptly pointed out in his book *Beyond the Chindwin*, that they must take care not to get killed on the journey home This was an adverse reaction, though entirely human.

Wingate decided to re-cross the Irrawaddy at Inywa where he, his H.Q., and two columns, had crossed a few days previously. He hoped the Japanese would not expect such an obvious move. He hoped wrongly for, as the leading column began crossing, the Japanese opened fire. He then decided that the brigade should split up into parties, not exceeding forty in number, and make independently for India. That was at the end of March.

For the next month, and longer in some cases, little groups of men were scattered throughout the length and breadth of northern Burma. Most parties got out of the Irrawaddy-Shweli triangle, and naturally made for the Kachin country to the north. There they knew that they would obtain food and temporary protection from a most loyal and friendly race of people. The record of help given by the Kachins, at their own peril, to Wingate's first and second Chindit expeditions is as glorious as any in the whole war.

Just under 2,000 officers and men, or over sixty per cent, of the original brigade reached the sanctuary of India. Behind them they left some 1,500 dead Japanese, a blown-up gorge and railway line and a large number of disillusioned Burmese who had imagined the British had returned for good.

This brief explanation of the Chindit expedition gives no account of the stresses and strains, the dramatic and often sad moments, the most difficult decisions junior commanders had to make, or the extreme bravery of many officers and men of many different races. The leaving of wounded comrades and friends to the suspect mercy of the Japanese or unfriendly Burmese; the finding of great friends tortured and murdered by the Japanese; the terrible pangs of hunger and the character required to share even the last few raisins with one's comrades and not keep or steal something for oneself; all those things and many more can never be understood properly by anyone who has not experienced war at its grimmest. If heroism bespoke success then Wingate's Chindits were successful. Unfortunately heroism does not necessarily bring with it material achievements.

On the face of it the Chindit expedition was not a success. It was a small-scale and lone operation in the heart of a big country. It dovetailed with no other operations and thereby lost a great deal of its purpose. What it did achieve in demolitions or the killing of Japanese could have equally well been achieved by air strikes and bombing. It lost considerably more men than the attacking air forces would have done in achieving similar results. It gave very little assistance to the building of the Ledo road because that

THE ARRIVAL OF WINGATE 83

had not really reached Japanese-controlled north Burma, and it is doubtful whether the Japanese would have made any serious effort to stop the building. It did not hinder supplies and troop reinforcements to north Burma for long. It did not divert a great many Japanese troops. It served as an irritant but not a bad one.

It is even doubtful whether it proved that British troops were better than Japanese in the jungle, for after only two months the Chindits were emaciated and fatigued. Its effect on the morale of the troops waiting to fight in Burma was only transient. At first the propaganda boost attached to the expedition buoyed up morale. Later the lurid stories of individual Chindits lowered it again.

But like a number of pioneer efforts it was productive. It was the birth of an idea which had greater effect later on. At the least Wingate had proved that courage and enterprise, and boldness and leadership could, given all material help possible, find a way to do something that maps and paper and arm-chairs could not do. No man succeeded in so many activities in war as Wingate.

Almost immediately after the return of this Chindit expedition Wingate began planning another and much more ambitious long-range penetration into Burma. This time he found fewer opponents, for the glamour of his first show had impressed a number of people. Moreover, the theory he wished to exploit—the theory of a two-way air supply—was by then considered within the bounds of reality.

Wingate had seen where and how his troops had suffered. Air drop had not yet been perfected; the inability either to take out wounded and sick or to take in heavy equipment had been a limiting factor. If his columns could build and hold rough airstrips inside Burma, if in the initial stage they could be flown in and landed at some selected spot, then many of his problems would be solved.

The troops could be flown in, the landing-place could be

improved as an airstrip, others could be built and could serve as bases of operations for Chindit columns. All this pre-supposed air supremacy to permit transport planes and gliders to run in unmolested. There were other problems of rations and clothing and equipment to be solved, but they presented few difficulties, for by then Wingate, had captured the world's imagination and through Churchill and President Roosevelt he was given the benefit of American ingenuity. And, above all, just as he had found a friend and believer in Wavell for his first expedition, so he found Admiral Lord Louis Mountbatten, a man whose vision was as wide as Wingate's, as a backer for his second.

From Quebec in August 1943 came the announcement of the formation of South-East Asia Command with Mountbatten as its Supreme Commander. The reasons were straightforward.

Events in Europe foreshadowed the possible defeat of Germany within a year. The budgets for manpower in Europe had been made and it was considered possible that later British divisions might be released for duty in the East. There was also a considerable increase in the number of trained and available Indian divisions while, on the Burma front, there was enough force to permit an offensive with, it was thought, little risk.

The conduct of current operations and the planning of those in contemplation required more vigorous direction than hithertoo. So far the British had achieved nothing in the reconquest of Burma and, in fact, had played a particularly passive role except for Wingate's one mission. A new theatre, principally a British one and under a figure such as Mountbatten, might convert South-East Asia from a publicity starved backwater into one able to bring prestige to Britain to compare, but in a smaller way, with the prestige already gained by the Americans in the Pacific. There were other reasons.

The theatre of British operations in the East, based on India, was geographically very large. Though the defence of India was vitally important, any offensive action must take armies and fleets far beyond the boundaries of India into Burma, Malaya, Singapore, Siam, and even the Dutch East Indies. To ask General Auchinleck, who had succeeded Wavell as C.-in-C., to train and equip a new Indian Army to produce and supply divisions for the Middle East, to defend India and also to mount an offensive against the Japanese, was considered something almost beyond the powers even of that general. Therefore it was decided to split the command into two. India Command was to remain as a base for training, equipping, and supply; the new South-East Asia Command was responsible for all operations on land, sea, and in the air.

Admiral Mountbatten, at forty-three, was by far the youngest Supreme Commander in any theatre of war. His earleir war record as a commander of a destroyer flotilla and as Chief of Combined Operations is well known. He had a good record for courage, vision, and boldness. Though in seniority only a Captain R.N. he was promoted Admiral, with the corresponding ranks of General and Air Marshal.

Mountbatten had his critics, many inspired by jealousy at seeing so young a man in so important a job. Though in parts of America where he was personally known—Philadelphia, Boston, and New York—he was admired by the Americans, there was a large press of the less dignified and reputable kind which unjustifiably denigrated him as a Mayfair playboy, while among the upper heirarchy of the Admiralty there was at least one admiral who was opposed to Mountbatten, integrated commands, and anything likely to disturb the personality and traditional workings of the Royal Navy. This admiral unfortunately remained a confirmed opponent of South-East Asia from its birth to the end of the war.

In Delhi, where he set up his first headquarters adjoining

G.H.Q. (I), Mountbatten was not free from rivalry. Here it must be said that he was given all possible assistance by the new Viceroy, Viscount Wavell, and by General Auchinleck. It was from the lesser lights of G.H.Q. (I), who felt their position being undermined and their thunder being taken from them, that the opposition came.

It was at the end of 1943 that an attempt was made to make the world conscious of the atrocities which the Japanese had and were committing against Allied prisoners, civilian internees, and the people of occupied countries. A considerable amount of data had already been collected by G.H.Q. India, and information was coming through of the terrible plight of the prisoners whom the Japanese were forcing to build the Burma–Siam railroad, known afterwards as the 'Railroad of Death'. This railway line ran through the jungled and hilly wilderness between the southern strip of Burma and south Siam. 260 miles long it linked the Moulmein–Ye line in Burma to the Bangkok–Singapore line in Siam. It was to serve as a line of communication for the Japanese. It was completed early in 1945.

Without sufficient or proper food, clothing, equipment, or medical supplies, thousands of British and Australian officers and men and native labourers brought from Japanese-occupied countries were being forced to cut through this wilderness. Already, after a year of working—the railway line had been begun at the end of 1942—hundreds of men had died. The Japanese were for the most part brutal and quite unsympathetic in their handling of their 'slaves'. Sick men were ordered to perform physical tasks that would never be undertaken by a stronger Westerner on normal Western rations. Men were herded together in jungle camps, those with dysentery, beri-beri, pellagra, and malaria living cheek by jowl with those living skeletons who were considered fit. Jungle sores, which grew and ate away the flesh, weakened and incapacitated thousands. The pus had to be scraped out daily with bits of tin. Amputations were performed with little or no anaesthetics. The Japanese strutted and gloried in his power and beat the white man to his knees for any and every offence, however minor. Some men were bayoneted, others shot and some beheaded for trying to escape. Escape from the frontier region of Burma and Siam was a virtual impossibility.

After consultations between the Governments of Britain, America, Canada, South Africa, Australia, and New Zealand, it was agreed to release accounts of atrocities committed by the Japanese. At first America and Australia were unwilling for they feared for their own prisoners and civilians in Japanese hands. Britain with the most, however, was willing to take the chance, although Auchinleck and others considerd the likelihood of any captive remaining alive was small. Finally all countries agreed to a limited publicity campaign.

It was the author's unenviable task to sift, sort, check, and finally produce for public reading the tales of Japanese atrocities. In three weeks forty-seven different forms of atrocity were produced, ranging from the frequent and common beheading of Chinese in Singapore to the vivisection of British prisoners in Japanese officers' messes, as an after-dinner entertainment, and the murdering by pouring boiling water over a British soldier staked to ground in the bazaar area of a north Burma town. In the latter case the British soldier and a Chinese were tied together like a couple of cattle and dragged round the town as a parade for the inhabitants who were forced at the bayonet point to watch the execution. The story was brought back by a Burmese nurse who witnessed it and, escaping with the help of the Kachins and Nagas, reached the Allies in Assam.

Conditions in Stanley Camp, Hong Kong—and many others as well—were known to be terrible, and there was considerable doubt whether the civilian internees would survive. The case of Sir Vandelaur Graybourn, head of a

British bank, was no worse than many others though it was horrific enough. Taken from the camp Graybourn was confined for weeks in a small cell. He was beaten and tortured. His wife sent him food and clothes but heard no word of his fate until one day she was told to go to the camp gates with a wheelbarrow. There she collected the remains of her husband and the parcels she had been sending him but which he had never received.

Considering their primitiveness, their disregard for life, and their natural cruelty the Japanese were, however, no match for the Germans in mass atrocity and inhumanity. Japanese atrocities were widespread but not general or on anything like the scale of Belsen and Buchenwald. But they did commit atrocities, officers did behead captives with their Samurai swords and no one could prejudge the temper of any Japanese in whose hands he might fall. But it was not easy at the end of 1943 to persuade the world that the Japanese were a cruel and vicious enemy.

7
THE FORMATION OF SOUTH-EAST ASIA COMMAND

Arrival of Mountbatten—Japanese Offensive begins in Arakan

ADMIRAL Mountbatten arrived in India to form South-East Asia Command in October 1943. As he has said, he was given little with which to form it, and had to beg and borrow and rely on the generosity of the War Office, G.H.Q. (I), and the American War Department, for men, materials, and aircraft.

Here then is the position which faced Mountbatten when he first arrived.

The Japanese were in undisputed possession of Burma and had at least eight divisions. They possessed interior lines of communications, including roads, railways, and rivers, all leading to the port of Rangoon. In the north they held Myitkyina, Mogaung, Bhamo, and Kamaing. On the central front their advanced line stretched over the Chindwin river. In the Arakan they still held the Maungdaw–Buthidaung road.

In the air Japanese Army Air Force units had begun to return to Burma and Siam after retiring for the monsoon. Their fighter strength had been increased considerably and new medium bomber units were appearing in rear areas.

Though Allied fighter action—U.S.A.A.F. and R.A.F.—was taking a steady toll of Japanese aircraft, their combat strength remained reasonably high. Obviously they had reserves.

On the Allied side the Ledo road was still bogged down because of the monsoon. Brigadier-General Pick had arrived and was shortly to rescue it. The Chinese 38th Division, screening Stilwell's Ledo road builders, was at last deployed north of the Huwkawng Valley. On the central front, 4th Corps was being strengthened by the 20th Indian Division and preparations were being made for an advance as far as Kalewa (the original Wavell plan). In the Arakan 15th Corps included the 5th, 7th, and 26th Indian Divisions. A number of new divisions were being trained in India. Wingate was training his second Chindit expedition on a much larger and more ambitious scale. An American task force, known as Galahad Force, had arrived for training. It was the first all-American combat ground force in the theatre. In the air and at sea supremacy had been achieved.

Also in India there was an organization known as the 11th Army Group under General Sir George Giffard, who had served in the jungle campaigns in West Africa in the previous war, and held command in West Africa in this one. 11th Army Group was responsible for all land operations in the theatre and, upon the formation of S.E.A.C., came under Mountbatten's command.

Under the Army Group had been formed an Indian Expeditionary Force with the 2nd and 36th British Divisions as the spearheads and Indian divisions as the followers-up. This I.E.F. had disintegrated when it was known that the landing-craft allotted to the command were to be taken back to Europe.

Stilwell was appointed Mountbatten's Deputy Supreme Commander. He retained his several other portfolios, including that of commander of the China–Burma–India Command which, operationally, became surbordinate to S.E.A.C. As Chief of Staff, Lieut.-Gen. Sir Henry Pownall came from Iraq. As his Deputy Chief of Staff, Mountbatten had chosen Maj.-Gen. Albert C. Wedermeyer, an American. Admiral Sir James Somerville commanded the Eastern

Fleet, Air Chief Marshal Sir Richard Peirse the Allied Air Forces, and Giffard the Land Forces.

As Principal Administrative Officer Mountbatten was given Lieut.-Gen. Raymond Wheeler, an American who later became Deputy Supreme Commander. Wheeler had previously been Chief of Supply Services for the C.B.I. and had laid the plans for the building of the Ledo road. Wheeler's opposite number in India Command, under Auchinleck, was Britain's leading logistical expert, General Sir Walter Lindsell, whose first conference in Delhi, shortly after his arrival, was such an attack on the administrative ineptitude and bureaucracy that it was struck off the records.

In this grand gallery of commanders there was, for Mountbatten, one snag. While he was responsible to the Combined Chiefs of Staff for the conduct of operations and the carrying out of their orders, his three operational commanders, Somerville, Giffard, and Peirse all maintained their own links with the Admiralty, War Office, and Air Ministry. Thus it was possible for each one to signal his department in London if he did not agree with any orders given by Mountbatten. Moreover, though Stilwell had taken an immediate liking to his new Supreme Commander, he also had his various routes to the War Department in Washington and could, if he so wished, make matters difficult for Mountbatten. From this it can be seen that Mountbatten's responsibilities, strategical, political, and diplomatic, were considerable and his position far from easy.

Mountbatten's wish was to build up an integrated British-American command. While the ground and naval forces were to come primarily from the British Empire, the air forces were to be split between the British and Americans. He appointed Maj.-Gen. George E. Stratermeyer as Peirse's second-in-command. He was also fortunate in having Colonel Phil Cochran and Brigadier William Old, two notable American airmen, within the command.

His headquarters was to be a British-American unit, and always he hoped that by making it so he would found a better and more sympathetic relationship between the British and Americans under his command, not merely for the duration of the war but for always.

Though Mountbatten was at first regarded with suspicion by a number of the Americans who served under him, soon they were among his greatest supporters. His personality could win over anyone—even General Stilwell.

But lower down the scale, when his headquarters had moved to Kandy in Ceylon, the British and Americans moved apart and there was very little mixing of the two, even though the officers lived in the same camp. The only common ground for meeting was the office or at the officers' dances in 'Jacob's Folly', an officers' club.

It was a pity, and the fault lay principally in the Englishman's inherent quality of gradually forming his own little circle and keeping to it. The British, in fact, made very little attempt at entertaining the Americans, showed very little ingenuity in making their officers' messes anything like so attractive as the Americans', and, though they should have been hosts, gradually retired into themselves, as the British will. This was probably Mountbatten's biggest failure of the war.

On the operational side Mountbatten had already built up ideas for an amphibious war. It was only natural seeing his background. After the negative results of the past two years many others also considered the reconquest of Burma could only be achieved by a seaborne landing in south Burma. This school of thought had powerful opponents in Stilwell, Giffard, Slim, and Wingate, all of whom, in different degrees of time and space, considered that Burma could be liberated from the land.

The question was decided at the Sextant Conference in November when the Combined Chiefs of Staff ordered the

THE FORMATION OF SOUTH-EAST ASIA COMMAND 93

assault on southern France to be on a major scale. At the previous Quadrant Conference amphibious operations in the Bay of Bengal had been planned for late 1944, but these were postponed at Cairo, and the landing-craft allotted to S.E.A.C. diverted to Europe. This meant that 15 L.S.T.s and 6 L.S.I.s were released from S.E.A.C. They were later used in Europe and at Anzio.

Various plans were produced for a land offensive into Burma. The chief one was 'Capital'. It called for Stilwell to advance into north Burma as far as Myitkyina, for 4th Corps to advance into central Burma, for Wingate to disrupt Japanese communications in north-central Burma, and, it was hoped, for a Chinese advance from Yunnan. Fundamentally it was the original 1942 plan on a larger scale.

Though Stilwell was much in favour of this plan, Giffard was still doubtful whether the communications in Assam were capable of supplying the necessary force. They had been improved only slightly from the early days. The possibility of supplying the advancing troops by air on a really large scale was not contemplated. There was still a shortage of transport aircraft. The Americans maintained Giffard was being too cautious.

Mountbatten decided to militarize the Assam–Bengal railway system and asked for American railway companies to operate it, but not until a year later was the effect really felt. At the time the railway, which was Stilwell's and 4th Corp's life-line, was capable of carrying only 90,000 tons a month.

Mountbatten and Giffard decided the Eastern Army should be commanded by General Slim and be given a number. Slim did not create the 14th Army as is often supposed, although he was its first and, in battle, its only commander. The War Office gave the army the number 14 but ordered that it should be kept a secret in case the Japanese discovered they were fighting the 14th Army! This queer edict remained secure until 2nd Lieut. Frank Owen, former editor of the *Evening Standard*, and, at that time, editor of the Forces' newspaper, *SEAC*, published a goodwill message from Churchill and thus broke security, although what effect it had on the Japanese was never discovered.

For the troops the arrival of Mountbatten was a tonic, and they expected some immediate dynamic action in the theatre. The diversion of the landing-craft, and with them Mountbatten's hopes of a sea operation, was not publicized until some time after the event. By then the troops had become disillusioned. They wondered whether he had got 'lost' in India. Only personal appearances by Mountbatten, during which he talked frankly to the troops, gave them cause for hope.

Although it was considered the hard way, Operation Capital was accepted. By the end of the year Stilwell's engineer group had reached Shinbwiyang and his Chinese screen was in the Huwkawng. Early in the New Year Galahad Force, renamed Merrill's Marauders, was due to join him. The way lay down the Huwkawng and Mogaung Valleys to Myitkyina.

Manipur, where 4th Corps was stationed, provided the only other two lands routes into Burma. From Imphal to Tamu, on the Burma border, there was the old Assam Tea-planters' trail, built in 1942, which had been converted into a double highway by the army. From Tamu down to the Chindwin there were tracks and one dirt road down the Kabaw Valley.

From Imphal to Tiddim, in the Chin Hills, there was the 163-mile narrow mountain road which culminated, in front of Tiddim, in the 'Chocolate Staircase' rising 4,000 feet in eight miles. From Tiddim an old route straggled past the 9,000-foot Kennedy Peak, Fort White, the Bamboo Stockades (old British outposts) and down to the Chindwin Valley and

Kalewa. The 20th Division was ordered to advance its line down the Kabaw Valley and the 17th forward of Tiddim.

At the same time Slim ordered General Christison and his 15th Corps in the Arakan to clear the Mayu peninsula. This would give command of the Naf river and permit sea supply of forward troops while securing the Maungdaw–Buthidaung road, which crossed the Mayu range from west to east. This road runs through the famous tunnels, which were originally built some time in the last century for the purpose of laying a railway line. When the topographical section of both H.Q. Supreme Allied Commander and G.H.Q. (I) wanted to find out the geography of the tunnels, no one in Calcutta could remember who had actually built them.

The geography of the Arakan consists of a series of hill ranges, valleys, and rivers, running parallel to the coast There are half a dozen or more. The Mayu range is the first and most adjacent to the coast. Beyond it lies the Kalapanzin river which runs into the Mayu river. Between these valleys lateral communications are few. There are only three passes between the coastal strip and the Mayu Valley. They are the Maungdaw–Buthidaung road through the tunnels; the Ngakyedauk Pass (named 'Okey-doke' by the troops) and the Goppe Pass to the village of Bawli Bazaar.

General Christison's 15th Corps consisted of the 26th Indian Division, the 5th Indian, which had returned from the Middle East, the 7th Indian, and the 81st West African. The latter had arrived earlier in 1943 as the first of several divisions from East and West Africa. In reserve were the 25th Indian Division and the 36th British Division, which was intended for any seaborne landing on Akyab. 224 Group of the R.A.F. supported the Corps.

While the 5th and 7th Indian Divisions cleared the Mayu peninsula the West Africans, who had spent several months jungle training on the Wingate pattern, were ordered on an independent mission in the Kaladan Valley, some 60 miles inland from the coast. This was mainly to insure against a flank attack on the main forces such as had disorganized the 1942–3 Arakan campaign, but it had as its secondary objective the clearing of the valley and occupation of Kyauktaw, which would open up a fairly easy route to the Akyab delta. Akyab was still the carrot in front of the horse's nose.

Though numerically much larger than Wingate's first Chindit mission, the West Africans were to be supplied by Old's Troop Carrying Command, the most ambitious air supply project yet conducted in the campaign.

By New Year's Eve 1943 the Ngakyedauk Pass had been secured and the 5th Division were within range of Maungdaw and Razabil. At Razabil the British-Indian troops found the Japanese in a stubborn no-surrender mood, and after a week's fighting only one outpost was captured when the Japanese slipped away in the night. Maungdaw fell, but a hill dominating Razabil from the south refused to give in for several days. When at last it was captured it was found to be a complete underground fortress. Meanwhile the 7th Indian Division had secured a foothold in the tunnels and the King's Own Scottish Borderers, who held it, were cut off for some days. That, however, was all that this particular offensive in the Arakan achieved, for the Japanese began their counter-offensive, striking towards Chittagong.

During the early part of January the Japanese air forces did their best to hinder Allied supply dropping and close-support, and also to disrupt the straggling lines of communication by fighter-bomber attacks. But in the middle of January fighter sweeps over the forward positions increased in scale and intensity. On 15 January three groups of twelve Japanese fighters each were intercepted by fighters of

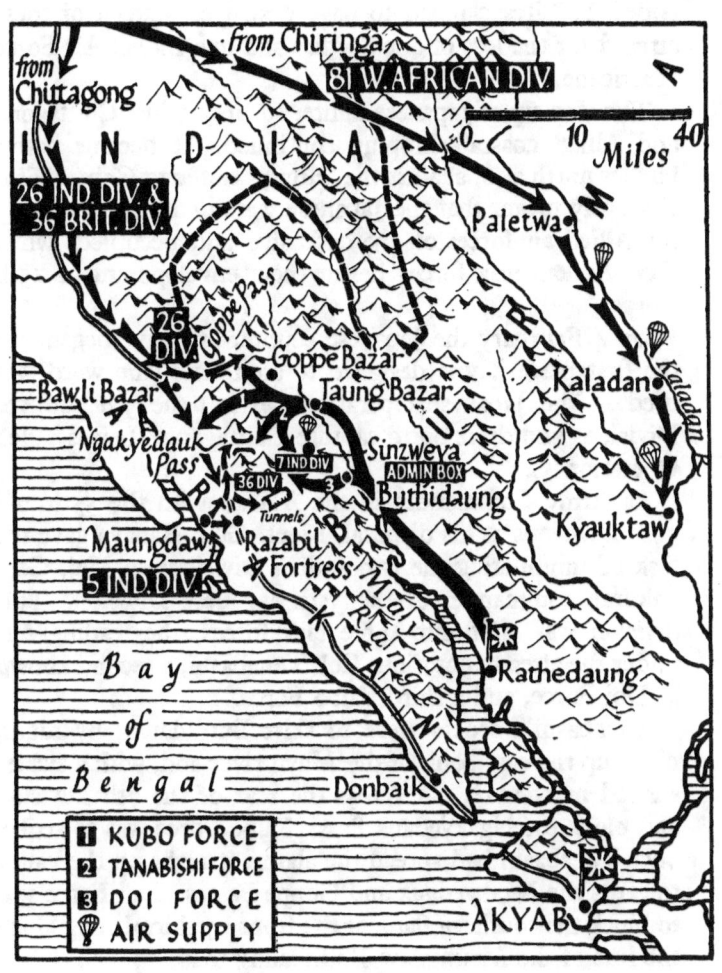

JAPANESE OFFENSIVE IN ARAKAN—JANUARY–APRIL 1944

224 Group over the Naf peninsula and the Buthidaung area. Allied Spitfires claimed to have destroyed sixteen of these aircraft for the loss of one Spitfire and one Indian Air Force Hurricane.

The step-up of Japanese fighter sorties against Chittagong and Allied coastal shipping continued. It became active farther north also, against the 'Hump' traffic to China. This obviously meant that the Japanese were determined to keep the Allied air forces on the defensive and occupied, while their Arakan task forces began their envelopment of 15th Corps.

On 4 February the Japanese counter-offensive began. In the first place it was designed to annihilate (the word was used in the Japanese Operation Orders) the 5th and 7th Divisions and drive on to capture Chittagong. It was called Operation C.

As Army Commander in the Arakan with the 55th and 54th Divisions at his disposal, Lieut.-Gen. Hanaya gave the task of annihilating the two Indian Divisions to Maj.-Gen. Sakurai, commander of the 55th Japanese Division. This division was split into three task forces, the leading one under the already notorious Col. Tanabashi, a second known as Doi Force, and a third Kubo Force.

Tanabashi's orders were to skirt Buthidaung by night, move up the east bank of the Mayu river and, with a sickle-shaped manœuvre, cut across the rear of the 7th Division and block the Ngakyedauk Pass. Kubo Force was to strike, once Tanabashi had spread the alarm, straight up the valley towards the Ngakyedauk and Goppe Passes. Doi Force was to block the southern flank of the front by skirmishing along the line of the Maungdaw–Buthidaung road.

The plan envisaged complete encirclement of the two divisions and a blocking of their rearward escape or supply routes. It was bold; the leadership was aggressive and energetic. And, in typical Japanese manner, the three task forces were given seven days to do the job. After that they would live, like a snake, off the mass they were crushing in their belly.

The initial onslaught was swift. Tanabashi struck at Taung Bazaar, a little village nestling in the range separating the Mayu and Kalapanzin Valleys. Crossing the river, he reached the Mayu range and attacked the administrative area of the 7th Division at Sinzweya. At the same time Kubo Force attacked General Messervy's main divisional headquarters, causing it to disintegrate. The general escaped with most of his staff by wading a 'chaung' while wearing pyjamas and carrying only a Bible. This was not the first or last time General Messervy had suffered such misfortune. He had been captured in the desert and, when interrogated, had told the Germans he was the general's batman. He had then escaped.

Finding the route to the Goppe Pass blocked, Kubo Force (which showed considerable strength and stamina) crossed the Mayu range and blocked the west side of the Ngakyedauk Pass and the road linking Maungdaw and Bawli Bazaar, thus cutting the land lines of communications of the 5th Division.

General Messervy decided to mass what troops he could gather together in the administrative area, known afterwards as the 'Admin. Box'. When he escaped from his H.Q. he was only four miles away but it took him four hours to reach it. Here he decided to stand the siege, for already Mountbatten had announced that he would supply the besieged by air with everything required from mail to food, ammunition to beer. It would require an air lift of 4,000 tons a month if the siege lasted that long.

The battle of the 'Admin. Box', its eventual relief, and the shattering of the Japanese task forces, is chiefly notable in history not so much for the actual staunchness and heroism of the British and Indian troops as for the complete success of the air supply under Brig.-Gen. Old, chief of the Troop Carrying Command, and the excellent, even if partially improvised, organization of producing, packing, and sending of everything required by Maj.-Gen. Snelling, M.G.A., of the 14th Army. During his career as general, Slim's 'A' Officer, General Snelling, was asked to do a great many difficult things, and his usual reply was, 'What you ask, sir, is impossible, but I will arrange'.

The three weeks' siege along the Kalapanzin river consisted of several phases. General Messervy in the Box had to hold out against the most determined and vicious attacks from Tanabashi. His forward brigades, also supplied by air, had to hold Doi Force, and his reserve brigade had to recapture Taung Bazaar and clear the north end of the valley.

Over on the Naf river side of the Mayu range, where the 5th Indian Division were cut off by land from their rear, Maj.-Gen. R. Briggs had the task of clearing his communications and then the Ngakyedauk Pass to relieve the siege in the Box. He was supplied by air and sea, as the Japanese had omitted to close the coastal transport route.

In the air as many as eighty Japanese fighters were over the battle area in a single day, operating from central Burma. Few bombers appeared and it was obvious that the Japanese were determined to hinder Allied supply dropping. They failed because the Allied air forces increased their fighter escort. Eventually the Japanese air force gave up the job in the Arakan and turned their attention to assisting their Manipur invasion, which was about to begin.

During the battle the Japanese overran a field hospital and, after bayoneting the patients, lined up a number of doctors and shot them. One doctor escaped by feigning death and another, who was operating at the time, by having his surgery foxhole so well-blacked out that the Japanese missed it. As this atrocity happened at night, it was difficult for the main body within the Box area to counter-attack

THE FORMATION OF SOUTH-EAST ASIA COMMAND 101

effectively, though they did try. They were met by walking wounded, forced to march in front of the Japanese as a screen. This was one of the few atrocities that occurred from then on in the Burma war.

Finding the British or Indians in no mood for surrender, and the fact that they were battering up against solid walls of defence undoubtedly angered the Japanese. Moreover, the continual presence of Allied supply and fighter planes—9,000 sorties were flown in three weeks—and the growing absence of their own, demoralized them. Their time-table had been thrown out of gear, over ten days having elapsed since Tanibashi made his first thrust. They were without rations and short of ammunition. Foraging among the rugged countryside and stricken villages was unprofitable. The Japanese became exhausted.

Despite their propagandists' joyous pronouncements that the 'March on Delhi' was succeeding, the Japanese commanders in the battle zone realized that to masticate and digest two Indian divisions, supplied as they were by air, with less than 12,000 men was by then beyond them. General Hanaya decided to concentrate on the 7th Division, thus freeing the 5th Indian Division from some of its embarrassments in the Naf peninsula.

General Slim's plan for the relief of the 7th Division and eventual destruction of the Japanese Task Forces was eased by the growing weakness of the Japanese. The 26th Indian Division, concentrated at Chittagong, was to hold the western approaches to the Ngakyedauk Pass until relieved by the 36th British Division, *en route* from Calcutta. Then the 26th would descend into the northern part of the Kalapanzin valleys through the Goppe Pass. The 5th Division was to sweep over the Ngakyedauk Pass and join forces with the besieged garrison.

What had been a battle of defence and improvisation, of hurried action, and urgent all-round co-operation by everyone, began to turn into a limited counter-offensive designed to free the trapped forces, some of whom were soon to be needed in the central front, and generally to stabilize the Arakan. It was the King's Own Scottish Borderers who made the eventual link-up with the 5th Division after a ten-days' battle for the last Japanese dug-in position at Hill 1070, in which the use of tanks, aircraft, and artillery testifies to the stubborness of the Japanese.

It took General Christison another couple of weeks to complete the job. His 5th Division, assisted by some 200 guns in mass formation and non-stop dive-bombing, captured Razabil, which they had been in the process of doing a month before. The 36th Division hammered away at the tunnels, still resolutely held by the Japanese, and the 7th Division set about cleaning up what remained of the Japanese forces in the Mayu Valley.

Five thousand of the original Japanese task forces escaped, leaving 7,000 of their comrades behind dead, except for one—the first prisoner taken during the war in this theatre. He was unconscious when captured. Tanabashi was among those who escaped, and it is worth noting that he remained a colonel and did not achieve promotion for the remainder of his time in Burma. Our own casualties, though much smaller in the numbers killed, amounted to no less when reckoned in figures of wounded and sick.

The West Africans had begun their mission smoothly. It had taken them a couple of months to build a road from Chiringa, their base, to the Kaladan Valley but that had had been finished in the middle of January. A week after the division had begun their advance it had occupied Paletwa without opposition. The air supply by free drop had drawn the following remark from one African soldier: 'Sir, bullet no fear, mortar no fear. But if one bag rice come chop me my wife think I be very foolish man.'

As part of the propaganda build-up of this West African

Force it was made known to the Japanese that should they be taken prisoner the Africans would eat them which, if true, says something for the West African stomach.

Kyauktaw was occupied two weeks after the Japanese had attacked the remainder of the corps on the peninsula. From there an all-weather road ran down to the Akyab delta. But circumstances changed plans, and the Japanese began to react violently. Kyauktaw was lost while a Japanese thrust at the African's tail cost the division some 1,500 casualties. The division withdrew into a 'box' formation at Kyringi, where an airstrip was built. The box was protected on three sides by water. It was held for two weeks. The division was then ordered to withdraw from the Kaladan as the Japanese, having reoccupied Kaladan village, were threatening the flank of the rest of the corps. The Japanese garrison melted on being challenged by the Africans but reappeared nearer Taung Bazaar. The division crossed into the Kalapanzin Valley in April.

Though this Arakan battle was claimed by the British as a great victory, the first over the Japanese in the theatre, it is better described as a successful avoidance of defeat. No side with such vastly superior ground and air forces could claim a victory when it was compelled by a small force to coil up and defend itself. Against 12,000 Japanese were arrayed first two Indian divisions. A third Indian and a British division was added, while a West African division had to be deflected from its original purpose. The disparity between four or five divisions and a Japanese task force the size of one, is too great.

If anything it was a victory for the morale of the British-Indian troops who, for the first time against the Japanese, realized that when attacked and encircled they did not need to retreat.

That it was, at the time, claimed as a victory was propaganda, for had Mountbatten, Giffard, or Slim been forced to admit defeat the repercussions within India and Bengal would have been equalled only by the severity of the criticism abroad. From their viewpoint it had to be a victory irrespective of the number of divisions employed in gaining it. It was, as Churchill pointed out, a challenge to the enemy, but whether, as he also said, the Japanese were beaten in the jungle was another matter. Could the Allies, given the same resources as the Japanese and set the same task, have done as well? It is doubtful.

8

THE JAPANESE INVASION OF ASSAM

Air Supply—General Slim's Plans for Offensive—Japanese Invasion of Manipur Begins

A GREAT deal has already been said about air supply and much more will be written before the story of these campaigns is finished. During the war in Burma much was written separately about the R.A.F., its allied air forces, and the Army. Each, through its Public Relations Officers, patted itself on the back, but generally it was supposed that the Army, and the Army, alone, won the battle for Burma. At the time it was not easy to integrate the tale of co-operation, liaison, and mutual assistance rendered by one service to the other which resulted during this year of campaigning, 1944, in the formation of vast organizations in which the Army and R.A.F. worked completely together for the purpose of keeping nearly one million men in the field of battle. That each maintained its right of grumbling at the other was only natural. That the beleagured garrisons in the Imphal Plain came near to disintegration through lack of supplies was the fault of neither.

Therefore, as the whole problem of air supply had become, by 1944, one of considerable importance, it might be useful to digress for a moment on this subject.

It was not Mountbatten or Wingate or Slim who 'invented' the supplying of jungle armies by air. They, seeing its widespread possibilities and control over the destinies of jungle-bound armies, exploited and expanded it to the limit of their resources; and sometimes over the limit.

It was back in the days of the Burma retreat that 31

Squadron of the R.A.F. and the 2nd Troop Carrier Squadron U.S.A.A.F. pioneered air supply while the Airborne Forces Research Centre in the Punjab devised methods of training and experimental development. Though it may now seem obvious, it had then to be discovered that a sufficiency of transport aircraft and crews was by no means the only requisite. Lessons had to be learned in packing, housing, loading, and disposing of the paraphernalia required by the Army. A great deal depended on the location of railway lines and stations, their proximity to airfields and ability to supply the transport aircraft with the materials to fly to the troops.

For the Army it was the ubiquitous Royal Indian Army Service Corps who took on the job. They had their base depots near airfields and railway stations and worked in effective liaison with the R.A.F. Units of the R.I.A.S.C. were formed into air supply companies. Five were in existence in the autumn of 1943 and many more of far greater size were operating a year later.

All through the experimental stage a great deal was being learnt, so that when this last Arakan campaign was fought neither the army nor the air forces were caught napping, as was so frequently imagined during the war. At the beginning of 1944 these Air Supply Companies and the Troop Carrier Command had widespread commitments ranging from General Stilwell's Chinese and Americans in north Burma on the Ledo road, down through the frontier region where several Allied clandestine organizations were operating against the Japanese, to the West African Division in the Kaladan Valley. They were also concerned with the new Wingate expedition, for which was planned an airborne send-off into Burma in March. Then came the encirclement of the 7th Division and the reassuring discovery that the whole air supply organization was flexible enough to deal with this while not starving its other infants.

For the whole task there were four British and four American squadrons of Dakotas, plus a few Commandos lent by the American Air Transport Command when the emergency arose. Unfortunately most squadrons were short of crews and the number of aircraft available was never what it appeared to be on paper.

The air evacuation of wounded was becoming an adjunct of this supply organization by the time the Arakan battle was fought. As, however, it was not always possible to build Dakota strips in the middle of a battle-field—during the two months' Arakan campaign some twenty-five airstrips were built—individual ingenuity had full play and one R.A.F. officer organized a shuttle service with light planes, which carried over 800 wounded men out of battle to safety. Later, when casualty evacuation by air became a highly organized service, links between the battle-field and the Dakotas were maintained by light American planes known as Piper Cubs or Ls. 4 and 5, depending on their size.

There were bound to be difficulties in any theatre of war, but none more so than in Burma or Assam, where railways and roads were few and precarious, where jungle and mountain ranges covered the face of the land and made it a hostile wilderness, and where a monsoon raged for five months. It was this monsoon which was the greatest menace to air transport and not the Japanese Air Force, which, except for spasmodic raids, was adequately subdued by the Allied air forces. It was this monsoon which so nearly won the forthcoming battle for the Japanese in Manipur, for it rendered the transport aircraft and crews helpless. And the army lost its life-line.

The battle of which the Japanese expedition into the Kalapanzin Valley was a prelude, moved up the frontier some 400 miles to the central Burma front, known also as the Manipur or Imphal front. The Japanese had not been deterred by their lack of success in the Arakan. They had made their plans some time previously and were determined to carry them out. From the prestige viewpoint it seemed almost as important for them to bring some action into the Burma war as it was for the British. It was still more important, however, for the Japanese to strike before the Allies launched anything like a major offensive against Burma. Numerically inferior, the Japanese knew the time was approaching when they could no longer hold the Allies. They could only postpone events. A foothold on India, however expensively acquired, was worth a great deal of 'face' in the East. It had considerable propaganda value. The Allies caution and hesitation gave them the chance of striking first.

Imphal is a saucer of fifty square miles, flat and, in the monsoon season, partially waterlogged. It is situated among a great mass of hills and possesses only one connecting road with Assam and two with Burma. The first runs northwards to Kohima and Dimapur, Imphal's nearest railhead in Assam. The other two ran east and south to Tamu and Tiddim in Burma. All cut into and through hill ranges. Imphal was the biggest Allied base along the Burma front. Geographically it was sound for offence, for it permitted twin drives into Burma. But it was something of a death-trap if the Japanese chose to invade on that front, for its one road to India ran parallel to the front. This link, being a winding, tortuous road through hills, was not very difficult to cut and cut again. And, as it proved later on, it was a very difficult road to clear.

But there was no other more suitable base on the whole 800-mile front which, apart from the Imphal Plain, was a great mass of jungled mountains with few known passes and fewer roads.

The Imphal Plain and its straggling bamboo and mud-hutted township was the centre of the state of Manipur, over which ruled an impoverished Maharajah whose chief complaint in life was that he did not possess as many wives as his father. He was guided by a British Prime Minister, and watched over by a British Resident.

In normal times, the European population of this distant isolated state was confined to these two Britishers, a District Officer who looked after the Nagas, in the Naga Hills, and a few foreign missionaries. Neither Imphal nor Manipur was on the normal visiting list of senior British officials in India, and Lord Curzon was the only Viceroy ever to visit the State.

That the British of his day were of tough fibre was proved when Lord Curzon made the journey from Silchar, in Assam, to Imphal in a palanquin over a mountain track so narrow in parts that it would not even be traversed by mules. That was before the Imphal-Kohima-Dimapur road was built. Even when the Silchar track was developed by Col. Chapman and a group of ordinary soldiers and native labourers in 1942, it was unusable by jeeps, and was therefore useless for army purposes. It was an exit from the plain which could only be used as a last resort.

The strategic importance of Imphal was that, in our hands, it could maintain forces in the Chin Hills or along the west bank of the Chindwin river. Some 200,000 troops used it as a base.

In the hands of the Japanese, Imphal was of even greater significance. It would constitute Japan's first real foothold on Hindu India, and would cause confusion and alarm throughout the Hindu world which might rock the foundations of Britain's rule. As it was, the fact that the Japanese did isolate the plain caused more alarm within India than it did to the British-Indian troops who were isolated.

It would give the Japanese a base for operations against Assam, with its growing number of Allied airfields and its railway line. It would give them a stepping-off ground into Bengal. It would isolate General Stilwell in the north, and

Wingate, whose second Chindit expedition was just about to fly into Burma. It would cut off China from its air supply. Finally, it would end Mountbatten's newly formed South-East Asia Command, for at that time his theatre of war began east of the Brahmaputra and he would have had no land territory left. The battle for India would pass to General Sir Claude Auchinleck and India Command. For all these reasons the battle of Imphal which began in March 1944 was of far-reaching importance to the world in general.

By February 1944 the Japanese had increased their divisional strength in Burma to eight. During the previous four months four new divisions had appeared—two from central China, one from Java, and one from Guadalcanal. At the same time came an army headquarters and an independent brigade. The total number of combatant battalions was seventy-five, more than double the number of men, divisions, and other units which had captured and held Burma for nearly two years. Forty-eight of these battalions were brigaded under the 15th Army (Lieut.-Gen. Mutagachi) ranging across the north and up and down the east bank of the Upper Chindwin river. To strengthen their left flank the Japanese had, at the end of 1943, occupied Falam in the Lushai Hills, a base from which British-led Lushai guerrilla forces had been operating against the enemy.

Though at the end of February the Japanese had withdrawn some of their fighter formations to rear areas, it was apparently only for the purposes of re-grouping for, by the first week in March, a strong force of bombers and fighters moved up to the series of airfields in the Shwebo area. Also during the early weeks of 1944 an increasing number of river craft were reported to be lining the Chindwin and its offshoots. It was clear the Japanese were preparing for action irrespective of what was the fate of their Arakan expedition.

On the Allied side three Indian divisions, the 20th, 17th, and 23rd, and one tank brigade, the 254th, were deployed over the whole Imphal area. Maj.-Gen. D. T. Cowan's 17th, who had been in the original Burma retreat, was based on Tiddim in the Chin Hills and, as a line of communication, had the 163-mile Tiddim road back to Imphal. He had maintained outposts as far forward as the Bamboo Stockades and Fort White but had withdrawn them to the region of Kennedy Peak, the 9,000-foot king peak of the hills.

Maj.-Gen. Douglas Gracey's 20th Division ranged down the Kabaw Valley from Tamu and had wrested the patrolling initiative from the Japanese, while Maj.-Gen. O. L. Roberts's 23rd was assigned to the defence of Imphal and the Imphal–Kohima road. These three divisions covered some 25,000 square miles of hills, jungle, and valleys. Lieut.-Gen. G. A. P. Scoones, the 4th Corps commander, had his headquarters first in Imphal and, when the battle began, on a wooded hill just outside the town.

Imphal also was the headquarters of 221 Group of the R.A.F. At the several airstrips, only two of which were all-weather, were two squadrons of Spitfires which had only arrived in this theatre in November 1943, some Hurricanes, and three squadrons of Hurribombers, all of which came under 170 Wing. This group comprised part of Air Marshal Sir John Baldwin's 3rd Tactical Air Force which, in turn, was part of the British-American integrated Eastern Air Command. Apart from local and air transport route defence, they were assisted in the overall air strategy by the 14th U.S.A.A.F. based in China, the 10th U.S.A.A.F. in the north, and the Strategic Air Force in India.

Despite what was happening in the Arakan, Mountbatten's basic policy was still to recover north Burma and push on the road into China. Everything had to be subordinated to that single idea. It was the prime task given him by the Combined Chiefs of Staff in London and Washington.

Therefore, irrespective of what counter-action the Japanese took, Wingate's second Chindits were to be launched to coincide with the advance of the Ledo road into and across the Huwkawng Valley, while General Scoones pushed his 4th Corps to the line of the Upper Chindwin.

From the beginning of March until well into July the events on this central and its closely correlated fronts, Stilwell's and Wingate's, remained completely obscure to the outside world. So many things happened at one time, many of them top secret, the pattern of warfare was so intricate and the censorship so rigid, that even that brilliant military correspondent and commentator, Hanson Baldwin of the *New York Times*, could make little of what was happening. He remained, however, both optimistic and uncynical and did his best to paint a picture to a sensitive American public of the true position, which was rarely as bad as was made out.

When finally the facts were known Baldwin described General Slim's conduct of the whole 'Assam Valley Operations' as the most brilliant of the war.

Therefore, in describing the events of the next few months it is best to take each separately and occasionally place them all in chronological perspective.

On 5 March Maj.-Gen. Wingate's second Chindit expedition was launched on 'Operation Thursday', a glider-borne expedition into his old hunting-ground in north Burma. This time he took not a brigade but a division-plus in strength. A month before, Brigadier Fergusson, leading a brigade column of the Chindits—the only one to march on this occasion—had begun his advance from Ledo on Stilwell's west flank.

General Stilwell with the 22nd and 38th Chinese Divisions and Colonel Rothwell Brown's Chinese-manned American tanks left Shinbwiyang to cross into the Huwkawng Valley, joined by a new long-range penetration group, Brigadier

Frank Merrill's Marauders. 'Y' Force, otherwise the Trans-Salween Chinese, should have begun their advance into north-east Burma by way of the old Burma road from Yunnan, but again defected. 4th Corps probed down the Kabaw Valley or past Kennedy Peak in the Chin Hills.

All these operations, those of Stilwell, Wingate, and Scoones, came under the overall command of General Slim. Simultaneously the Japanese 15th Army began crossing the Chindwin and flowing into the Chin Hills for their attack against Assam and India. They moved with considerable speed.

The Japanese 15th Army, comprising the 15th, 31st, and 33rd divisions with attendant troops, amounting to nearly 100,000 men, moved in three directions on three different tasks which were to take not more than ten days if successful.

The 31st Division crossed the Chindwin around Thaungdut and Homalin, passed through the Naga Hills and made for Kohima, Dimapur, and the railway, Stilwell's life-line. The 15th Division advanced up the Kabaw Valley with the object of cutting off and wiping out the 20th Indian Division. The 33rd Division, infiltrating into the Chin Hills, was entrusted with the annihilation of their old enemy, the 17th Indian Division. They would then join the 15th in Imphal. General Mutagachi bestowed the divine blessing of the Japanese Emperor on the whole operation, exhorting his men to conserve ammunition and live by capture when their own stocks had run out.

The attempted envelopment of 17th Division by the 33rd Japanese took place first. It was called by the Japanese, 'Operation White Tiger', for the crack 33rd Division had a white tiger as its sign. The 17th Indian had a black cat as its divisional sign.

It was at the end of February when 48th Brigade of the 17th Division fought the battle of Milestone 22, a domed peak overlooking Fort White and dominating the immediate area as far as Kennedy Peak, which was the 17th Division's most advanced secure point.

Milestone 22 had been burrowed by the Japanese as if they were rabbits. There was a tunnel running back to Fort White. Foxholes with camouflaged lids on them covered the hill. Except for a few skeleton trees it was completely bare and open. The battle is chiefly interesting since it was the last, in this sector, of the original offensive plan. It aimed at capturing Fort White when the division could advance to Kalewa.

Two companies of Gurkhas were ordered to take the hill and hold it. After a preliminary barrage to keep the Japanese within their holes, the bandy-legged little Gurkhas swarmed over the hill, looking for, but not finding, many foxhole entrances. Despite well-placed machine-guns on the reverse slope of the hills, the Gurkhas' casualties were not heavy. One company wired itself in for the night. The other failed to do so.

During the night pandemonium broke out. In the dim starlit night men wearing Gurkha hats or tin helmets could be seen moving over the barren hill shooting and shouting. The company within their wire perimeter could do nothing for fear of shooting friends. The company without a perimeter knew little of what was happening except, it seemed, their own men were shooting at them. In the morning not one Gurkha or British officer not within the wire perimeter remained on the hill. All had disappeared during the night. The Japanese, disguised in British uniforms and with darkened faces, had emerged from their foxholes and killed or captured the surprised Gurkhas. Then they had dragged them into their underground fortress. It may sound incredible but it was, nevertheless, true.

48th Brigade never captured Milestone 22. Instead other units of the division besieged and eventually forced the Japanese to withdraw from two crests known as Lophei and Vaona which were the Japanese outpost wings. Here again was an example of the peculiarities of hill warfare, because the Japanese had dug themselves complete underground fortessses, each capable of holding a battalion in a very small area. Each had tanks holding sufficient water for several days and was surrounded by wire and booby traps. Water was the answer, and the division trapped the incoming supplies until the Japanese were forced to break out and withdraw.

By the end of February it became clear that the Japanese were on the move into Manipur even if the strength and full intentions of their thrust were unclear. With two divisions out on limbs, very long limbs too, and only one in defence of the Imphal Plain and the Imphal–Kohima road, the military position of 4th Corps was tactically unsound. It would not be difficult for even a small force of Japanese to cut across each limb and isolate the 20th Division in the Kabaw Valley and the 17th in the Chin Hills. What should have been a complete corps group would then have split up into at least three sections each fighting an individual battle to free itself and permitting any further Japanese forces to move where they pleased. Scoones had no choice but to call in his outlying divisions, though from the point of view of prestige and morale withdrawal was odious.

On 12 March, General Cowan received orders to withdraw from Tiddim within forty-eight hours. His division was strung out forward of Tiddim for some twenty-five miles and out on limbs which required at least twenty-four hours to reach. It was one of the characteristics of hill-fighting that a platoon on one crest might be within shouting distance of another on a crest next door, yet for one to reach the other meant a trail down into the valley, perhaps 3,000 feet below, and up again.

Anticipating events, General Cowan had his withdrawal

plan ready made and it is one of those strange incidents in a man's life that he awoke during the night of the thirteenth convinced that he should begin right away. He ordered the withdrawal to begin immediately.

The Japanese made for Tongzang, a hill village on the road from Tiddim to Imphal. The village was lightly held by the West Yorks and, if the Japanese captured it, they would lie directly in the division's path of retreat. They moved so fast that the affair became a race. The West Yorks were actually fighting as the general, marching in traditional style at the head of his troops, filed past. Behind him strung out the divisional column.

During the first day of retreat the 17th Division made forty miles, every officer and man except sick and wounded marching on foot. Unfortunately the Japanese had sent another prong to Milestone 109, where lay one of the several large supply bases along the road. Held only by administrative troops and situated in a cup in the hills, Milestone 109 was vulnerable. The Japanese descended upon it from all sides, whereupon the garrison was forced to retire. Sick and wounded were carried out on bamboo stretchers and at times the senior officer, known as the 'Admin. Commandant', who possessed a black spaniel as his ever-present companion, was forced to keep the Sikhs at the revolver point from dropping their loads of wounded.

Farther down the road, at Milestone 82, was another large supply base. This, too, the Japanese threatened, setting up a road block between it and Milestone 109 and sending out nightly jitter parties to stir up panic within the perimeter of Milestone 82.

Events were moving so fast that little was known of what was happening until a brigadier, going forward from Milestone 82 to reach 109, found his way barred and the telephone line cut. Leaving their jeep and hiding in the jungle from Japanese patrols, the brigadier and his orderly managed to tap in on the open telephone line and send a message back to 82 that 109 was captured and the Japanese were moving down the road.

Another officer taking forward his monthly rum ration was fired upon, and jumped over the side of a hill out of his jeep. When the Japanese passed he recovered his jeep but was chagrined to discover they had absconded with his rum!

As the 17th Division fought for the recovery of Milestone 109—fortunately the Japanese occupation force was not large and was primarily engaged on eating as much tinned fruit as possible in a short time—Milestone 82 fought one of those typical battles that flared up all over the Burma front until men became used to the jungle, the night, and the Japanese.

The road divided Milestone 82 into two halves, containing in all some 5,000 men and 2,000 vehicles. The great majority of men were untrained in fighting. The 37th Brigade of 23rd Division, which had arrived from Imphal to assist clear the road for the 17th Division, was operating in the hills outside the perimeter of the supply camp.

A few Japanese, armed with tin cans loaded with stones and shouting English and Urdu, caused pandemonium among the inhabitants of the 'box'. One side of the road fired on the other and the night was lit up with red and yellow tracer darting into the hills on either side and, in some cases, straight up in the air. It was quite impossible to stop these 'jitter parties' once they had begun, and only weariness and a lack of ammunition ever caused them to die down. For those whose nerves were hardened by experience the only place of safety was well down in a slit trench or on the floor of a basha. That such 'jitterings' should occur in 1944—they happened again and again—proved that only actual war and not training could steel men's nerves.

For three weeks the Japanese held on to positions and road blocks in the area of Milestones 109 and 82 with the 17th

Division hammering them from one side and the 37th Brigade from the other. Frequently the Japanese announced the annihilation of the division, but it remained almost completely intact with all its guns and vehicles. Every vehicle at Milestone 109 was recaptured undamaged.

At the beginning of April the division reached the supply base at Milestone 82 with only one block between it and Imphal. When, on 2 April, General Cowan moved out of his headquarters mess for the final march back to Imphal, a despairing Japanese shell hit the mess 'basha' a few minutes after the cook sergeant had cleared away the last plates. The division lost few men on its journey and reached Imphal with all its guns and wounded and ninety per cent of its transport. Behind it came the tanks of the 33rd Japanese Division.

9
THE SIEGE OF IMPHAL

Withdrawal of 20th Division—Fly-in of 5th Division to Imphal—Siege of Imphal—Hazards of Air Supply

THE withdrawal from the Kabaw Valley of General Gracey's 20th Indian Division took place about the same time as that of the 17th from Tiddim. In its case, however, the retreat was to be slow and stubbornly fought, whereas for the 17th it had to be as fast as possible. The reason was that along the Palel–Tamu road, which wound through the hills for some forty miles, were several most defensible and dominating positions on peaks and spurs from which the 20th Division could impede the Japanese advance while digging similar positions farther back. Ultimately the division was to stop short of the Palel entrance to the hills in an attempt to prevent, if possible, the Japanese from overlooking the Plain and the Palel airstrip. Palel was some twenty miles south-east of Imphal, at the base of the hill range separating the plain from the Kabaw Valley.

It was on Japanese Army Day, 10 March, that an Indian jemadar of the Frontier Force Regiment spotted an armoured patrol of Bren carriers moving up the valley from the area of Htintzin. He naturally accepted the patrol as Allied until he was fired upon. Replying with a couple of grenades, he retired with the information.

A week later, just as the division was about to pull in its outposts, the second Japanese prisoner of the Burma War was taken in a foxhole near the Uyu river, a tributary of the Chindwin. He was dazed and quite useless, like so many later, to the intelligence officers who interrogated him. He did, however, have the distinction of saluting and being spoken to, through an interpreter, by Mountbatten in Imphal.

Gurkhas and a Border battalion met the leading elements of the Japanese 15th Division while other units of the 20th Division formed defensive boxes nearer Tamu, at Charing Cross and Moreh. The Borders, retiring from Witok, were ambushed by the Japanese at night and in the resulting panic both the C.O. and the padre were kicked over the side of the hill by an angry mule. The battalion, except for one isolated party including wounded, found its way in small bands back to the Charing Cross 'box', where stood the 32nd Brigade.

Pressing upon the heels of the withdrawing troops, the Japanese brought up tanks and also their biggest artillery piece, the 155-mm. gun, which out-ranged anything the British had in Burma. One 155 was directed with some accuracy on divisional headquarters while the tanks set ambushes along the jungled parts of the Witok–Tamu road.

It was on this road that the first tank-*versus*-tank battle was fought quite fortuitously. Unbeknown to the Japanese, General Lees and Grants of the 3rd Carabiniers had arrived in Tamu disguised, on their tank tractors, as canteen stores. They had driven all the way down from Dimapur and few people had known what actually lay hidden under the giant tarpaulins.

Eight Grants and a company of Gurkhas emerged from the Charing Cross 'box' under one of the finest tank officers of the whole campaign, Major Teddy Pettit, who was later killed in an air crash, to rescue an isolated party down the valley. After a few miles the jungle on either side of the dusty track broke away into a fair-sized plain. At the junction the Japanese had laid an ambush consisting of half a dozen tanks and a company of men.

As the leading Grant tank reached the ambush the Japanese opened fire and hit the one vulnerable part of the tank, the petrol tank. The other Grants opened fire into the jungle and then chased the Japanese tanks into the open, where they destroyed five tanks and their crews and captured one tank virtually intact. This latter was driven off the battle-field by a British corporal. On investigation the Japanese tanks proved to be copies of 1928 Cardon-Lloyds armed with one 37-mm. gun and holding a crew of three in very cramped conditions. Against Grants or Lees they had no chance whatsoever.

The Japanese attempt to cut across the 20th Division's withdrawal at Sebang in the hills coincided with their efforts to break the Charing Cross and Moreh 'boxes' which guarded the division's only exit from the Kabaw Valley. They were beaten to Sebang by the leading troops of the withdrawing division, who found the Japanese ensconced in foxholes but not in large numbers. The division's main objective was the Shenam Saddle, which they were able to consolidate without any serious Japanese threat, thus showing that their withdrawal had been timed correctly.

Unable to force the direct route into the Imphal Plain and failing to cut off the division, the Japanese lay back in the hills, looking for opportunities to make entrance to the plain, or, at least, to make part of it untenable for aircraft. This they succeeded in doing and Palel airstrip was evacuated.

In the Imphal Plain, during these two withdrawals, the 23rd Indian Division, under General Roberts, was given the ubiquitous role of not only blocking up the holes into the plain, but also maintaining at least one brigade as a mobile reserve. Roberts established his headquarters on one of the few excrescences rising out of the plain, from which he could see as far as Bishenpur, near the Tiddim road entrance, Wanjing and Palel near the Tamu road, as far as corps headquarters, which covered the exit to the Kohima–Dimapur road, and finally the other principal entrance or exit, the road to Ukhrul in the Naga Hills.

It was at Ukhrul that one of the major disasters of the Imphal campaign occurred. The fighting manpower situation was considered so serious that the 50th Parachute Brigade consisting of Gurkhas and British officers—one of the only completely trained parachute units in the whole theatre—was transferred to Imphal to fight a ground action. It marched to Ukhrul and formed a very tight box near the village. Its task was to stop or hinder the Japanese 31st Division moving across the Naga Hills and upwards towards Kohima. The perimeter of the box was so small that aircraft could not drop their supplies with any accuracy and most of the food and ammunition was collected by the enemy.

The 50th Parachute Brigade's operation, which should have been offensive, became a siege. The Japanese surrounded the 'box' and gradually starved the brigade into a position of surrender or disintegration. No help was available in Imphal, and the brigade was accounted as a dead loss, eventually breaking out in small parties and attempting with moderate success to reach Imphal. The young brigadier in command fell down a hill-side, but, despite a fractured spine and several other serious injuries, struggled back to Imphal.

Whereas 4th Corps should have turned on an offensive to aid Stilwell's drive in the north, it had been forced to recoil and was then in a very serious military position. Stilwell's right flank was exposed and his main line of communication threatened. As Stilwell was, as he called it, 'at the end of the line' some bitterness was natural and he displayed antagonism towards Giffard. Mountbatten, thereupon, assumed all responsibility for land operations and Giffard retired. Mountbatten maintained direct contact with Slim, who was responsible for fighting the battle and, for this operation, was also over Stilwell.

Mountbatten and Slim realized that three divisions were

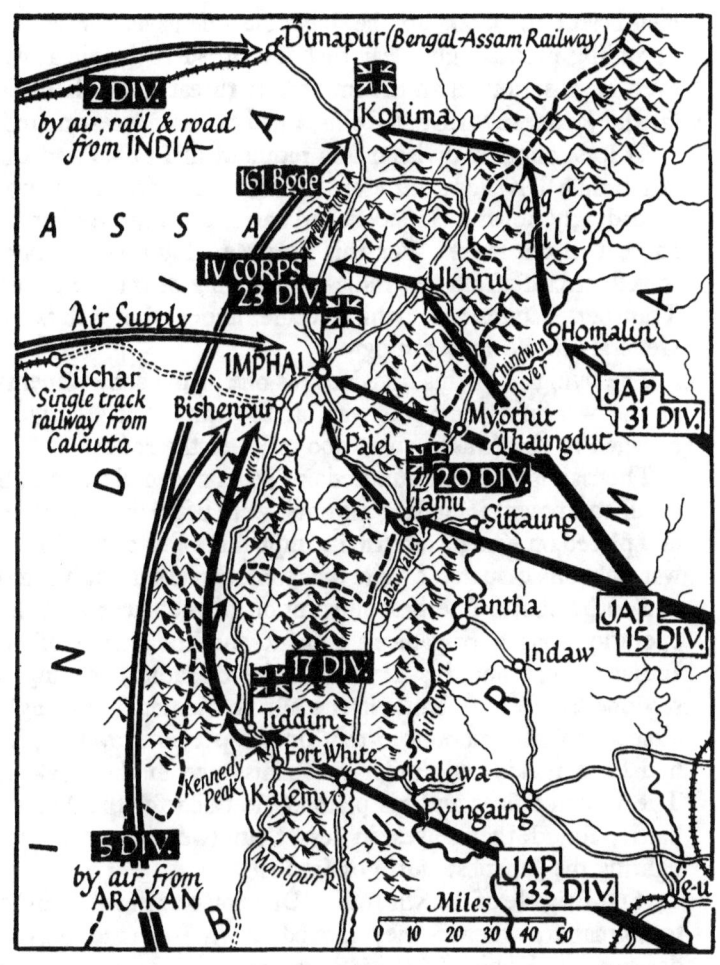

THE SIEGE OF IMPHAL—MARCH 1944

Showing retreat of British-Indian Divisions, Advance of Japanese, and Counter Measures

insufficient to break up the Japanese offensive, for it was becoming increasingly clear that the threat to Kohima was even more serious than the immediate threat to Imphal. So far the Japanese thrust at Kohima had been underestimated.

At least another division was required in Imphal and the 5th Indian Division, of desert and Arakan experience, was accordingly flown lock, stock, and barrel from the Arakan to Imphal in one week. For this purpose Mountbatten 'borrowed' aircraft from the India-China wing of the American Transport Command, which came under the orders of General Arnold in Washington.

The flying in of this division was one of the achievements of the war in Burma. It was, at the time, fairly actively engaged in the Arakan some 400 miles to the south.

Thousands of men, hundreds of jeeps and mules, and all small equipment including mortars, were lifted into the skies and placed on Kangla airstrip in Imphal in a few days. There was only one casualty; a mule that went berserk in the air and had to be shot. The best illustration of the success of the operation was a brigadier's remark and the action of an Indian officer and his platoon. The brigadier, making a reconnaissance for a battle in the hills to the north of Kangla airstrip, calmly announced that on the previous evening he had been making a similar reconnaissance in the Arakan. The Indian officer and his platoon, destined for the Arakan battle, found themselves in less than twenty-four hours, fighting the Japanese north of Imphal.

161st Brigade of the 5th Indian Division was flown straight to Dimapur, whence they moved down the road to the defence of Kohima, which was being harassed by the leading elements of the 31st Japanese Division.

With the increase in numbers in the Imphal Plain it became imperative that all unnecessary ('soft') mouths should be hastily evacuated. Transport aircraft could handle fair numbers but General Scoones wished to be rid of at least 50,000, for his ration list exceeded 165,000, which was more than the British Army in peacetime. Therefore every man not considered necessary for the impending siege—the Japanese had already cut the Imphal-Kohima-Dimapur road thus isolating Imphal completely—was dispatched by air or along the Silchar and Haflong tracks, two mountain trails, which wound their way westward to Assam proper. Neither of these tracks was usable by vehicles and the men, carrying their food, had to march. The Japanese made a determined effort to cut the Haflong track but succeeded only in damaging a water station.

The siege of Imphal had then begun. Inside the plain were the 17th, 20th, 23rd, and 5th Indians Divisions, less one brigade, the 254 Tank Brigade under General Scoones's brother, and tens of thousands of other troops who were considered able to fight with rifle and bayonet, though before they had driven trucks or bulldozers or wielded picks and shovels in hacking out roads and tracks.

On the north, east, and south of the plain, were the Japanese 15th and 33rd Divisions, astride the few roads entering the plain, and constantly probing down little-used tracks to find some weak spot. Kohima had become completely separated and was, by then, a battle on its own. All these things happened in the brief space of a few weeks.

The outpourings of the Japanese radio, claiming the annihilation of Indian divisions and the capture of Kohima and Imphal, had considerable demoralizing effects in India. They brought criticism of the British from America and caused bewilderment in Britain. However, the seriousness was, as yet, unrealized by the troops caged in Imphal. Only the senior commanders, especially Mountbatten, who stood trial on the success or failure of this operation, knew what could happen. In Delhi, General Auchinleck, while allaying the fears of the Assembly and Chamber of Princes with a very calm speech, was preparing for the final eventuality:

the evacuation of the Brahmaputra Valley by 4th Corps and the passing over of command to himself and a strained India Command already drained of its best troops.

The battle which developed on the Imphal sector was not so much a fight between British-Indian soldiers and Japanese, or a match between the cunning and appreciation of Slim or Scoones and that of Mutagachi, as a battle for keeping 4th Corps replenished with food, ammunition, and petrol. It was fought by transport aircraft against many handicaps, the major one being the weather. From the purely military point of view the chief ground action was being fought up at Kohima with the object of recapturing the village and opening the road to Imphal.

Imphal had two chances provided that Scoones used his divisions and brigades successfully in blocking the plain from any major Japanese incursion. The first chance was supplied by aircraft and the second by the speed with which 33rd Corps, under Lieut.-Gen. M. Stopford, cleared the road.

The siege of Imphal became a battle of air supply. It turned out to be the biggest operation of its kind carried out up till that moment.

General Scoones inhabited an eyrie of his own on the top of a hill and when all the divisions had collected round him like chickens round the mother hen, Mountbatten arrived from a tour of Stilwell's northern front. He sensed the growing disillusionment of the British troops at the series of retreats and the apparent failure to cope with the Japanese. Man for man the British soldier was confident of his own personal superiority, but he was not always confident of his commanders.

Mountbatten toured round the battalions, trying out his newly learnt Urdu on the Indians and speaking in intimate and confident terms to the British. As a personality he was, and still is, an unqualified success and in those gloomy days, with the monsoon clouds already forming away over and above the hills, he did a great deal to alleviate the fears of the troops. He told them quite frankly the position and its difficulties. He told of the shortage of aircraft and how he had signalled to Maitland Wilson (he added no title to the Mediterranean Commander) and how he had borrowed from the 'Hump' route—a fact out of which the American correspondents later tried to make critical capital—and how, having won a similar but smaller battle in the Arakan by air supply, he hoped they would win this one. The troops were impressed with the forthright man-to-man nature of their Supreme Commander.

Here it is worth recording one of several incidents which prove Mountbatten's ability to overcome personal scepticism on the part of individuals. There was a cook in the Border Regiment who did not believe in Royalty and titles and who considered that Mountbatten's appointment had been the result of his family relationship to the King. The cook had no wish to meet such a man, nor did he believe he was capable of pulling the battalion out of the trouble it was already in.

The Commanding Officer therefore gave the cook permission to miss Mountbatten's talk to the officers and men but took good care that it should take place near the cookhouse.

Mountbatten had not been speaking long, but already there were laughs from the crowd when the C.O. saw the cook emerge from his cookhouse and join them. The expression on the cook's face altered, one gathers, from cynical dislike to grinning pleasure as he, too, was captured by the personality of the speaker. From then on the cook became one of Mountbatten's most loyal and devoted servants.

If Mountbatten could be light-hearted in the open he was deadly serious within. Though his main headquarters were, at that time, on the move from Delhi to Kandy in Ceylon, at the cost of two million pounds, he maintained a private headquarters in Assam so that he could more readily keep in touch with his various land and air commanders.

Extra stocks of petrol and ammunition had been brought into Imphal before the Japanese cut the road to Dimapur. The situation, however, was likely to become so grave that a general redistribution of air transport resources was necessary within the whole theatre.

The root difficulty was that of balancing the needs of the Imphal garrison, and anticipating its length of siege, against those of all the other Allied groups supplied by air. The eight Dakota squadrons and a small number of loaned Commandos were still responsible for all air supply and transport commitments from the Huwkawng Valley in north Burma to Maungdaw in the Arakan, including by then, quite apart from Imphal, General Wingate's Chindits, who had been launched into north-central Burma, and the 81st West African Division still in the Kaladán Valley.

In mid-April several conferences on the supply problem took place in Assam, closing with one at 14th Army H.Q. at Comilla, at which was represented everyone of importance. It was decided that the daily tonnage required by the troops of 4th Corps and the R.A.F. was 540 at the minimum, or 16,000 tons a month. It was agreed that the troops' field ration scale should be cut to 65 per cent and that two of the hospitals in Imphal should be flown out to relieve the congestion. But it was also suggested that up to the end of the month the quantity flown in should be large enough to build up at least thirty days' stock in Imphal itself.

The policy, from 1 May onwards, was to reduce the quantities so that the reserve should never be lower than fifteen days, and so that air supply could be stepped-up to other sectors, primarily to the Chinese-American one where General Stilwell was advancing on Myitkyina. This, it must be realized, was the conference table theory. In practice things did not work out.

THE SIEGE OF IMPHAL

Soon afterwards some of the aircraft earmarked for the supply of Imphal were diverted to fulfil urgent requests from Wingate's Chindits. The West Africans' requirements proved heavier than anticipated. To build another all-weather airstrip in Imphal—Kangla was the only all-weather one—over 300 tons of bithess had to be transported by air from Calcutta at the expense of food and ammunition. And, much worse, the weather broke earlier, and with greater violence, than expected.

For the rest of April and throughout May the monsoon gathered momentum. It converted any but all-weather airstrips into bogs. Its cloudbanks covered with an unbroken shroud the vast area of hills and plains and not only cut down the hours of flying but cut out whole days as well. For pilots, flying over the hills surrounding Imphal, looking for some tiny crack or break in the cloud banks through which they might descend into the plain, it was a nightmare. A fifty-square-mile plain among 25,000 square miles of hills and valleys is not easy to find on a clear day. Under monsoon conditions it was wellnigh impossible. Pilots sometimes made three or four attempts from different directions. A few, fortunately a very few, made their descent through a break and, misjudging their position, hit the side of a hill. It was a perilous task.

Often transport aircraft were forced to land not at their own base but at the nearest available landing-strip. To avoid the scattering of stores and supplies a staging-post was established at Kumbhirgam, just west of the hills surrounding Imphal, on the normal route. Aircraft could dump their supplies there and move off. At favourable moments these stocks were flown into Imphal.

4th Corps speeded up its evacuation of 'soft-mouthed' troops, while the R.A.F. dispensed with all possible administrative staff and brought down their number of air squadrons based in the plain to a minimum of two squadrons of Spitfires, I.A.F., a squadron of ground attack Hurricanes, and two of Hurribombers.

Despite the reinforcement of air transport planes, including six squadrons from the Mediterranean (five American and one British), and retention over their term of the Commandos from the China run, the backlog in Imphal continued to mount up. During May only 5,000 tons were flown in to Imphal against an estimated requirement of 16,000 plus the increasing size of the backlog.

The end of May and the beginning of June was the critical period of the whole campaign. The weather still prohibited flying for days on end. The calls for transport aircraft to all sectors became urgent and incessant. Stocks in Imphal were reduced to two weeks' amount of food, on reduced rations, a week's supply of petrol on the absolute minimum scale—it was a court-martial offence to drive an empty vehicle—and ammunition was down to nothing except what was carried by the troops and gun vehicles.

As a final measure of self-help Strategic Air Force Wellingtons and Mitchells were withdrawn from bombing duties to carry in ammunition, and bomber crews were transferred to relieve the overworked and understaffed Dakota squadrons.

What amounted to a final blow at Mountbatten's hopes of holding out in Imphal came when the six Dakota squadrons were ordered to return to the Middle East for the invasion of Europe. It was then that he sent his urgent personal signal to Maitland Wilson requesting the retention of the aircraft against the growing crisis.

Though he did not stress the point, Mountbatten realized that he was within a few days of facing the ultimate and disastrous alternatives: leaving 4th Corps in Imphal to surrender, or ordering them to leave everything and fight their way back to Assam and India. In either case the Japanese would have scored a momentous victory. It was within the space of a few hours that the reply came from Maitland

Wilson that the Dakotas could remain. It was a matter of a couple of days before the weather cleared and the tonnage rose suddenly from as low as five per day to over 300. The day of judgment had been postponed.

10

THE BATTLE OF KOHIMA

An Allied Error of Judgment—Japanese Claim Capture of Kohima—Arrival of 2nd Division—Battle of Kohima Develops

COINCIDING with the movement of events and divisions in Imphal came the advance of the Japanese 31st Division on Kohima, a little hill town some 6,000 feet above sea-level and perched on several peaks. Residing there was a British District Commissioner, Charles Pawsey.

The advance was no less swift than any of the others. The division crossed the Chindwin at Homalin and Thaungdut, infiltrated through the Naga Hills, forced the disintegration of the 50th Parachute Brigade at Ukhrul, thus ensuring its main line of communication—one road motorable in good weather back to the Chindwin—and continued on to Kohima's two outposts, Jessami and Phek.

The initial part of their advance was watched by a British officer of 'V' Force. Unfortunately he was unable to communicate with his headquarters as his wireless set had broken down. The Jessami garrison, manned by troops of the Assam Regiment, were in similar plight and did not receive the radio, telephone, or air-dropped messages to retire. It put up a gallant stand, several times being forced to move position, until finally a British officer got through from Phek, twenty miles away, with the order to retire on Kohima. By then it was all but too late. The Japanese had swept on.

The Japanese objective was not principally Kohima. The 31st Divisional Commander was entrusted with the task of capturing Dimapur, railhead for Imphal and junction of

THE BATTLE OF KOHIMA 133

Assam's only railway. It lay fifty miles to the west of Kohima and dominated not only the railway line but also the road running north through Assam.

Dimapur was a valuable prize, for its capture would isolate General Stilwell and his Chinese and American troops in the north. It would also cut off the great air-base airfields such as Chabua, Jorhat, Dinjan, and Ledo, in North Assam, which relied on the railway for their heavy supplies. To the Imphal garrison its capture would be the key being turned in the door.

The capture of Kohima would seal off Imphal, but nothing else. The Japanese occupation of Dimapur would make it extremely difficult for the Allies to bring up a relief force, for there was not another rail base for miles. When, and if, a relief force arrived, it would have to recapture Dimapur before advancing on Kohima, which was a place easy to defend.

If the railway line was cut every Allied unit, big and small, in north and east Assam would be dependent on air supply, a commitment far beyond the resources of Troop Carrying Command even in the best of weather. The Japanese had only to hold on for a month or so and they would succeed in starving the Allied garrisons into surrender.

There is no doubt that the Japanese threat to Kohima and Dimapur was misappreciated by the intelligence department of the 14th Army, which was then responsible for the land fighting in this theatre. General Stilwell and General Wingate were, for the purposes of this phase of the war, under the command of General Slim, though Stilwell was still in the peculiar position of being Deputy Supreme Commander and in that capacity above Slim.

The investment of Imphal and the rapid movement of the Japanese 15th and 33rd Divisions must have blinded the 14th Army staff to the more serious aspects of the Japanese crossings at Homalin and Thaungdut, while the difficulties of obtaining sound intelligence led them to under-estimate the strength of the Japanese.

Kohima was garrisoned by 161st Brigade of the 5th Division (who only just arrived in time), and by administrative troops and men of the Burma and Assam Regiments and Assam Rifles, 3,500 men in all. Dimapur was held by administrative and railway troops, some of whom were armed with wooden rifles! A Japanese division, prepared to accept losses, which the Japanese always were, would have little trouble in overcoming this opposition by isolating it. The difficulties of supplying by air small garrisons or defensive 'boxes' perched on hills is apparent.

While Slim's question, 'Where will the Japanese strike next?' was being answered by their advance on Kohima, orders for a new British-Indian Corps to come to the rescue were being carried out. The seriousness of the position at Kohima and its possible implications was, by then, thoroughly clear. The cutting of the railway line had to be prevented and, so it seemed, only the reopening of the Kohima–Imphal road would save 4th Corps. Such apprehension was understandable, for it was obviously unknown at the time that both the weather and the transport aircraft position would improve in May and allow the air lift to Imphal to increase from starvation to subsistence level.

The order for Lieut.-Gen. M. Stopford's 33rd Corps to come part from the far side of India—2,000 miles away by road—and part from the Arakan did not go out until the middle of March, and the first units did not arrive at Dimapur until one day after the Japanese claimed the capture of Kohima, 4 April.

It was one of those fortunate coincidences of the war that an under-appreciation of the enemy's strength and intentions by the Allies was cancelled out by a grave error by the Japanese commander. Instead of investing Kohima and sweeping straight on to Dimapur, the 31st Divisional commander decided first to complete the capture of Kohima. It is probably a Japanese characteristic, just as it is a German one, to finish one affair before beginning another.

By concentrating on Kohima this Japanese officer lost all the advantages of rapid movement and surprise, and eventually his mistake cost the Japanese 15th Army its life and the whole campaign. Even one battalion pushed straight on to Dimapur as advance guard would have been a most serious embarrassment to the arrival of Maj.-Gen. John M. L. Grover's 2nd British Division, which came forward as the spearhead of 33rd Corps.

Kohima was dominated by a series of spurs and ridges, all of which soon acquired appropriate and sometimes picturesque names: Jail Hill, Kohima Ridge, Aradura Spur, Garrison Hill, G.P.T. (General Purpose Transport) Ridge, the District Commissioner's Bungalow, the Detail Issue Store. Through this maze of hills and ridges ran the tortuous winding road, so easy to cut, so difficult to clear.

The Japanese fell on Kohima by way of Kohima Ridge. The garrison of 3,500, besieged by 12,000 determined Japanese, was gradually forced to evacuate its outposts and strong-points and, greatly reduced in numbers through casualties, finally gather together for the last stand on Garrison Hill. There the Royal West Kents achieved immortal fame. They were the only battalion of 161st Brigade actually to reach the Hill and supplement the defenders. The other two battalions, the Rajputana Rifles and the Mahratta Light Infantry, had been cut off on the road leading into Kohima. There, too, Lance-Corporal John Harman, R.W.K., won his V.C. for knocking out one enemy machine-gun post with grenades and another by bayonet assault. In this battle one platoon of the R.W.K.s was reduced to four men. Once, it has been said, a Japanese digging his foxhole threw the earth into a foxhole occupied by a British soldier a few yards away, so close was the fighting.

For two weeks this little garrison hung on to their last foothold in Kohima. The rest of the town, battered and blasted by incessant mortar fire, was occupied by the Japanese. Doctors and stretcher bearers worked unceasingly bringing in and treating the casualties, of which there were hundreds. Often they had to pass through the Japanese lines; often they were fired upon by both sides; and always the wounded had to be carried by manpower, from hill to hill, ridge to ridge. The only water supply was in the hands of the Japanese, and the garrison was reduced to a pint a day for all purposes. But so staunch was their defence and so sure their aim that the Japanese gave up daylight infantry attacks on Garrison Hill.

While this was happening the 2nd British Division was moving across India and General Frank Messervy's 7th Division was preparing to leave the Arakan. Brig. L. Perowne's 23rd Brigade, trained in long-range penetration, was moving up for the task of cutting the Japanese lines of communication in the Naga Hills.

When the call came the 2nd British Division, which had seen no fighting since Dunkirk and had only a few of the original division left, was training in the area of Bombay and Belgaum. One brigade was, in fact, on its way to a leave centre in the Nilgiri Hills in southern India. All units were at least 2,000 miles away. This division had arrived in India two years previously and had been maintained as an Imperial force for emergencies in the Middle East, Iraq, or Burma. It had been trained in combined operations and jungle warfare and maintained all its vehicles modified for desert warfare.

The move of the 2nd Division took place by road, rail, river, and air, and while the head of the division arrived by air at Dimapur at the beginning of April, the tail did not wind up until the middle of May. Its column length was 2,000 miles.

On arrival at Dimapur the 5th Brigade (Dorsets, Camerons,

and Worcesters) found little transport and had to be shuttled down the road towards Kohima. Camerons and Worcesters were first into action on April 14. The first man killed was the Worcesters' padre, Father O'Callaghan, who was with the leading elements of his battalion.

On 14 April the Camerons, with Grant tanks, broke a Japanese road block and captured a hill which became known as Cameron Ridge, a feat not dissimilar to the capture of Cameron Ridge at Keren by another battalion of the same regiment. They made contact with 161st Brigade two days later.

The contact was a prelude to the relief of the small garrison by the Royal Berkshires of 6th Brigade, which followed on 19 April after Red Cross Ambulances had run the gauntlet of enemy fire to get through to the wounded on Garrison Hill. The besieged garrison was dazed but cheerful when the Berkshires arrived. They had withstood a terrible pounding by mortar and light guns for three weeks.

The majority of their air-dropped supplies either remained at the end of their parachutes just outside the perimeter or had been captured by the Japanese. Men had lived for three weeks without thought of shaving or washing. Mostly they had existed in foxholes, the only protection from the continuous Japanese barrage. But they had held the last uncaptured portion of Kohima, thereby making possible their own relief and giving the relieving troops time and room to manœuvre for the eventual recapture of the town.

The relief of the garrison was by no means the end of the Kohima bloodbath, for on all the remaining spurs and ridges the Japanese were well placed in foxholes and the underground earthworks which they are so adept at building. The next stage of the battle was the clearing of the Japanese from the high ground dominating Kohima in almost a complete circle—the only break in the circle being held by the garrison and relieving troops.

General Grover decided to push the 6th Brigade (D.L.I., Royal Welch Fusiliers, Royal Berkshires) farther and more firmly into the centre slice, move the 5th Brigade eastwards across a valley and on to a ridge giving access to Naga village, and send the 4th Brigade (Royal Scots, Royal Norfolks, Lancashire Fusiliers) round the west flank. The manœuvre constituted a centre punch and two hooking movements.

To reach the ridge to Naga village the 4th Brigade had to cut their way over a most precipitous ridge and bring up their supplies by Naga porters, as mules could not make the journey. The brigadier reported that his men were hanging on by their eyelids. The 5th Brigade had to advance right through Japanese positions to reach their objective, a feat they achieved in daylight before the Japanese took any serious counter-action. For nearly three weeks the brigade was out on a limb. Both brigades held firmly on to the flanks while the main assault went in on Jail Hill in the centre.

The initial assault on Jail Hill was unsuccessful, too few troops being employed. The second attempt, in the middle of May, was made with three brigades, the 4th and 6th and the 33rd Indian Brigade (Queen's Royal Regiment and two Gurkha battalions). The Queen's stormed 'Jail Hill' and took it, being then reinforced for the consolidation by two Gurkha companies.

It was, however, the clearing away of the Japanese minefields by the 2nd Divisional sappers, permitting tanks to come forward and work with the infantry, that settled the fate of the battle in mid-May. Kohima was back in Allied hands, although the Japanese were dug in among the surrounding hills.

The bare description of this phase of the battle for Kohima gives little idea of the blood-red colour of the fighting which, considering the terrain and the difficulties, was never again equalled in Burma. Some illustration is required.

THE BATTLE OF KOHIMA 139

Often battalions and companies were led into action by their commanding officers in the old style. Once the C.O. of the Norfolks (Lieut.-Col. Robert Scott) led his men on to the top of a hill held by the enemy and had a personal battle with a Japanese soldier. The C.O. won because he had a better aim with a grenade and, according to one of his men, because the Japanese was visibly shaken by the flow of language that came with the grenade. 'The C.O.,' said the soldier, 'had a way of expressing himself in his own vernacular.'

C.S.M. Cook, Cameron Highlanders, fought a duel on a hill with a Japanese officer. Cook was armed with rifle and bayonet and the Japanese with his sword. The Scots sergeant-major won, relieved the officer of his sword, and then killed him. British and Japanese watched this ghostly battle from their holes in the ground and, on one side, applauded. C.S.M. Cook was killed soon afterwards.

The Camerons, as is the tradition and habit of Highlanders in full cry, showed no mercy to the Japanese. Their ferocity at close quarters exceeded that of the famed Gurkhas and caused the Japanese to howl over their radio that the battalion had been specially trained in murder tactics, branding them 'Churchill's Murderers'—a compliment gratefully accepted.

In a strange battle on the tennis court of the District Commissioner's bungalow a Grant tank drove up to the front door of the Japanese-held bungalow and pumped shells into it. Outside on the fringe of the court men from the Dorsets lay perched on a little terrace above a position held by the Japanese. They improvised fishing-rods and dangled grenades into the Japanese positions below.

Forsaking their vehicles, the Reconnaissance Battalion fought on foot and, having executed a most arduous march across the hills and valleys, sat on a ridge for nineteen days, to the complete embarrassment of the Japanese.

The Royal Scots held the record bag for snipers with

thirty-five credited kills. Once the gunners—the terrain made normal artillery deployment almost impossible—had four medium guns, eight twenty-five pounders, and eight howitzers, firing from an area of less than a hundred square yards.

If it is generally conceded that senior officers are in safer positions than private soldiers, Burma must be excepted. At Kohima three brigadiers were killed and one severely wounded in the first few days. The general was often fortunate to escape death or wounds, for he was always up with his men, urging and inspiring them to greater efforts.

Such was the battle for Kohima itself. The opening of the road to Imphal had still to be achieved while the 7th Division and 23rd Brigade were playing a less spectacular but equally important part in the battle among the Naga Hills.

By the beginning of June the beleagured Imphal garrison had settled down to a tough routine of bare existence and short fierce skirmishing on the perimeter where Japanese sought entrance to the plain. The monsoon was in full swing by the last week in May. The one all-weather airstrip was crammed full of supply aircraft, queues circled in the air waiting to land, and queues waited on the side runs of the strip to take off. As the wheels of the aircraft touched down or those of offgoing aircraft raced along the concrete, great sprays of water covered anything within fifty yards. From dawn to dusk, except on really bad days when no planes came in or left, the traffic continued. Troops and R.A.F. ground personnel worked without rest to move the supplies.

The 20th Division held the Shenam Saddle, some forty miles from Imphal on the Palel–Tamu road, but failed to prevent the Japanese in the hills from rendering Palel airstrip unusable. However, they held the road, which was the only real entrance to the plain, although to do so they had to fight an unending series of hill battles.

Round Shenam was a series of 5,000-foot pimples known by such names as 'Nippon Hill', 'Scraggy', 'Malta', 'Crete', and 'Dead Mule Gulch'. So strange were the dispositions of the 20th Division and Japanese that in one instance a British soldiers' cookhouse was situated on a spur between friend and foe. Yet the Japanese could not overlook it.

Once a Japanese sniper tied himself to a tree commanding a bend in the mountain road. He scored an officer and two British N.C.O.s. An artillery barrage failed to remove him, and tanks firing at short range failed to hit his tree. Finally an officer, armed with an anti-tank Piat gun, crawled forward at the risk of being sniped and with one shot removed tree and sniper.

In one hill battle the Japanese had dug in on the top and surrounded their position with wire. The Devons attacked and reached the rim of the summit. At night they dug in and added a further layer of wire below them. During the night more Japanese arrived and they too added a third layer to the sandwich. For several days Japanese, British, and Japanese, wrestled and sniped from a few yards' range until finally the lower layer of Japanese were killed by Gurkha and the upper layer buried by mortar fire.

The Devons took and consolidated the peak. Two days later a sergeant-major, walking across the summit, noticed a half-buried Japanese who had been taken for dead. He kicked the Japanese in the face. The Japanese wriggled free of earth, brought up his rifle, and aimed at the sergeant-major before an officer killed him with his revolver. For an opportunity to escape this Japanese was prepared to remain immobile for days. Finally all the Japanese bodies were placed together in a pile and burned, British and Indians keeping their distance as grenades in the clothing of the Japanese began to go off.

Across on the Tiddim side of the plain the Japanese had succeeded in reaching the area of Bishenpur, a village at the edge of the foothills. There they were locked in combat with the 17th Division. The division's stragglers had mostly returned. Two officers who had been captured by the Japanese had lived for several days in an enemy officers' mess, underground. They had been treated well by officers of the 33rd Japanese Division, so well that soon they were able to escape. Three N.C.O.s from the Border Regiment had got cut off in the retreat and, despite being new to jungle life, had trekked through the hills and jungles for twenty-one days, living on acorns, Indian corn, and an occasional egg from friendly hill folk. Somehow they found their way back to their division.

On the north side of the plain the 5th Division probed up the Imphal–Kohima road and fought among the foothills in an attempt to clear the road for the link-up with the 33rd Corps from Kohima.

The 5th Division and the 254th Brigade invented a new method of bunker fighting. Their tanks, which could not be used in a normal role, fought in ones and twos and became hill climbers. Driven with great nerve and accuracy, tanks crawled up the side of a hill on a razor-backed approach, lay as near a Japanese bunker as possible, blasting it with their guns as the infantry waited below the crest to attack.

Sometimes tanks toppled over the edge. One once fell 500 feet and, apart from a bruising and a shaking, its crew were unhurt. Others did not fare so well. But the record height ever climbed by a tank was over 6,000 feet. It was easier to go up than down, for there was no room for tanks to turn round.

The ubiquitous 23rd Division sent patrols and sorties everywhere. Every time the Japanese appeared to have found some soft spot in the perimeter the 23rd Division sent a battalion or a brigade to block it. This division, including the 1st Battalion Seaforth Highlanders, had been in the area

THE BATTLE OF KOHIMA

of Imphal longer than anyone. They arrived in February 1942 and without a single break fought there until late in 1944. In no theatre of war were troops exposed to such long periods without rest or respite as in Burma. In no theatre of war were the rests and respites so inadequate when they came.

Once, on the receipt of a report that the 15th Japanese Divisional Commander was in the Naga Hills with three wives impressed from among the local inhabitants, General Roberts sent out the 1st Brigade, including the Seaforths, a battalion of Punjabs, and a battalion of the Parialas—a native state force of Sikhs—to give chase. For three weeks Brigadier Robert King and his brigade searched for the elusive general, but without success.

Unfortunately this brigadier could not speak Urdu or Hindustani and, in one action, he repeatedly tried to stop Lieut.-Col. Balwant Singh's Sikhs from going on. The Sikhs, however, pretended that they could not understand a word, and continued to chase a party of Japanese from hill to hill.

Colonel Balwant Singh, a grey-bearded patriarch of the Sikh race, bemedalled as much as General Auchinleck, was one of the legendary figures of this campaign. Though nearly sixty, he personally taught every man in his battalion to patrol by leading them against the Japanese. He had no British officer in his battalion, which he ruled with a rod of iron. Such Indian officers were rare, but proof that India can produce sons of iron and steel.

All through April and May, the Japanese air forces attempted to intercept the Allied supply aircraft. Usually they came over in groups consisting of six bombers and about thirty Oscars. Their targets were invariably the Imphal airstrips and, when the weather or the Japanese had put all but one out of commission, the single Imphal airfield at Kangla. Imphal-based Spitfires claimed a fair number of

Japanese, but the intruder sweeps of the American aircraft over the Japanese-held Burma airfields kept the number of missions and aircraft down to a minimum.

Owing to the occupation of the hills surrounding Imphal by the enemy, the aircraft detector systems were unable to function fully. It was therefore possible for Japanese planes to sneak into or over Imphal. In May alone the Japanese mounted twenty-two missions over the Imphal and Kohima areas, but their overall losses were heavy, American P38s and P51s claiming 78 destroyed in the air and 135 on the ground.

In the middle of the month Myitkyina airfield, in north Burma, was captured by Stilwell's Chinese-American group. This reduced Japanese air effectiveness, although they made one despairing effort just before the monsoon broke, sending forty Tojos over the Bishenpur area of Imphal. This was the first time the Tojo fighter had been seen over South-East Asia Command.

Defensive patrolling by Spitfires was found to be too expensive in petrol which, like everything else, had to be flown into Imphal, but a successful tactic was developed whereby, whenever Japanese aircraft did fly into the plain, Spitfires would haunt the two exit areas and wait for the Japanese to depart. On one occasion a Spitfire on a test flight reported the arrival of Japanese aircraft from the Tiddim direction. Other Spitfires joined this one and when the Japanese retired by the same route they ran into the ambush and lost six destroyed and several more probably destroyed or damaged.

For those thousands of troops not engaged in direct fighting or keeping aircraft in the air, the months were dull, tense, and depressing. Entertainment of any kind was virtually non-existent. One film was flown into Imphal and shown on the only two available mobile cinemas. It was that moving picture *This Above All*, and was first shown in a little clearing among some hills while Gurkhas fought a ghostly battle not far away. Over the sound of the music could be heard the unmistakable rattle of a Bren gun and the equally unmistakable 'phuttle' of a Japanese L.M.G.

Food and cigarettes were scarce. The local Manipuri villages were combed for vegetables and sweet popcorn which, though fly-blown, alleviated the sugar pangs. Eggs rose to the equivalent of five shillings each. Money meant nothing.

Mud and rain soaked clothes and made them filthy. Although this plain was held by over 100,000 troops, constituting more than a corps, there was not a single mobile bath unit. India Command had completely neglected such necessities of life.

A few hundreds of miles away in north Burma, within sound of the battle, Americans had a different film show nightly and a monthly case of beer per man. Less than a hundred miles away, as the 2nd British Division fought down the road, their own home-made bath unit bathed and provided clean dry clothing for a whole battalion every few days. Moreover their fighting columns were accompanied by their own cinema, concert party, and mobile printing press, bought and built into a lorry by the Division. This press, until the two compositors were wounded, produced a daily paper in battle.

Such, unfortunately, was the difference between the Americans, a British division under energetic command, and units equipped and maintained by India Command. The neglect of welfare of the Indian and the British troops was one of the misfortunes of the Burma war. Not until some time after the arrival of Mountbatten did things improve. It was, however, always Delhi and not H.Q.S.E.A.C. at Kandy, which maintained the Indians in the field.

11

THE RELIEF OF IMPHAL

Relief of Imphal—Junction of 33rd and 4th Corps—General Grover relieved—Fly-in of Wingate's Second Chindits

ON 22 June 1944 the road from Kohima to Imphal was cleared. The Japanese retreat had begun and plans were already in operation for the blocking of their escape and, if possible, the decimation of the 15th Japanese Army. Only the 33rd Japanese Division, still strong and compact enough to form a formidable fighting force, held to their positions in the monsoon 'lake district' of Bishenpur.

During the last three weeks of this part of the campaign the morale of the fighting troops in Imphal had decreased considerably. They saw no end to the battle except surrender or disintegration. They lost confidence in the ability of their commanders to extricate them from the situation they were in. Only those at the various headquarters had any exact information of the movement of the 2nd Division down the road, and of the battles fought at Merema, Viswema, and among the foothills. Their morale was bolstered up by the daily movement of the allied blue lines on the maps showing advances, often extremely small but nevertheless advances.

Having lost their hold on Kohima and its surrounding hills and suffered casualties amounting to 4,000 men, the Japanese hung grimly on to their hill positions overlooking the eighty-mile stretch of the Kohima–Imphal road. Every Japanese position had to be winkled out at the point of the bayonet or blasted by guns and tanks. One of the fiercest battles was fought at Merema, where the Worcesters captured a 75-mm. gun which had been causing considerable damage and cleared a Japanese position in thirty-six hours when the enemy had been ordered to hold out for ten days.

The surge of the 2nd Division down the road was irresistible, for the troops were in high spirits, despite severe losses, and appreciated the urgency of their task. Away eastwards among the Naga Hills, across the Japanese escape routes, marched the 7th Division. Farther away still, down towards Ukhrul, advanced the 23rd Brigade (Essex, Duke of Wellington's, Borders). These two left-hooks were designed to block the escape path of the 31st Division and elements of the 15th.

The 20th Division moved from Imphal up towards Ukhrul while slowly, too slowly it often appeared, the 5th Division fought its way up the Kohima road from Imphal. The whole was a series of divisional movements planned to lock up the 31st Japanese Division in the hills. Already the Japanese were suffering from disease, starvation, and shortage of ammunition in the inhospitable monsoon-soaked hills.

Brigadier Perowne's 23rd Brigade march was a fine feat of endurance, for the country through which he moved was amongst the wildest on the front. Sometimes moving up gradients of one in two for 7,000 feet, his men had to cut steps for the mules and manhandle the mountain guns. One column with eighty-pound loads scaled an 8,000-foot peak. All had to cross successive ranges of hills. There was no rest from continuous climb or descent. The geography of the Assam front strained the hearts of even the fittest and toughest men.

The junction of the 33rd and 4th Corps occurred early on the morning of the twenty-second. The 2nd Division column was impressive, for General Grover was in the leading tank and General Stopford in the second one, while behind trailed most of the 6th Brigade. For 4th Corps' part, witnesses of the junction were one tank from the 7th Cavalry, manned by Indians, and three British Military Observers who had walked forward across the advanced line of the 5th Division and left a battle being fought behind them: 4th Corps had not expected the junction so soon. The Military Observers, sensing news, had anticipated correctly.

The first priority for the Imphal garrison was rum, beer, food, and cigarettes. In the wake of the relieving column was a large convoy of lorries laden with all these requirements. Within a few hours of the relief they rolled down the road into Imphal and that evening, if the rum and beer had not reached every unit, those that did possess some celebrated. The three months' siege of Imphal was over. For only the second time in the whole Burma war, from its beginning in 1942 to June 1944, the initiative had passed into the hands of the Allies. The first time has yet to be described, for it was General Stilwell's advance in north Burma, which resulted in August in the capture of Myitkyina. The two together meant that the whole trend of war in this theatre, and not just one phase, could at last be switched to offence.

On 1 June, as 33rd Corps began their clearance of the Kohima–Imphal road, 4th Corps held reduced rations for sixteen days, aviation spirit for seven days, and no ammunition reserves. The corps had asked for 475 tons of supplies daily, but the 3rd Tactical Air Force, part of Eastern Air Command, had refused to commit themselves to more than 363 tons and fell far short of this figure at the beginning of the month.

The critical days were thus those at the start of June. During the last week of June, however, the daily tonnage flown in increased to 517 and was thus reducing the backlog, and with the improved weather—still monsoon, of course—that figure could have been maintained. The overall figure of air-lifted tons from mid-April to the end of June was

18,000. In May alone, when supplies fell short of requirements, 5,000 tons were lifted into Imphal, several times the quantity flown into the next highest consumer of air supplies, the West Africans in the Kaladan Valley.

During the four months over which the Manipur campaign was fought defensively, the 3rd Tactical Air Force made 24,000 offensive sorties. The Strategic Air Forces, concentrating on railway communications and Japanese bases throughout South-East Asia, reduced the effectiveness of all lanes so much that to move reinforcements from Siam to Burma took weeks, not days, a fact which had a tremendous effect on the morale as well as the military position of the Japanese forces invading Manipur.

The air forces, which approximated fifty per cent British and fifty per cent American, were completely integrated. The two worked in such amicable conjunction that, during the critical period of the air supply of Imphal when even one transport aircraft grounded made a difference, the two shared all spare parts. Everyone had learned to expect efficiency and one hundred per cent effort from the R.A.F., and it was gratifying to find the Americans as wholehearted, as gallant, and sometimes even more ingenious. It is one of the incongruities of the two races that the Americans would always give a ride to any British officer or man and the British would do the same for the Americans. For their own folk, however, each required the necessary passes and forms.

The Kohima battle produced its post-mortems and aftermaths. When it was realized that the need for the opening of the road had not been so vital as anticipated, there were those who claimed that the sacrifices of the 2nd British Division had been too great, the losses too severe. The battle was described as worse than Hill 60 in the last war. It was described as the Flanders of Burma.

In the six weeks from the time the 5th Brigade first hit

the Japanese at Kohima to the day the 6th Brigade opened the road to Imphal, the 2nd Division lost 2,500 men, killed, wounded, sick, and missing. The Japanese lost nearly double that number. In Flanders or at Passchendaele as many men were lost per hour, though this is not offered as an excuse but merely as an illustration of emotional over-statement.

The principal result was the relief of General Grover from the command of the 2nd Division, which later had its own rather serious repercussions within the division itself. Grover was sent home, ostensibly to be Director of Military Training with the object of training men for this theatre. His only rival for the job was, perhaps, General Frank Festing, of the 36th British Division. Curiously enough, their careers had run parallel throughout the war and both were Old Wykehamists.

Grover left South-East Asia shortly after the conclusion of the Kohima–Imphal battles. When he arrived in England he was reduced to the rank of colonel and told to take a holiday. Later he was restored to the rank of major-general and given a job as Director of Welfare and Amenities at the War Office, a position he has held with distinction.

With regard to the 2nd Division's casualties, which were admittedly high, two points are worth bearing in mind. In the first place, the relief of Kohima was a matter of vital urgency justifying heavy losses in the relieving force, for nobody then knew the air-lift would increase to Imphal in mid-June. In the second place, no general who wasted his troops' lives ever won their devotion as General Grover won and kept that of the 2nd Division.

When Lord Munster, representing Mr. Winston Churchill, toured the theatre to investigate the welfare arrangements and hear the men's complaints, he received none from the 2nd Division except 'Where is General Grover? We want him back.' One sergeant-major harangued his lordship for nearly half an hour on the general's merits. Others took less time, but made their point with equal vehemence. Lord Munster, astonished at this loyalty, mentioned it in his report without, however, any effect.

One must now return over the months to consider the parallel operations that were going on in Burma, the operations of Generals Stilwell and Wingate, who, despite the Japanese invasion of Manipur, were able to continue with their long-planned enterprises—the building of the Ledo road and the freeing of upper north Burma. By the time the Kohima-Imphal road was clear the Chindits, except for those already flown out, had come under General Stilwell's command and were attacking around Mogaung. Stilwell's Chinese and Americans were investing Kamaing and Myitkyina.

Though originally two separate, though complementary, missions, the Chindits had, by then, become merged with the Stilwell group for the purposes of capturing Myitkyina, Mogaung, and Kamaing, three of the main centres in north Burma. Earlier, however, Brigadier Fergusson's brigade had afforded some flank protection to Stilwell's advancing Chinese when the Japanese advance into Manipur had exposed his right flank.

'Operation Thursday' was the airborne landing of the second Chindit force, this time six brigades strong, comprising some 15,000 men from Britain, America, India, Nepal, and Africa. They were trained as thoroughly as the first Chindits were in 1943. They were equipped with all the ingenuity of the Americans, and at the Quebec Conference, to which Wingate and Mountbatten had accompanied Churchill, the whole expedition had been blue-printed.

Wingate had said: 'On my return to India in the autumn of 1943 I found there was a great deal of doubt as to the feasibility of the proposed operation. . . . My plan was to go where the enemy was not. Previous airborne operations have always gone where the enemy was waiting and established.'

In spite of doubts in India, Churchill and Generals Marshall and Arnold, the American Chief of Staff and Chief of Air respectively, were as whole-heartedly behind Wingate as Mountbatten and Slim, under whose command the Second Chindits would come, once committed to Burma. General Arnold appointed, as organizer of the airborne landings, thirty-three-year-old Colonel Philip Cochran, one of the finest American airmen, and, as Cochran's second-in-command, Colonel John R. Alison. The force that Cochran built up became known as the 1st Air Commando or, more popularly, as Phil Cochran's Circus. Brig.-Gen. Old had the task of supplying the Chindits with his Troop Carrying Command once they had landed inside Burma and hacked out and built their airstrips.

If the second Chindit expedition was much larger and more powerful than the first, it was also more revolutionary in conception. Wingate's idea was to fly in an advance brigade by glider and land it at two known possible landing-places just north of the Irrawaddy between Katha and Bhamo. These two clearings in the jungle were called 'Broadway' and 'Piccadilly'.

The first troops to land by glider would, with the help of American engineers and bulldozers, also to be glided in, clear the ground and make landing-grounds for Dakotas, which would fly in other brigades and evacuate the wounded. On the second night of 'Operation Thursday' more gliders would descend upon Chowringhee, another clearing south of the Irrawaddy. 'D' Day was 5 March.

Once established, the two brigades, with the help of Brigadier Fergusson's marching brigade, which had started from Ledo a month previously, would capture Indaw East airstrip. This would be garrisoned by another division from the 14th Army, not necessarily one trained in long-range penetration.

The Chindits would then mill round north-central Burma,

once more cutting the Mandalay–Myitkyina railway line, blocking the road to convoys, and destroying all Japanese food and ammunition dumps they could find. Wingate did not design or equip the Chindits to fight long pitched battles, though as it happened they had to do so. He reckoned that two months would be the limit of their endurance. After that the Chindits would be taken out for reconditioning and others flown in to take over.

This plan failed to work for several reasons. The original Chindits of six brigades were reduced to five by the transfer of Brigadier Perowne's 23rd Brigade to the Kohima front, and to four when the West African Brigade (Brigadier Gillmore) was split up for airstrip defence. The four brigades were commanded by Brigadiers Fergusson, Calvert, Lentaigne, and Brodie. Even if Indaw East airstrip had been captured, no outside division was available for its defence since all were locked up in combat in the Arakan and Imphal.

On the evening of 5 March, the airfield at Lalaghat in Assam was crammed full of gliders, their tow-craft, and the troops who were to act as spearhead for the Chindits on Broadway and Piccadilly. Gliders were loaded with bull-dozers, jeeps, and other machines. Colonel Cochran was giving last instructions to his American pilots, who were to fly over Burma by moonlight, using no lights or signals, and were to release their gliders over the landing-grounds.

As 'Operation Thursday' was about to begin, a photograph of the two landing-grounds arrived. One, Piccadilly, was seen to be covered by tree-trunks. It would be impossible to land any gliders on it. The immediate reaction was 'Had the Japanese advance information of the proposed air expedition?' and 'What should be done with the gliders destined for Piccadilly?'

It was reckoned that the Japanese, knowing that a Dakota had once landed at Piccadilly, were ensuring against its happening again, and that the tree-trunks had no association with an intelligence leak. As to the cancellation of part of the project, Colonel Cochran would have none of it. He strolled up to his Piccadilly-bound pilots and calmly said: 'Boys, we've found a grand new place for you to land. It's called Broadway.' Cochran and his staff took little time in describing the whereabouts and lay-out of Broadway.

Twenty-six transport aircraft and fifty-four gliders took off for Broadway on 'D' night. In them was Brigadier Calvert's 77th Brigade (King's Liverpool Regiment, Lancashire Fusiliers, South Staffs, and Gurkhas). Thirty-seven gliders came down on Broadway. After the first wave had skidded and crashed at all angles into the jungle or across the clearing, others piled in on top. In the darkness it seemed that only a few men could have escaped death or injury and that from the first moment the expedition was wrecked. Brigadier Calvert had no choice but to signal failure. But when daylight came the men (King's Regiment) and the American engineers began to clear up the landing-ground and prepare it for incoming transport planes. The brigadier was able to signal success before the day was out.

The morale of the troops when first they crash-landed into the jungle dropped considerably. They imagined, quite wrongly, that many more had been killed than was actually the case. When the brigadier held a burial service for the thirty-three killed he pointed out that had they been forced to march into Burma casualties would, by the time they had reached Broadway, have been much higher.

Within twenty-two hours of the first landings, Broadway was ready for the next sixty gliders. Besides thousands of men, including West Africans, half a million pounds of stores and over 1,250 mules and ponies were landed that day.

Of those gliders that never reached Broadway some landed in friendly country west of the Chindwin, others in Japanese-held territory. One, in fact, landed on a Japanese headquarters and caused much consternation among the Japanese before its occupants made off into the jungle. Another, carrying Gurkhas, having circled round for some time, landed at what it took to be Broadway. Actually it came down on 4th Corps H.Q. at Imphal.

The Gurkhas, being well trained in action drill, immediately disembarked and took up a perimeter defence. Corps headquarters officers and staff, investigating this strange occurrence, found a very hostile and aggressive little band of Gurkhas, who refused to believe they were not in the middle of a Japanese hornets' nest and being fooled by the Japanese talking English. It required considerable tact on the part of the invaders' officers finally to convince them otherwise. This was about the nearest 4th Corps H.Q. ever came to being overrun.

With Piccadilly useless as a landing-strip, plans were reshuffled for the next landings. On 9 March, Brigadier W. D. A. Lentaigne's 111th Brigade (Cameronians, King's Own, King's Liverpool, and Gurkhas) were glided into Chowringhee on the south side of the Irrawaddy. Following them came the Chindits H.Q.

In the meantime Brigadier Fergusson's 16th Brigade (Royal Artillery, without guns, Queen's Regiment, Leicesters, Reconnaissance Regiment) was performing what *The Times* described as the greatest feat of human endurance in this theatre of war.

The brigade began their march from Ledo in February, moving southwards across the hills parallel to the Ledo road and General Stilwell's troops. Two columns of Fergusson's men, mostly gunners, left the main body of the brigade and attacked a Japanese staging-post at Lonkin with success, rendering assistance to the Chinese who were advancing towards Myitkyina.

The rest of the brigade made for the area of Banmauk and Indaw, a rail junction just west of the Irrawaddy on the dividing line of north and central Burma. Their object was to secure a position for a landing-strip in the Meza Valley and hold it while Brigadier Brodie's 14th Brigade (Black Watch, Beds and Herts, York and Lancs, Leicesters) were flown in. Then, together, they intended to attack and wrest Indaw East airstrip from the Japanese.

'Aberdeen' was the name given to the landing-strip which was cleared out of the jungle. On 23 March the 14th Brigade began their ascent into Burma. Immediately they joined forces with 16th Brigade and began a pincer movement on Indaw but, despite heavy fighting, failed to capture the airstrip. It was claimed that 2,000 to 3,000 Japanese were holding Indaw and, with Fergusson's brigade still split up and Brodie's taking some days to complete its fly-in, the attack went off at half-cock and was finally called off.

Thus by the end of March, Chindits were, with few exceptions, completely installed inside Burma. On 24 March Maj.-Gen. Orde Charles Wingate, creator, inspirer, and leader of the Chindits, was killed in an air crash over friendly territory. With him died two British war correspondents, Stuart Emeny (*News Chronicle*), creator of the tag 'The Forgotten Army', and Stanley Wills (*Daily Herald*).

12

WITH STILWELL IN NORTH BURMA

*Wingate—Chindits in Burma—Come under Stilwell's Command—
The Marauders—Advance in N. Burma*

THE death of Wingate was not only a national tragedy but an international one. Few men in this world, even during and after a war that threw up great men, could claim to be mourned sincerely by so many diverse races and communities. To the Jews of Palestine, the Abyssinians, the British, the Indians, the Gurkhas, the Burmese, and many Americans, Wingate was almost a god. Moreover he was a man who fought for ideals—his own ideals—with a fervour which, when added to his military genius and powers of personal leadership, made him a tremendous, if in certain quarters sometimes an unpopular, personality.

Anecdotes there are by the dozen of his eccentricities. Tales are told of his intransigence and intolerance. Sometimes he would not shave for days, even when in Delhi, and would interview the Commander-in-Chief or Viceroy unshaven. He would carry around an alarm clock to remind people that time marched on. He would dogmatize and brook no argument, however reasoned, from anyone. In upbringing he was a Puritan.

Once Wingate shut himself in his hotel room in Delhi and played symphonies to himself on the gramophone for days. Another time he 'disappeared' with a mass of books from the library of G.H.Q., Delhi—books which, by the way, were never returned. He munched raw onions on the march. He scrubbed his back every morning with a rubber brush. Once he voiced a complaint in writing to the King, an ancient privilege of a British officer. He would harangue seniors on their mistakes, and naturally incurred their dislike.

When, in 1941, Wingate returned from his successful exploits in Abyssinia he had worked out a scheme for the reconquest of North Africa. He was ill-received in Whitehall and posted to a gunner unit in Gibraltar as battery commander. But such a man, who had so little fear of authority, could not lie fallow for long, and at the request of Wavell he was sent to India. He joined Wavell in Delhi. There the general reaction to Wingate was that he was mad, or 'puggled', as the Indians say; to which he replied: 'You know I'm not half so crazy as people make out.'

Perhaps the greatest compliment ever paid to Wingate, and a good many appreciations have been written of him, came from a Palestinian leader during the crisis of El Alamein. When told that a number of divisions would defend Palestine against any German invasion, he said: 'Send us Wingate and we will do without troops and additional arms.'

On the formation of S.E.A.C., Wingate came under Mountbatten. These two accompanied Mr. Churchill to Quebec and convinced the sceptics of the possibilities of airborne invasions of Burma. Mountbatten could not have been given a field commander nearer his own somewhat piratical heart.

There are people who, in attempting to appraise the strength of Britain's leadership in the Far East, try to compare Wingate with Mountbatten, and even with Slim. Unquestionably those three represent the best leaders Britain put into the Far Eastern war, but comparisons are really impossible. Each man was so utterly different. Would Wingate have been happy to be a Supreme Commander, conducting affairs from an office in Kandy, with only occasional trips to the front? Could he have dealt with the

OPERATIONS IN NORTH BURMA—FEBRUARY–AUGUST 1944

terribly difficult tasks of diplomacy between the British and Americans, as did Slim and Mountbatten? The answer in both cases is no. On the other hand, both Slim and Mountbatten could have led long-range penetration groups, though not, perhaps, with the same inspired skill and genius as Wingate. Each of these three great men—the word 'great' is not loosely used—played his own part in his own way. Wingate was, perhaps, the most spectacular. But, after all, Britain produced only one Wingate between 1939 and 1945.

Leadership of the Chindits devolved on Brigadier Lentaigne, who was promoted Major-General. He had originally flown into Chowringhee airstrip with his 111th Brigade, which he handed over to his Brigade Major, Lieut.-Col. J. R. Masters. Lentaigne's task was most difficult, as it would have been for anyone who followed such an outstanding personality as Wingate. He could hardly be expected to infuse the same fire into the Chindits. This became more noticeable at the end of the Chindit expedition, when except for those columns already flown out, it had come under Stilwell. Then the Chindits were very tired, and it is doubtful whether Wingate would have tolerated their extended tour.

The movements and cross movements of the Second Chindits were as varied and complicated as those of the first expedition. For two months, from mid-March to mid-May, Calvert's brigade, assisted by Gillmore's West Africans and later by Brodie's brigade, held the 'White City' airstrip clearing and, for a time, the Henu road-block so that no train passed along the line to Myitkyina. Six battalions of Japanese were pinned down to that little front, while reinforcements, a regiment in strength, were stopped and harassed by Brodie's brigade operating as floating columns.

The battles for White City were fought by both sides with intense ferocity and often man to man. The Japanese strained themselves but never succeeded in capturing it, though at times they employed suicide squads. When, in mid-May, Calvert's brigade evacuated the strip, Masters's 111th Brigade had established a block on the railway line and road farther north, at 'Blackpool', near Hopin. By the time Blackpool was evacuated—there was a general movement northwards towards Mogaung by then—the roads were almost impassable owing to the monsoon and the Japanese garrisons in north Burma were existing on their fast-dwindling stocks.

The demolition of Japanese dumps by ground troops and the air forces, who were given a large number of targets by the Chindits, and the bombing and cutting of the railway line, produced grave stock and supply problems for the Japanese 'Q' staff. In monsoon weather, living off the land, unless ample provision has previously been made, is virtually impossible.

Not only was northbound Japanese traffic interrupted and reduced to a trickle, but 111th and 16th Brigades, operating on the Indaw front and demolishing all dumps and rice supplies, virtually cut the principal Japanese line of communication to Homalin and the Manipur front and denuded the area of food. This 'scorched earth' policy had its effect later on when the Japanese, retreating from Manipur, had to divert many of their troops south down the Chindwin, since so many who tried the Homalin-Banmauk-Indaw route died of starvation and disease. Skeletons of hundreds were found by the 14th Army units which advanced into Burma later in the year.

In the Indaw area 123 storehouses were destroyed and 200 truckloads of ammunition were blown up or captured by ground troops, while the air forces destroyed trains, rolling-stock, animals, lorries, and thousands of gallons of petrol. Doubtless small convoys did get past the Chindits' blocks and ambushes, but when the Kamaing-Mogaung-Myitkyina area was freed the Japanese store cupboards were found to be very bare indeed.

A force of Gurkhas, under Lieut.-Col. J. Morris, landed at Chowringhee and moved independently in the direction of Bhamo, in the bend of the Irrawaddy as it straightens out to run north to Myitkyina, to lay ambushes along the Bhamo-Namkam and Bhamo-Myitkyina roads. By mid-May, 'Morris Force' was in contact with the Japanese only thirty miles south of Myitkyina, where the Chinese and Americans were then fighting for the town and its airstrip.

Having covered Calvert's evacuation of White City—everything, including heavy equipment, was lifted by air—Brodie's brigade tried to get through to act as floating columns to the newly established Blackpool garrison. There Masters's brigade was being besieged by considerable numbers of Japanese. The weather beat Brodie. At times, as he was advancing through the Indawgyi Lake Valley, progress was reduced to four miles a day. Almost hourly mules had to be unloaded and loaded again, and men dared not sit down because of leeches, which were bad enough in their boots and on their legs, let alone all over their bodies. Everyone lived, ate, and marched in mud. Many slept in jungle hammocks.

Brodie's brigade took over the Kyusanlai Pass, controlling the southern reaches of the Indawgyi Lake. Through this pass the casualties of 111th Brigade at Blackpool were evacuated. It was their only route of contact with the rest of the columns and the aircraft which flew them back to base hospitals. It was a race between Brodie and the Japanese for the pass, but the Leicesters reached it first and held off a violent Japanese attack. Brodie held the pass until the last week in June.

On Indawgyi Lake, some fifteen miles long, two Sunderland flying boats normally used on coastal and sea reconnaissance landed to assist in the evacuation of wounded. These two Sunderlands, named 'Gert' and 'Daisy', flew out over 500 wounded and sick men without a single loss,

WITH STILWELL IN NORTH BURMA

avoiding any action with the enemy through the skilful use of valleys and hills.

The weather conditions in June prohibited any further casualty evacuation by the Sunderlands. There remained, however, some 300 men waiting to be flown out. The Chindits formed a navy with an assortment of craft, christened after battleships and cruisers, from shallow draft country boats to sapper assault craft. Fifty rubber engine-powered boats were dropped from the air on the Indawgyi Lake 'naval base'. Technicians were parachuted down with them. The fleet sailed north across the lake and up the waterways, often under very rough conditions, to Kamaing, whence the casualties were flown out to Assam. Supplies, mules, and even jeeps, were ferried across the lake or up the waterways and rivers.

It is worth considering the route taken by a casualty from the point where he received his bullet to a hospital as far back, perhaps, as Calcutta. Unless he was wounded near where the Chindits had cut out a landing-ground for light aircraft, the casualty had to be carried by bamboo litter or mule over hills and through jungle to the nearest strip. From there the plane, with an official load of two sitting or one lying case, transported him to a strip at which Dakotas could land. He would then be flown to Assam and later to Calcutta. In all, a casualty's journey extended over hundreds of miles.

This does not mean that the Chindits possessed no field hospitals of their own. They did, and major operations were carried out by oil lamp under the most exacting conditions. On one occasion the staff for a hospital was parachuted into Burma. In all over 3,000 Chindit casualties were flown out of Burma during the first three months of the campaign.

At the end of April, Fergusson's brigade, weary after two months of continuous marching and fighting—they had been the only brigade to march into Burma—was flown out, having completed its last task of capturing Indaw West airstrip and temporarily rendering it unusable.

The brigade had fought for Indaw East airstrip, formed the 'Aberdeen' base, destroyed dumps in the Indaw area, harassed the enemy south of Calvert's Henu road-block, and laid a successful ambush in the railway corridor between Mawlu and Pinwe. It had marched over 500 miles, much of it over unknown, unmapped country. Possibly the greatest compliment it received had been from Wingate himself, who exclaimed 'Hannibal eclipsed' when Fergusson's men crossed the Chindwin by means of local craft and boats dropped by the air force. On that occasion, during their advance from Ledo, the troops had been without food for several days since the supply aircraft had been unable to locate the columns moving through the jungled hills.

Though these actions did not complete the operations of the Chindits, they can be described as Phase One, for on 17 May, the day Merrill's Marauders gained their first foothold on Myitkyina airstrip, Lentaigne's men passed under the command of Stilwell, and from then on their movements became more closely linked to those of the Chinese and Americans.

Stilwell's forces consisted of the 22nd and 38th Chinese Divisions, his engineer and labour battalions, a Chinese tank regiment under the direct command of Colonel Rothwell Brown, an American, and also the all-American task force, Merrill's Marauders.

The Marauders were a compact brigade unit entirely composed of combat men and about 2,500 in strength. Every man was a volunteer from America or from other theatres of war. Under Brig.-Gen. Frank Merrill, who had been with Stilwell in the retreat from Burma, they had been trained with the Chindits in long-range penetration and then assigned to Stilwell and not Wingate, as originally intended.

Like a lot of Americans, when first they arrived in South-East Asia the Marauders were not only sceptical of the British effort against the Japanese but also suspicious of Mountbatten. Both these facts were the result of adverse propaganda in America to which Britain offered no effective reply.

It was possibly with a picture of Mountbatten as portrayed in one of the American strip cartoons—the 'I say, chaps' sort of man—that the Marauders arrived for training.

Just before joining Stilwell in north Burma the Marauders were told Mountbatten would be visiting them. Instructions were forwarded by Mountbatten's Deputy Chief of Staff, Maj.-Gen. Wildman Lushington, R.M., as to the form of the visit. The general, a man for detail, ordered a bath to be ready in a special tent for Mountbatten to use on his arrival by air. This, to the Americans, who considered bathing in war a decadent pastime and thought that even in back areas a soldier should sleep in his pants, was like a red rag to a bull. However, the bath was constructed.

With his flair for informality, Mountbatten arrived and, leaving his staff to attend to details, wandered into the large marquee which served as a mess. Here he found a group of American officers standing rigidly at attention and looking uncomfortable. On the table was laid out food and drink.

Mountbatten walked over to the youngest-looking officer and said 'Have a drink', at the same time pouring one out. Having told everyone to relax, someone said: 'Say, who are you?' Mountbatten replied that he was Mountbatten and received the answer: 'Jeez, we thought you were his A.D.C.' After that everyone was thoroughly happy and the Marauders and the Supreme Commander became firm friends.

As the Chindits were being flown into Burma, Stilwell's forces were crossing the into Huwkawng Valley. By mid-March they had broken the main Japanese defence line at Maingkwan and Wallawbum and were fighting in the bottleneck of the pass between the Huwkawng and Mogaung Valleys. At Maingkwan and Wallawbum, Stilwell employed the tactics of encirclement and, with the aid of his tanks, slaughtered some 2,000 Japanese. Already the Ledo road had progressed 180 miles and his force was well inside Burma. These events coincided with the withdrawal of the 4th Corps divisions on the Chindwin or central front.

At the beginning of April, Stilwell, much concerned for the safety of his line of communication, flew to a conference with Slim at Dinjan. Stilwell wanted, because of the Japanese incursion into Manipur, to use one of his two Chinese divisions for its protection but realized full well that its withdrawal would compel him to abandon, or postpone, his advance on Myitkyina. He reckoned he would have to consolidate north of Kamaing, fifty miles west of Myitkyina.

General Slim was reluctant to agree to Stilwell's proposal. Seeing that the whole of the Japanese striking force was committed to action against Wingate or 4th Corps in Imphal, he considered there was little likelihood of an attack on Stilwell's line of communication. Moreover the moment seemed propitious for an all-out advance on Myitkyina, and he urged Stilwell to push ahead, promising that his line of communication would never be cut for more than ten days at the most. It was never cut.

In April the rains were starting and Stilwell's advance down the Mogaung Valley was slower than he had hoped. Though they had fought successfully in the Huwkawng, his Chinese divisions were not showing the confidence necessary for an all-out drive to Mogaung. At the end of the month Stilwell decided to compose a force of the Marauders, a Chinese regiment, and artillery, and send it on an independent mission to try to capture the Myitkyina airstrip. Should this be captured, a new Chinese division would immediately be flown over the 'Hump' to land there.

The force was split into three combat teams. The route

lay over the 5,000-foot Naunhyit Hills. Executing a remarkable twenty-day march under extremely arduous conditions, the force appeared on the airstrip on 17 May. The Japanese were completely surprised and before they could react the Marauders had established themselves there, several miles south of the town. As fighting was going on round the perimeter American transport planes and gliders brought in Chinese reinforcements. The exploit, however, exhausted the Marauders, whose value as a fighting force deteriorated from then on.

May 17 was a significant date in the Burma campaign. Stilwell took the Chindits under command, the Chinese closed on Kamaing and, thirty miles to the south, Masters's 111th Brigade was holding out at Blackpool despite frantic efforts by the Japanese to dislodge him. In Manipur, 4th Corps had their backs to the wall.

The battle of north Burma was developing into three separate actions, the battles for Kamaing, Mogaung, and Myitkyina, all of which merged into a tactical whole and meant the clearance of all north Burma except the railway corridor and the area of Bhamo and the northern Shan States. The capture of Myitkyina airstrip, though it could not properly be consummated without the capture of the town, meant the leg of a new air route from Assam to China, by-passing the hazardous 'Hump' run.

The monsoon had broken when Calvert's brigade trudged northwards towards Mogaung, having evacuated White City. They marched through mud and monsoon streams, cut their way through jungle and over hills. Always it rained. Men got trench feet, their clothes were ragged, and they had to fight to clear the hills to the east of Mogaung before they finally saw their objective a couple of miles away. With the closest of air support, the brigade cleared a series of Japanese strong-points dominating the town from the east but, though its battle casualties were fairly light, its sickness rate was rising and by itself the brigade was not strong enough to tackle the final assault.

The Chinese were still fighting around Kamaing where, with characteristic stubbornness, the Japanese held out in their foxholes while, with characteristic plodding, the Chinese made only a few yards a day.

A Chinese regiment was ordered to assist Calvert, but it failed to arrive until late June. Calvert was ordered to withdraw, but when his Gurkhas reported a slight Japanese withdrawal in their sector he decided to hang on.

With the arrival of the Chinese regiment Calvert decided on the final assault on Mogaung. It was prefaced with mortar barrages and air attack and was carried out with flame-throwers and Piat guns as well as all normal infantry weapons. The air forces' close support was within 200 yards of the leading British and Chinese troops. Under such pressure, the Japanese withdrew, though some committed suicide in their foxholes rather than retreat.

On 26 June, two days after the Chinese radio had announced the Chinese capture of Mogaung, Calvert's brigade entered the town. The Chinese regiment had, in fact, fought outside the town at the village of Ywathit and were not the troops that actually entered Mogaung. It was not the last occasion when Chinese claims proved inaccurate.

That virtually ended Calvert's part in the 1944 Chindit expedition. His brigade was very weak by then and the men were in no condition to continue fighting, though Stilwell was sorely pressed for men. Kamaing held out for a few more days and, for the only time during the Burma campaigns, the Japanese dropped food and medical supplies from the air to their garrison. Myitkyina held out for five more weeks.

Brodie's and Masters's brigades fought among the hills south-west and west of Mogaung for several weeks, thus cutting a possible Japanese retreat route. Brodie's brigade having spent five months inside Burma was withdrawn in August, and was the last Chindit force to withdraw. Others, including Morris Force, were evacuated in July.

The Chindits claimed the killing of 5,000 Japanese. They were unable to assess the casualties caused by air bombing and strafing of targets they had pin-pointed, or the number of Japanese who died of starvation or disease, causes attributable to the presence of the Chindits across their supply lines. Their own overall casualties were 3,500, excluding sick, who numbered several thousand more.

Had it not been for the Japanese invasion of Manipur and the determination of the Japanese opposing Stilwell, the Chindits would have made their airborne sorties into Burma and withdrawn in a couple of months. As it was, they were a very ragged, weary group of men who needed months of rehabilitation and reconditioning after living without rest or comfort on Army 'K' rations for four or five months.

Having to fight on in the monsoon after already completing two months inside Burma was a strain which few commanders would dare to impose on their troops. Fortunately few commanders in any theatre of war had to make such decisions as were made during the critical first six months of 1944 in Burma. Men, whether Chindits or not, had to go on fighting. There was no respite, no way of retreat. The Japanese accepted such strain and impositions. They went on fighting without food until death or suicide claimed them.

The battle for Myitkyina went on into August. There were 1,500 Japanese inside the town invested by two and a half Chinese divisions, tanks, and the Marauders. Moreover they were hammered day and night by Maj.-Gen. Howard C. Davidson's 10th U.S.A.A.F., which was responsible for all aerial combat in this zone.

For twenty-four hours a day this American air force group

took part in strategic bombing, tactical bombing, strafing, and close support to the infantry. With Vengeances and Lightnings, the dive-bombing and close support was, at times, so accurate that it was less than a hundred yards ahead of the allied infantry. On one occasion British troops stood up a hundred yards from the Japanese positions and watched the strafing.

For seventy-eight days the 1,500 Japanese held Myitkyina, though their number was gradually reduced by the bombing and air strikes. The lack of decisiveness and dynamism of the Chinese reflected itself in criticism of Stilwell and doubts as to his capability of ever capturing Myitkyina. Doubtless the Chinese, because of their philosophical and psychological outlook, needed to be prodded into action. Time mattered little to them and there were many stories of how they were persuaded to advance, some of them undoubtedly apocryphal.

It was said that, in order to persuade a Chinese general to advance, Stilwell would pitch his tent in front of him. The Chinese general, considering he was losing 'face' by being behind a senior commander, leap-frogged Stilwell and pushed his troops forward. Another supposed method was for the supply aircraft to drop their supplies several hundred yards in front of the Chinese lines. The Chinese, who claimed anything found in their area, naturally moved forward into the dropping zone.

Worried by the slowness of the Chinese and the exhaustion of the Marauders, Stilwell ordered two battalions of American combat engineers to be flown in for the battle of Myitkyina. Though these engineers were supposed to have had combat training, they proved very green in the arts of infantry fighting.

Stilwell also ordered hospital cases from the Marauders back to the line, so pressed was he for British or American combat troops to stiffen the Chinese. But this act merely

WITH STILWELL IN NORTH BURMA

precipitated the final Marauder crisis for, reduced by sickness and casualties from 2,500 to a few hundred men, they dissolved completely. For both these actions Stilwell came in for severe criticism from his own people. A man of extremely tough fibre himself, and determined to prove the Japanese could be beaten, he probably failed to appreciate the more common frailties of his fellow creatures.

For the final attack on Myitkyina the Americans called for 200 Chinese volunteers. None was forthcoming. As an inducement, the Americans offered a thirty-rupee bonus per volunteer and a double rise in rank (e.g. from private to corporal). This simple expedient had the desired effect.

Though ostensibly ringing Myitkyina, the Chinese conveniently left a gap through which, on 3 August, the surviving Japanese escaped. This ancient tactical manœuvre was repeated at Bhamo.

The Chinese had been fighting in Burma as long as the Chindits. They, too, had relied on air supply and carried with them not only their military equipment but also their life's goods and chattels. They, too, were tired.

There is no gainsaying the praise due to Stilwell for these operations. He had fought the sceptics who claimed he would never capture Myitkyina. With Chinese troops and one small American task force, he had fought terrain, climate, and the Japanese, while considerably greater numbers of British and Indian troops were surrounded and harried by the Japanese in Manipur. His was a lone operation out on the longest limb in a large theatre of war. But what of the Chindits?

Though spectacular in method, there were doubts whether the Chindits produced a sufficient return for the effort required. Pownall, Mountbatten's Chief of Staff, has said that they gave only a five per cent return. He had hoped for more. Stilwell and others claimed they were used in the wrong way; that Wingate's idea of blocking and moving, of sparring and shadow-boxing, was exhausting and gave no results. It would have been better, Stilwell said, if the Chindits had been used as the Marauders were—to fight in conjunction with a main body of troops, though used on special missions. As it was, the Chindits were completely independent and, though claiming to have mauled five Japanese regiments, they did not prevent parts of the 53rd Japanese Division from reinforcing north Burma and finally, with elements of the 18th, escaping.

The answer was surely the events in Manipur. Had the 14th Army been quicker on the offence instead of being pegged back by the Japanese, the three operations of Stilwell, Wingate, and the 14th Army, advancing into central Burma, would have synchronized. Eventually all would have linked up. Having prepared for his second Chindit expedition, Wingate was not a man to have his plans thwarted by a Japanese thrust elsewhere although they might have a direct effect on his own operations. Had not Wingate's Chindits flown into north-central Burma in March it is possible that Stilwell might not have captured Myitkyina in August.

13

ANGLO-AMERICAN RELATIONS

August 1944—Review of Whole Battle Front—Mountbatten speaks to the World—Anglo-American Relations Strained—36th Division join Stilwell—Widespread Japanese Withdrawal Begins

IN August of 1944 it still rained. The battle was still on. Only the see-saw of the battle had, by then, come down on the side of the Allies. For the only time since the Burma war began the Allied Commanders could determine their own course and actions and make their plans with the reasonable assurance that the Japanese would neither interrupt nor disrupt them.

The Japanese 15th Army, invaders of Manipur, were, by August 1944, quite definitely a disintegrating force. What was left of the Japanese 18th Division in north Burma had fallen back on Bhamo. The 2nd Japanese Division, so long held in reserve in the Rangoon area, was split up into regimental and even battalion packets and parcelled out to the several and weakening commands and armies, of which there were still three, the 28th, 15th, and 33rd. There was no Japanese air activity on sixteen days during August.

The position of the Allies, strung out in the form of a shepherd's crook from Myitkyina to Mayu over an area considerably greater than Great Britain, needs some brief explanation.

Stilwell had recovered the first strategic landmark in Burma, Myitkyina. Myitkyina's airfield, which soon accepted a traffic of 250 planes a day, was not only a plank for the air offensive against the Japanese in central Burma but gave the Americans and the few British planes on the

China run a shorter and safer route to China. Myitkyina was the capital of north Burma. Its recovery had prestige value. The Ledo road had reached Warazup in the Mogaung Valley.

Farther eastwards the Trans-Salween Chinese Expeditionary Force, under General Wei-Li-Huang, had crossed the Salween in May and was fighting among the 11,000 feet Kaoli mountains, an eastern spur of the Himalayas. This expeditionary force, known as 'Y' Force, had been trained under Stilwell by Brigadier Frank Dorn and other American officers in China. It was also equipped by the Americans.

On the Manipur front a twin drive by Brigadier Perowne's 23rd Brigade, after months of laborious fighting which included cutting lines of communication among the Naga Hills, and by 20th Indian Division from Imphal, had recaptured Ukhrul and straddled the main Japanese 31st Division's escape route back to Burma by mid-July. The 23rd Brigade had counted nearly 900 Japanese casualties to its credit.

The 23rd Indian Division had taken over from the 20th on the Palel front—the entrance to the Imphal plain from Tamu—and with the 2nd British Division had chased the Japanese 15th Division, or what was left of it, to the Chindwin. The 11th East African Division, veteran askaris from the Abyssinian and Eritrean campaigns, newly arrived in South-East Asia, then took over in the Kabaw Valley and advanced south to Kalewa. They fought their first action on 8 August.

In the south of the Imphal plain the 33rd Japanese Division hung on to the village of Bishenpur and several satellites. In the monsoon lakes formed in the plain they fought bitterly personal and bloody actions with the 17th Indian Division. The lakes became so deep that Gurkhas and Japanese were often too short to stand in them. They fought in boats or sniped at each other with only their heads above water.

The bamboo village of Ninthouthong was atomized by a force of Liberators and Mitchells, yet somehow the Japanese still lived in it and the Punjabis, following through with the bayonet after the bombing, were machine-gunned from a few yards' range. Casualties were floated out of battle on bamboo rafts. Once during the night the Japanese overran a mule park, killing many and causing panic. The battlefield, when daylight came, was littered with dead Japanese and mules. British bulldozers swept the lot into open graves as a housewife might sweep dust into her pan.

Across the rear of 33rd Division came the Lushai Brigade —Chins and Nagas and Lushias under British officers, the guerrillas of the hills.

In the Arakan, General Christison, without the 5th, 7th, or 36th Divisions, who had previously gone north, had re-grouped his 15th Corps. The 26th Indian Division lay in reserve. The 25th, having taken over the Maungdaw–Buthidaung area from the 36th British Division in April, held their ground throughout the months of the monsoon. The 81st West African Division, having rested after its first Kaladan expedition, re-entered the valley by the same route in August.

During the months after the affair of the 7th Divisional 'Admin. Box', continuous sampan sweeps were made along the broken coastline and up the many rivers and waterways (chaungs) of the Arakan. It was called 'Chaung warfare'. There was little rest for any formation in the line, for one of Mountbatten's principles, expressed soon after his arrival in South-East Asia, was that fighting should go on throughout the monsoon.

During the preceding months the Eastern Fleet had been strengthened by the addition of *Renown*, *Queen Elizabeth*, *Valiant*, the aircraft carriers *Illustrious* and *Unicorn*, the French battleship *Richelieu* and, for a time, the U.S.S. *Saratoga* and six U.S. destroyers.

Sabang, in Sumatra, was raided first in April and later its port installations were completely destroyed in July by air strikes from an Eastern Fleet Task Force. In May the fleet had sailed into MacArthur's territory as far east as Sourabaya, on the eastern tip of Java. In June, Port Blair in the Andaman Islands had been raided.

Some of these strikes formed part of the strategical policy of the Combined Chiefs of Staff, and were designed to assist MacArthur by creating a diversion as much as to help Mountbatten in South-East Asia. Others aimed at destroying Japanese oil plants and storage tanks. The frequent trips to Sumatra, which governs the Malacca Straits, were designed to keep down to a miminum Japanese shipping in the Straits and along the coastline to Rangoon. They succeeded, for the Japanese sent only small craft on coast-hugging expeditions, and many of them fell prey to Allied submarines.

The Japanese had given up the Indian Ocean and Bay of Bengal without a fight. Their shipping was needed in the Pacific, where events were moving faster than they had anticipated. Burma and its allied commands in Japan's South-East Asian empire were being relegated to the same position in Japan's overall strategy as Burma was in the Allied; that of lowest priority front.

The navy did, however, have one domestic setback when the 50,000-ton floating dock, built in India, capsized in Trincomalee harbour in the middle of 1944. It was the only British floating dock in the East and was one of the largest in the world. It docked the *Valiant* when it capsized and descended to a depth of twenty-five fathoms. It was never salvaged during the war and its loss necessitated the larger naval units going back to Durban for repairs.

During the so-called 'March on Delhi' the Japanese had reinforced Burma to ten and a half divisions. But when their Manipur invasion had proved a failure they informed

General Kimura, C.-in-C. Burma Command, that there would be no more reinforcements except from within the theatre and that the troops holding the country could rely on no outside help. They would remain in conquest or die in defeat.

Though some Japanese bombers were removed to the Philippines area for convoy protection, the chief reasons for the lack of air activity were the monsoon and the need for a period of refitting, when the Japanese squadrons moved as far back as Indo-China. Later the Japanese Naval Air Force returned revitalized.

It was in August that Mountbatten flew back to London and, among other things, gave a report on his command, which was barely nine months old, to a gathering of newspaper correspondents representing all the allied and neutral countries. At this moment in the story of this unknown war it is fitting to quote from it, for the Supreme Commander placed before the public the difficulties and achievements, in succinct form and in their proper order, which continuous reporting and commenting on events were unable to do.

'My object in this conference is to try and put before the Press of the world that every effort has been and is continuing to be put into the South-East Asia campaign; that my plans are made in close consultation with my deputy, General Joseph Stilwell, and that we carry them out with a common end in view,' he began.

He went on to say that South-East Asia Command was one big Allied effort and, as such, was going well. 'I go round and talk to the men, and what worries them is that their wives, their mothers, their daughters, their sweethearts, and their sisters don't seem to know that the war they are fighting is important and worth while, which it most assuredly is.' He explained that the chief reason for this neglect was the climax of the war in Europe and the advances of MacArthur and Nimitz in the Pacific.

'Enemy-held territory in S.E.A.C. extends 2,500 miles southwards from the north of Burma. The front on which we are at present fighting in Burma alone extends some 700 miles and is second only in length to the Russian front. It is the hard land crust which protects the Japanese conquests in China and Indo-China. It is Japan's land route to India and, more important, the Allies' land route to China. Both offensively and defensively Japan has strained and is straining, every nerve to hold Burma. . . .

'Before 1943 there were no roads into Burma from the north, while the lower reaches of the Brahmaputra are unbridgeable. Assam is a logistical nightmare. . . . We are fighting against the grain of the country. In 1943 . . . a small force of British and Indian troops, under Brigadier Wingate, made the first experiment in long-range penetration and proved that we could out-fight the Japanese in the kind of war which he had made his own and under conditions which were to his advantage.

'At Quebec, the British and American Governments decided that the time had come to form an Allied operational command to take over the British command from G.H.Q. India, and include the American command in Burma and India and be responsible for land, sea, and air operations against the Japanese in South-East Asia.

'In view of my original association with Combined Operations, a lot of people, myself included, jumped to the conclusion that large-scale amphibious operations would at once be the order of the day . . . the landing-craft and ships originally allotted had to be withdrawn for more urgent operations in the West. . . . The order to us in Burma was to carry on with what we had left. Our plans had to be recast on a less ambitious scale, but there was one thing we could do, and that was to drive the Japanese out of the north-east corner of Burma, and so improve our communications with China.

'A concerted plan was therefore made for the whole of the Burma front to enable the forces of the north-east to advance. General Stilwell commanded the forces on the Ledo front.

'An advance in Burma is a different affair from an advance in France or Russia, since it has largely to be carried out along a single axis of your supply line and a relatively small force can thus stop the advance of a much larger one, however resolutely led. It thus became important that the overall plans for Burma should prevent Japanese reinforcements being able to bar the progress of the Chinese-American forces.

'There were two ways the 14th Army could most materially help . . . first by cutting the communications of the Japanese 18th Division . . . and, secondly, by engaging a greater number of Japanese divisions elsewhere in Burma. The first task . . . was given to General Wingate's long-range penetration forces . . . the second would have proved a more serious problem if it had not been for the Japanese plan to advance into India, through Chittagong on the Arakan front and Dimapur on the Imphal front.'

First Mountbatten mentioned the advance into the Arakan and the surrounding of the 7th Indian Division. 'The importance of the battle of the 7th Division "Admin. Box", was twofold,' he said. 'It was a victory of morale by men who refused to withdraw when their lines of communications were cut; the hitherto successful tactics of outflanking and infiltration were thus defeated. The second factor was the exploitation of air supply by American and British transport aircraft, which enabled our forces in the "Box" to be fully supplied throughout the siege.'

Then Mountbatten recapitulated the events around Imphal; the cutting of the supply road from Dimapur to Imphal; the air supply to the beleagured garrison; the arrival of the 33rd Corps to clear the road, and the battering received by the Japanese 31st Division.

'In point of numbers engaged this must have been one of the greatest land battles fought between Japanese and British forces and, I am glad to say, the Japanese have now been flung out of India.'

From recounting the efforts of Stilwell and Lentaigne's Chindits in north Burma, Mountbatten passed to casualties. 'All these impressive results have not been secured without heavy casualties. Allied forces in 1944 (up to August) have suffered 10,000 killed, 2,000 missing, and 27,000 wounded. But these have been amply avenged by the killing of no fewer than 50,000 Japanese. Even more deadly and persistent in inflicting casualties is the mosquito. . . . American and British medical services have succeeded in reducing the ravages of malaria by no less than forty per cent (of what they were in 1943). More than ninety per cent of patients report fit for duty after three weeks. All the same, the Allies have suffered close on a quarter of a million casualties from sickness.' Among other striking figures he quoted were that from May to the beginning of August 70,000 tons and 93,000 men, including 25,500 casualties, had been moved by air. These figures excluded the men and tonnage flown to and from China.

Except when measured against territory recovered, Mountbatten's claims of success looked good. But Burma was, except for parts of the north, still in Japanese hands. By laying stress on the diverting of amphibious equipment he made it appear as if South-East Asia was starved of most things (this was intended), which was hardly correct.

Air superiority having been achieved for some considerable time, the main things required for land fighting against the Japanese were trained men and transport aircraft. The former were there when Mountbatten arrived. He did not mention the numerical superiority of the Allied ground forces, which was so great that the number of men he quoted as being moved by air alone was equal to the number the

Japanese employed on their Arakan and Manipur expeditions.

For some time Mountbatten had been in overall command of all land operations in the theatre as well as being Supreme Commander. There were several reasons for this, one of which was that Giffard was waiting for his relief and was therefore playing no part in the current operations.

Giffard was an unspectacular man who had achieved distinction in the first world war. He was a very senior general. Though he always maintained Burma could be recaptured by land, he had displayed a caution whilst in the East which evoked considerable criticism from many quarters, especially from the Americans. As he was responsible for all land operations, until relinquishing his command, their limited scope and slow progress were directly attributable to his planning.

Giffard was, perhaps, a less ambitious man than Mountbatten or Stilwell. While they wanted quick victories he preferred to play a waiting game, building up strength and confidence before embarking on any offensive.

The moment had arrived in South-East Asia Command when great things were possible for, for the first time, the British and Indians were beating the Japanese. The opportunities were there for the taking and Mountbatten no longer had to consider alternative means of defeating or starving the Japanese in Burma as he had done when producing his plan for 'Operation Axiom'. ('Axiom' called for a by-passing of Burma with landings on the Andaman Islands as preludes to a full-scale invasion of Sumatra and Java.) The battle for Burma could be won on the land.

In achieving this victory, Slim might grind the retreating Japanese armies in central Burma and Stilwell might advance across north Burma and open the land route to China. But the ultimate responsibility lay on Mountbatten's young shoulders.

Lastly, relations between the Americans and British had become strained over the recent events in Manipur, the way the Chindits were used, Giffard's caution, and the refusal to give Stilwell a British formation in north Burma. Quite logically, the Americans, within and without the theatre, pointed to Burma and said: 'What has Britain done or achieved? What has she recovered of her own possession?' Their criticisms gained weight when Myitkyina fell to the Chinese and Americans at the end of August. By then Stilwell had ceased to come under the operational command of Slim and the two commands had separated. All these things made it necessary for Mountbatten to assume immediate command with Slim and Stilwell as his field commanders.

Mountbatten attempted to restore the strained Anglo-American relations in S.E.A.C., especially in Stilwell's Northern Combat Area Command, by injecting fresh troops into that area. He ordered Maj.-Gen. Frank W. Festing's 36th British Division, consisting of two brigades, the 29th Independent (the Madagascar landing brigade) and the 72nd, for duty under Stilwell in July.

At the time the 36th Division was resting in Shillong after a spell in the Arakan. Their previous training history since they were formed in the Bombay area had been similar to that of the 2nd British Division. The 29th Brigade, having cut its operational teeth as an amphibious force in Madagascar, formed the basis of a Combined Operations training team. The 36th Division had been formed round the brigade, whose commander, Brigadier Festing, had been elevated to the command of the division.

The choice of the 36th Division was wise and diplomatic. It was completely British and its commander was a most colourful character and personality who became an immediate favourite with every American in Northern Combat Area Command from Stilwell to the lowest G.I. The operation on which the 36th Division was bound was called 'Exercise Propaganda'—propaganda for the British in an American Command.

The leading elements of Festing's division arrived in north Burma by air while the battle for Myitkyina was still in progress. Other parts of the division followed by road, rail, and air. Those parts arriving at Mogaung found it a sea of brown mud through which they had to manhandle all guns and heavy equipment. It was so hot that three men died of heatstroke. Yet the men had to live in foxholes full of water or build above ground.

Stilwell urgently required a fresh combat formation to permit him to regroup and reform his Chinese divisions for the final strike on Myitkyina and the subsequent advance towards Bhamo.

There is a story, which Festing tells with delight, that on arrival in north Burma he reported to Stilwell, who was pondering over some maps in a tent. Festing saluted and said: 'Festing reporting for duty, sir.' The crusty Stilwell, without looking up, laconically replied: 'Take Taungyi' and no more. Festing turned about and took Taungyi. The significance of this little north Burma village was that its capture provided a screen for the Chinese divisions, which were regrouping.

Following this and other preliminary operations, the division captured Pinbaw on the general's birthday, and then temporarily halted while the rest of the north Burma forces readied for a general offensive to open the road to China by way of Bhamo, Namkam, and on to the China border where they hoped to meet the Trans-Salween Chinese Expeditionary Force.

For this part of the north Burma operations the 36th British Division was given four tasks. First, the opening of the north Burma railway corridor, which ran through the jungle from Mogaung to Naba junction, where the railway split, one arm continuing to Indaw and Mandalay and the other ending at Katha on the Irrawaddy. The length of the corridor was some 230 miles. It was known to be held by the Japanese, though only a few months previously the Chindits had fought over considerable lengths of it.

The second task was to provide a firm base from which two Chinese divisions, operating on a parallel axis of advance, could debouch eastwards towards the Burma road. The third was to protect the western flank of the whole N.C.A.C. force; and the last, to link with the 14th Army, which had yet to cross the Chindwin over one hundred miles to the west of the corridor. On the move—it was never anticipated the division would remain stationary for long—the division would be supplied by air, an operation similar to but more difficult than the air supplying of the West Africans in the Kaladan Valley and the Chindits in Burma. The maintenance of air lines of communication during the monsoon for a mobile and aggressive operation was Festing's chief apprehension. Unlike the Chindits, his was a normally equipped division, only that his transport had been pared, as was the case with most Burma divisions, and his anti-tank units had been re-formed into mortar batteries. Otherwise his equipment was not designed for long-range penetration. The Americans were responsible for air supply, some of his gunners were Chinese, and he had under his command British, Chinese, Burmese, and later, Indian and Gurkha troops.

During the preliminary advance from Mogaung to Pinbaw in August, a battalion of the Royal Sussex led the division and fought the first two actions at Hill 60 and Thaikwagon. Though it dominated the surrounding country and the approaches to it, Hill 60 was thickly wooded and jungled. The Japanese in their bunkers had withstood a two weeks' siege by one Chindit column. The Sussex blasted their way to the hill in twelve hours. At Thaikwagon a group were caught in the open and pinned to the ground. So intense was the sun that several men died.

The rapid movement and hustling tactics of the 36th Division quickly renewed the Americans' confidence in the British as fighters. Festing, accompanied by his A.D.C., Capt. John Riddell, whose sister he had married before the war, was usually in the thick of a scrap. Even Lieut.-Col. Fred Eldridge, Stilwell's Public Relations Officer, who was very pro-Stilwell and critical of the British, eulogized Festing at length in an American journal as 'a legendary giant striding the jungles of north Burma . . .'

As a man, Festing was a giant indeed. He was often to be seen sitting up in a jeep and driving it at furious speed—he once drove into a river—or tramping through the jungle aided by a stick almost as tall as himself. He always carried an American carbine. He wore enormous American Ranger boots, an Australian bush hat, a fur-lined Air Force leather jacket when it was cold, and anything when it was hot. His was a restless, adventurous, and sometimes impish spirit.

At Winchester, he says, 'I was a bum. I didn't like discipline. I hated games and was no good at anything. At Sandhurst I found I was better than most people at soldiering.' An Irishman, he came from five generations of soldiers or sailors.

As a subaltern Festing sailed a 42-foot yacht across the Atlantic to race against the Americans. After taking a course at the Staff College he temporarily became an A.B. on a Finnish ship. Once he travelled down the Russian border by train, sitting on third-class wooden benches. He hates books on war or by women, but reads *The Scottish Minstrel over the Border* every night. Nearly always a prodigious pipe, in keeping with the man, dangles out of his mouth. He collects flintlocks, swords, and other weapons. If now, with no war to fight, he cannot find adventure, Festing wishes to retire to his bit of land. He may not be allowed to do so, because he is regarded in high circles as one of the 'coming young generals'.

That then briefly is the man. He was not always popular within his own division, but he did more for Anglo-American relations by personal contact than any one except, perhaps, Mountbatten. He was the type whom Americans admire.

Festing's division reaped the benefit of their popularity at Christmas 1944, when the Americans flew them thirty Dakota loads of Christmas food and drink. It is doubtful whether any front-line formation in the war had a better Christmas. By then, fortunately, the Japanese were retreating hard.

If the division faced a nine months' march through north and central Burma and the Shan Hills against a retreating enemy, it was, for the first part at least, an enemy prepared to fight.

Stilwell's Chinese, increased to five divisions by the addition of the 14th, 30th, and 50th to his veteran 22nd and 38th, and with the prospect of support from a new American Task Force, had months of gruelling fighting in front of them before the Ledo road could be built through to the China border where the Trans-Salween Force was battling between the Salween and the Shweli rivers.

Supporting these operations with increasing intensity in the air were Maj.-Gen. Howard C. Davidson's 10th U.S.A.A.F., based on Myitkyina, and Maj.-Gen. Claire Chennault's 14th U.S.A.A.F. in China.

Facing this concentration were the remnants of the Japanese 18th Division at Bhamo, the 56th Division on the Bhamo–Lashio line, the 53rd Division in the railway corridor, and the 24th and 34th Independent Motor Brigades. They were prepared for a slow withdrawal.

On the Imphal front the Japanese 15th Army was retreating in disorder. Its plight was terrible. Although incessantly struck and pounded from the air, the Japanese must have considered this one of the lesser evils, for to reach the asylum of central Burma they faced the implacability of the monsoon, the jungle, the mountains, the Chindwin river, and the rolling weight of the 33rd Corps.

The few main routes through the mountains on the Burma border were barred to them. The 15th and 31st Divisions had to split up into small parties and try to reach the Chindwin—and cross it, of course—by little-known, slippery mountain tracks. Food and ammunition they had none. The Nagas' rice stocks were looted when not hidden, but they proved insufficient.

Beri-beri, a starvation disease caused by a diet of polished rice, scourged the Japanese; malaria and dysentery were its sisters. How many thousands of Japanese died will never be known. Swollen bodies floated swiftly down the mountain streams and monsoon rivers. The Allied doctors reported dead groups of Japanese, their skin drawn tightly over their bones, with little bags of rice which they could not eat or digest hanging round their necks. Hundreds of bodies were found in Tamu alone. Many of the Japanese were too weak to carry out their normal practice of killing their sick and wounded. Near Tamu a complete hospital full of patients was captured. With a few exceptions, the patients were too weak to commit suicide. They lay in a daze on the ground or on rough bamboo stretchers. Some Japanese gave themselves up, while others were captured before they could blow themselves to pieces with hand grenades. All were numbed by the agonies of the last few months.

Even the 33rd Japanese Division, a fighting unit of which any nation, Allied or enemy, might be proud, cracked around Bishenpur after weeks of merciless fighting. They retreated up the Tiddim road, hoping to escape via the Chin Hills to Kalewa and across the Chindwin. They were chased by the 5th Indian Division, caught across their escape line by the Lushai Brigade, and had to take to the hills. Once a truckload of hands was found—the hands of dead men which their comrades had intended to cremate and send back to Japan.

On 25 August the last Japanese crossed the Indo-Burma border at Milestone 75 on the Imphal–Tiddim road. It seemed that the prophecy of the 33rd Divisional commander had proved correct. On receipt of General Mutagachi's order, 'The fate of the Empire depends on the result of this battle. You will take Imphal at all costs', he had added, 'You will take Imphal, but the division will be annihilated'.

14

THE RELIEF OF STILWELL

Second Quebec Conference—Relief of Stilwell—Change of Command in S.E.A.C.—Operations in North and Central Burma—Scrub Typhus

THE Second Quebec Conference in September 1944 was primarily concerned with the future course of the war against Japan. Events in Europe foreshadowed the defeat of Germany and a comprehensive plan, including the part to be played by both Britain and America, was required for what Mr. Churchill described as 'the destruction of the barbarians of the Pacific'.

For some time Britain's participation in the war against Japan, especially in the Pacific, had been the subject of much controversy in America. There were two schools of thought. The first had accused Britain of not wanting to give more than 'token assistance' in the war against Japan. The second suggested it would be wrong for Britain to figure too prominently in what some Americans regarded as America's war.

In general, the American public refused to accept the war in Burma, or Britain's effort in it, as much more than an Imperial knockabout in which a few British were prodded into action by General Stilwell. The reconquest of Imperial possessions, even though it might cause injury to Japan's war effort, was not popular across the Atlantic, while the fact that, by then, the arms of the British Empire had killed more Japanese in Burma than the Americans had in the Pacific was not known or was disregarded except by a very few.

These facts drew the following comment from Hanson

Baldwin of the *New York Times*. After pointing out that there was not, nor had there been, a single American division in Burma—why should there be?—he gave figures of the troops from the British Empire engaged and the casualties they had inflicted in the first six months of the year. He ended with: 'Thus Admiral Mountbatten's command cannot properly be accused of a "do-nothing" policy —as it is sometimes in this country—or of failure to employ a sizable land force on the borders of and inside Burma.'

Mr. Churchill stuck out for the fullest participation by Britain, and, among other things, Mountbatten's request for six extra divisions, an amphibious fleet, and other resources was accepted by the Combined Chiefs of Staff. It seemed that Britain meant to exert not only the fullest effort in South-East Asia but also in the Pacific under MacArthur or Nimitz, for in November—a month of many changes— Admiral Sir Bruce Fraser, who had taken over the Eastern Fleet from Admiral Sir James Somerville, became Admiral of the British Pacific Fleet, which was rapidly being increased in size. Admiral Sir Arthur John Power took over the East Indies Fleet.

Mountbatten, however, was unlucky with his six divisions and amphibious fleet, for the fluctuations in Europe permitted neither to go East for some considerable time. As before, S.E.A.C. had to do with what it possessed.

In October, Stilwell was relieved of his four portfolios in South-East Asia as (1) Commander of the U.S. China–Burma–India theatre, (2) Deputy Supreme Commander to Admiral Mountbatten, (3) Chief of Staff to Generalissimo Chiang Kai-shek, (4) Chief of Lend-Lease supplies to China.

The official White House announcement gave no reasons, but it was clear from the very start that his recall had nothing to do with any rift between Stilwell and Mountbatten. All the evidence pointed to a clash between Stilwell and the Generalissimo.

President Roosevelt answered the clamorous White House reporters with 'It's a simple fact. General Stilwell has done extremely well. I'm very fond of him personally. . . . Generalissimo Chiang Kai-shek and General Stilwell had had certain fallings out, oh, quite a while ago; and finally the other day, the Generalissimo asked that somebody be sent to replace him. And we did it.'

It was obvious, however, that there was more in it than two men taking a dislike to each other, for although Stilwell may never have been a very tactful man he was a great Sinophile, a powerful personality, and an extraordinary soldier. From a purely British viewpoint, any general who shared a tent with other officers, and slept in his shirt and pants even when out of the battle zone, must be extraordinary.

There were three probable reasons. First, a difference of opinion between Stilwell and the Generalissimo about the Lend-Lease supplies which were being flown over the 'Hump' to China from India. The Generalissimo was not entirely satisfied with the quantity. Stilwell was not satisfied with the use of the weapons and equipment. He openly expressed feelings on the Kuomintang-Communist situation, i.e. the antagonism between the National Government and the Chinese Communists.

The second reason was a proposal mooted by the U.S. Government that Stilwell should be in complete command of all China's forces against the Japanese. At first Chiang Kai-shek agreed, but then changed his mind.

The third reason was that neither Stilwell nor the American Government considered that China was putting a full or concerted effort into the Japanese war. China had been at war with Japan for seven years, but it was patently obvious that a great deal of the fighting was on a token basis. To give China her due, she was poorly armed and trained, but even as early as 1942, when a small but select band of British saboteurs and guerrillas under Major Gill-Davies, D.S.O., had gone from Burma 1,500 miles into China for railway destruction work, they were met by obstruction and frustration from all sides.

Taciturn, crusty, tactless, and critical of Britain's conduct and policy in the East though Stilwell may have been, he rendered great assistance to Britain's reconquest of Burma. Without his dynamic energy, forceful character, and superb field leadership the campaign in north Burma might well have proved abortive. Its importance to the whole strategy of the Far Eastern war can be judged by the priority placed on the Ledo road by the Combined Chiefs of Staff.

Stilwell 'drove' the bulldozers, the engineers, and the Chinese divisions and thus left an indelible mark on Asia, though one fears that it will one day be obliterated by the all-erasing jungle. Stilwell was one of the last British or Americans out of Burma in 1942. He was among the first to go back. With his Chinese and Americans he had captured the first big landmark in Burma proper—Myitkyina. In his own way Stilwell was as rare a jewel as Wingate. On his return to America he said little, but when asked what he thought of Mountbatten said: 'He's a great commander. He's such a personality he's dangerous.'

The U.S. China-Burma-India theatre was then split up into two, China becoming a separate command. Because of this Mountbatten lost another most capable American officer in Maj.-Gen. Albert C. Wedermeyer, who had been his Deputy Chief of Staff. Wedermeyer became head of the China theatre. Stilwell's place as commander of the India-Burma theatre and also field commander of the newly named Northern Combat Area Command in Burma—formerly Stilwell's North Burma Command—was taken by his deputy, Lieut.-Gen. Dan. I. Sultan, an expert military engineer.

Giffard's relief arrived in November. He was Lieut.-Gen.

Sir Oliver Leese, who had taken over the British 8th Army from Montgomery and had already built up a reputation for himself before coming to South-East Asia. His command, the 11th Army Group, was changed in designation to the Allied Land Forces South-East Asia (A.L.F.S.E.A.). His Chief of Staff was Maj.-Gen. G. P. Walsh.

Leese's command consisted of Sultan's N.C.A.C., Slim's 14th Army on the Imphal front, which had now geographically changed to the Chindwin front, and Christison's 15th Corps in the Arakan. Slim's two corps commanders were Lieut.-Gen. M. M. Stopford (33rd Corps) and Lieut.-Gen. Frank Messervy, who took over 4th Corps from Lieut.-Gen. Scoones. In December Slim, Scoones, and Stopford were knighted for their leadership in the Imphal campaign.

There was also a realignment of Air Command South-East Asia. Air Chief Marshal Sir Richard Peirse was replaced by Air Chief Marshal Sir Trafford Leigh-Mallory as commander of the Allied Expeditionary Air Forces, but he was lost in an air crash on his journey out East. Air Marshal Sir Guy Garrod, Assistant Air C.-in-C. South-East Asia, deputized until the arrival of Air Chief Marshal Sir Keith Park. Under these commanders, Lieut.-Gen. George E. Stratemeyer remained in charge of the Eastern Air Command, his assistant being Air Marshal Sir Alec Coryton, the man who taught the King to fly. Maj.-Gen. Howard C. Davidson still led the 10th U.S.A.A.F.; Air Commodore F. W. J. Mellersh the Strategic Air Force; Brig.-Gen. F. W. Evans took over the Combat Cargo Task Force from Brig.-Gen. William Old, and 221 and 224 Groups R.A.F. were commanded by Air Vice Marshal the Earl of Bandon. While the 10th U.S.A.A.F. operated on the N.C.A.C. front, 221 Group remained on the Chindwin front and 224 Group on the Arakan.

Lieut.-Gen. F. A. M. Browning, of Arnhem fame, became Mountbatten's Chief of Staff in succession to Lieut.-Gen.

Sir Henry Pownall. With Admiral Power commanding the East Indies Fleet, the Allied line-up for the reconquest of Burma and the destruction of General Kimura's Burma armies was complete. The team, to prepare for the invasion of Malaya, timed for just under a year hence, was assembled.

While the pursuit of the Japanese in the north and on the Chindwin front was being carried out, Mountbatten issued his orders for the next phase of the campaign. The completion of the Ledo road, the protection of the air route to China, the capture of Mandalay, the defeat of the Japanese armies in central Burma, and the clearing of the Arakan once and for all, were the immediate plans. The final prize was Rangoon.

The road and the capture of Lashio, on the old Burma road, were Sultan's tasks. The capture of Mandalay and the strangling of the Japanese army were Slim's. The capture of Akyab and Ramree, the landings along the Arakan coast, and the building up of air bases were Christison's. Admiral Power had to provide an amphibious fleet and its cover. Air operations extended from cargo flying and the close support of the advancing armies to the hindering of possible Japanese reinforcements to their Burma armies. The railway line from Bangkok to Moulmein, built by Allied prisoners of war, became the principal strategic target. The destruction of Rangoon's marshalling yards was another. The Japanese air forces, already driven back to rear bases, were to be driven farther still.

Slim's battle for Mandalay and in central Burma was the largest operation. It involved the complete 14th Army. But for the first time the 14th Army would, once across the Chindwin, be clear of the jungle. It could manœuvre, deploy, and employ tanks in their classic role.

The army required a gateway to the central Burma plain. Moreover the retreating Japanese could be given no respite.

Hence the monsoon operations of Maj.-Gen. C. C. Fowkes's 11th East African Division and Maj.-Gen. R. Briggs's 5th Indian Division.

The objective given to these two divisions was Kalewa, where a bridgehead could be formed over the Chindwin and the way opened for an advance by the 14th Army to another and even greater obstacle—the Irrawaddy. The date for Kalewa was Christmas 1944. By then the rains would have ceased, and the bulk of the 14th Army would have rested, re-formed, and be poised for action.

The East Africans took the route through the Kabaw Valley and the 5th Division advanced via Tiddim and the Chin Hills. Once Kalewa had been taken, the 2nd British Division, withdrawn to the area of Kohima for rest and refitting, would pass through the Africans and the 5th Indian Division, weary after two years' campaigning in Africa, the Arakan, and Imphal, would be flown out. Few members of the 5th Division believed that this would happen; too often had they been told of good things to come, and too often had they been disappointed.

The Africans fanned out in the Kabaw Valley, one brigade turning east of captured Sittaung on the Chindwin. The other two brigades moved south along the main valley track. The conditions beggar description.

What should have been roads and tracks had long since been washed away by the monsoon floods. New roads had to be built by the Africans as they advanced. Vehicles and guns were constantly being bogged and had to be winched out or heaved out by hand. Supply was by air. Somehow tanks joined in the advance against the Japanese retreat. They churned their way through mud, though as often as not they were bellied. For the Africans' first two months' campaigning in Burma, in this Kabaw Valley, it rained unceasingly.

At the beginning of October the Africans, having already

covered over sixty miles, were again split, one brigade being diverted towards Mawlaik, on the Chindwin, and the other two continuing on to Kalewa.

For three weeks this brigade fought for Mawlaik. The Japanese had temporarily recovered their balance and were attempting to turn their retreat from a desperate route to a slow, skilful rearguard action. Midway through November Mawlaik and Kaleymu, twenty miles south-west of Kaleymu, were taken.

As the 5th Division advanced along the tortuous 160-mile Tiddim road it closed the road behind it. There was no way back, only forward. Air supply of a moving force is never easy but the air supply of this division called for extreme accuracy and courage in the pilots. The road was so narrow in places it permitted only a single line of traffic. On one side hills rose up into the mist and on the other precipices sheered off into the valleys hundreds of feet below. Somehow along this narrow lane pilots had to drop food and ammunition to the troops as they trudged round bend after bend and always upwards among these massive hills.

The aircraft had to fly into the hills, not over them, and in the monsoon weather when clouds and mist often blanketed the whole mass of the Chin Hills it was well-nigh impossible. Yet, like so many other impossible things in the Burma war, it was achieved, though the division had to go teetotal for some weeks, since food and ammunition were so much more precious than beer and rum.

The Japanese did not neglect to destroy the bridges and causeways along the Tiddim road, built only just over a year before by the troops of the 17th and 23rd Divisions, 4th Corps Engineers, and thousands of Chin tribespeople. The 5th Division had to rebuild forty of them while pressing on to the tail of the Japanese 33rd Division—a tail with, at times, the sting of a scorpion.

To reach the 'Chocolate Staircase' the division crossed

the Beltang Lui river, which winds its way through the valley below the hills rising up to Tiddim.

Except for the final stretch of road from Burma into China —the 'zigzag to the heavens'—the 'Chocolate Staircase' is the most awe-inspiring stretch of road in South-East Asia. It rises through 130 hairpin bends, up 4,000 feet in 8 miles. At the top lies Tiddim, a typical hill township of palm, bamboo, or brick buildings with corrugated iron roofs. The Staircase was named 'Chocolate' because in the monsoon the golden colour of the dust turned a chocolate brown. When organized for defence, Tiddim is virtually unassailable from the direction of the Staircase. Yet the 5th Division approached from this direction.

Fortunately the Japanese, harassed in their rear by the Lushai Brigade, were not prepared for more than a temporary stand. Nor did they possess the cohesion effectively to counter any flanking moves. Showing considerable endurance, Indian troops scaled the hills to the flanks, and, in one case, to the rear of Tiddim. Tanks rumbled slowly under cover of cloud and mist up the Staircase itself. Overhead, Hurribombers maintained a continuous train of air strikes. The Japanese, demoralized, moved back from Tiddim to the 9,000-foot Kennedy Peak, where at the beginning of the year the highest troop of medium guns in the world had stood.

Grant tanks were winched up to an assault position near the Peak and with the aid of infantry and gunners took it, while the Royal West Kents and West Yorks moved across the Japanese main escape route and pressed on towards Kaleymu. The Japanese were forced once more to take to the hills and little-known paths through them, where they risked meeting the Chin guerrillas.

The East Africans and the 5th Division met in the area of Kaleymu in mid-November and parted again, for contrary to their expectations the 5th Division were immediately flown out for their promised rest. The fly-out was a fine piece of organization, for the aircraft were waiting for the leading 5th Division troops as they advanced into the southern end of Kabaw Valley.

One brigade of the East Africans crossed the Chindwin at Mawlaik and moved down the east bank. The others advanced into Kalewa from Kaleymu direction, reaching their objective at the end of November. On 3 December they captured the town and with it established a bridgehead over the Chindwin fifteen miles long. They were nearly a month ahead of schedule.

In mid-December the 2nd British Division, after a few months' 'rest' near their former battle-ground, Kohima, took over the bridgehead from the Africans. Engineers spanned the Chindwin with a 1,000-foot pontoon Bailey bridge, the longest Bailey in the world at that time.

Almost coinciding with this penetration into central Burma by the 2nd Division, followed by the 20th Indian, was the secret crossing farther north of a division new to this theatre of operations. For two years Maj.-Gen. T. W. Rees's 19th Indian Division had been training in South India. It had been a reserve division, and its training included combined operations.

The 19th Division crossed the Chindwin river at Nanthanyit and Sittaung at the end of November, assisted by landing-craft brought in pieces to the Uyu river, welded together on the banks, dragged by six elephants down river to the Chindwin crossing-place. In a few hours hundreds of men, seven hundred mules, and medical stores had been ferried across the river.

The general axis of advance for the division was across Burma to Pinlebu and Banmauk and then southwards, via Wuntho. Its ultimate objective, in this phase, was to link-up with the 2nd Division at Shwebo. The first part of the route was the same as that taken by the first Wingate expedition, part of the Japanese advance into Manipur, and the first part of the Japanese retreat from Manipur.

By the time the division had reached the Banmauk-Wuntho area—a distance of little more than a hundred miles as the crow flies—brigades and divisional headquarters had covered an average of 350 miles in a month's marching. Every one was on foot. One brigade had actually covered 382 miles, including twelve days in contact with the enemy rearguards and seven days static fighting.

All along the trail they passed derelict vehicles facing both ways, those of the refugee retreat of 1942 and those of the Japanese retreat of the current year. It was a wilderness, a foodless, friendless country, for it was out of the Kachin or Naga province and the local Burmese were terrified by the war that ebbed and flowed through their land.

A little farther north, in Sultan's Northern Combat Area Command, Festing's 36th British Division advanced down the railway corridor at the rate of two miles a day. To the east of him, along the same axis, moved the Chinese corps, 14th and 22nd Division under Lieut.-Gen. Liao Yo Hsiang, ready to debouch eastwards towards Lashio.

By the beginning of October, just before Sultan took over from Stilwell, the rains had almost ceased, and passing the bombed-out wreck of what once had been Hopin, a town over which the Chindits and the Chindit Africans had fought, the 36th Division disappeared once more into the jungle of north Burma.

At Mohyin a British sergeant killed a Japanese and secured his identity disc, which was proudly produced at Divisional Headquarters where Stilwell was holding a conference. It proved for the first time in Burma the presence of the 34th Independent Motor Brigade. Already the division had fought the 53rd Japanese Division and the 24th I.M.B.

The Japanese choose several places down the corridor for

determined stands. The first was at Mawlu, a village on the railway line. East Lancashires and Royal Scots Fusiliers of the 29th Brigade moved down the road to Mawlu, while the Royal Welch Fusiliers skirted the township to cut across the railway line. After several days of small but bitter scrapping, the general himself led the Scots into Mawlu and the Japanese withdrew farther down the corridor. For a time Mawlu became Divisional Headquarters while the 29th and 72nd Brigades probed forward to find the next Japanese line of resistance.

Almost immediately they hit the thickly jungled village of Pinwe. The Myitkyina–Mandalay road and railway converged at this point. It was ideally suited to defence, for the attacking side could see nothing and the defending side could hold their fire until the last moment.

The battle for Pinwe began on Armistice Day. For three weeks the divisional infantry, assisted by artillery barrages and air strikes, prodded, probed, and skirmished for the village. The gunners poured shells into the woods to clear away the branches and leaves, trying to make visibility greater. The Japanese dug into the ground, sited their automatics with characteristic cleverness, and picked off men by the dozen. It became a war of nerves. The Japanese planted snipers in trees as outposts. In what was possibly the thickest jungle in Burma they were unseen and it was certain death for anyone who came within their vision.

Where the winding, narrow track crossed the stream to enter the jungled mass of Pinwe, one Japanese sniper, 'Little Willie' he was called, lived for three weeks in a hole dug into the bottom of a tree. All manner of ruses were tried to persuade 'Little Willie' to show himself but none succeeded.

A mass assault on Pinwe was impossible. It would have been suicide. Platoons of men did creep over the stream by night, but when daylight came they found themselves ringed by fire and pinned to the holes they had scraped out of the ground. Once over 3,000 shells were poured into the woods in half an hour—a record barrage for north Burma at that time.

On the cold misty morning of St. Andrew's Day, 30 November, Royal Scots Fusiliers patrols found the area of the stream vacated. They moved farther into the woods without being fired upon and within an hour the Scots celebrated their day by marching into what once had been Pinwe, their pipers, under Pipe-Major McMenemy, playing 'Cock o' the North'. Pinwe was a burnt-out cinder heap. Only one Japanese was found, and he was shot by Brigadier Hugh Stockwell's batman. The Japanese had stayed their time and gone. The main Japanese forces had crossed the Irrawaddy.

By 10 December the 36th Division had advanced through Naba Junction, where the railway forks to Katha on the Irrawaddy and to Indaw for Mandalay, and consolidated the line of north and central Burma known as the Katha-Indaw line. There for a time they settled, though one brigade went some miles south to Tigyiang, a small Irrawaddy post. On 16 December, the 36th and 19th Indian Division linked hands west of Indaw. West of the Irrawaddy, north Burma was clear of Japanese.

During the advance of the 11th East African Division down the Kabaw Valley and of the 36th down the railway corridor, another war was fought and won, a war against what was for a time an unknown fever which struck down and killed the soldier. These two divisions were the principal sufferers.

Fortunately it did not take the doctors long to realize that this fever, which sometimes kept its victims in a state of semi-consciousness at a high temperature or at a low temperature apathy for as much as three weeks, was Japanese river fever, also known as scrub typhus. Scrub typhus had rarely been identified as far west as Burma. Its normal habitat was the islands of south Japan, the Dutch East Indies, and parts of the Malayan archipelago.

An outbreak of the fever had occurred in 1942 in Ceylon among a group of Africans. Over six hundred Africans had gone down with a mortality rate just below twenty per cent. The Australians had also suffered heavily in New Guinea. The doctors and scientists were therefore not completely unprepared. Preventive and recuperative measures were quickly taken.

At the time there was no known cure by drugs or inoculation. All that the doctors knew was that the patient had to be rapidly evacuated and nursed with the utmost care in white-sheeted beds, attended by nursing sisters. Comfort, gentleness, and quiet were the three things to keep down the mortality rate of scrub typhus.

When the outbreak first occurred, sufferers in the railway corridor or Kabaw Valley had to be evacuated over hundreds of miles to a base hospital. The means by which they were moved varied from bamboo litter and jeep over rough, muddy trails to light airplane and Dakota. Sometimes it took days to get a man settled down. This evacuation time-lag proved dangerous. Mortality figures during the very early period rose to over twenty per cent.

The solution was to take the nurses, the soft beds, and the sheets forward to the men so that within an hour or two of the fever being identified the patient was in hospital. So quickly were these measures taken that the fourteen per cent death-rate for August 1944 was reduced a month later to nine per cent.

Preventive measures were immediately taken in the field. Everyone (including nurses) was ordered to wear long trousers and boots and gaiters which had been sprayed with an insecticide. Scat (Di-methyl phthalate), and later the more powerful pest deterrent, DBP (Di-butyl phthalate), were used. As the troops advanced the area ahead of them was sprayed with DDT. Once the Japanese complained over Saigon radio that the British were using gas in the Kabaw Valley. Unfortunately DDT did not kill the Japanese.

The disease is not endemic over large areas. Mostly it is found in such places as jungle clearings which once were rice-fields but have become overgrown with long grass and scrub. Grains of rice remain on the ground and rats, the reservoir of the typhus virus, feed in the areas. From the rats the infection spreads to a mite which lives among the grass.

Such areas in Burma were easy to identify from air photographs and henceforth the army by-passed them. The whole of Burma through which the armies might be moving was photographed and maps issued with scrub typhus areas marked on them.

A tribute to the way the scrub typhus outbreak was tackled was paid by Brigadier Hawksley, consulting physician to the 12th Army and a Harley Street specialist in peacetime. He said: 'Without hesitation I should say the biggest single factor in saving lives (from scrub typhus) has been the work of the nurses. I was in the Middle East before coming to Burma. We had another type of typhus there—perhaps a more violent type—but from my experience of both theatres I consider what has been done in Burma by nurses and medical staffs, under incredible conditions, is nothing short of a miracle.' The Brigadier's remarks applied to the medical services throughout the later part of the Burma war.

The total sickness casualties during 1944, the peak year of fighting in the whole campaign, were half a million hospital admissions and another half-million treated but not bedded. The majority of the half-million admissions were sick with malaria. How the Japanese fared as far as sickness goes cannot be estimated with any accuracy. But since their medical services were not nearly so efficient as the Allied, it may be presumed their sickness rate was higher.

Compared with the sickness rates, battle casualties during 1944 were small. The 14th Army, including 15th Corps, lost 28,748 men, of whom 9,000 were killed or missing. Northern Combat Area Command had 19,832 casualties, of which 5,500 were killed or missing.

When broken down into casualties per British Empire division the figures were: 2nd British Division, 2,200; 5th Indian, 4,100; 7th, 2,800; 17th, 4,200; 20th, 3,200; 23rd, 2,500; 25th, 1,250; 26th, 2,400; 36th British, 1,000; 11th East African, 1,000; 81st and 82nd West African Divisions, 900; 50th Parachute Brigade (used in ground role at Ukhrul), 500; Chindits, 3,500.

For the same period the Japanese were estimated to have lost 72,338 killed, 98,261 wounded, and 1,211 taken prisoner of war. There is no reason for presuming the claims for killed to be incorrect. It is interesting to note that the total casualties for the year almost equal the number of Japanese said to be in Burma at the beginning of 1944 (the official figure was 185,000). At the end of 1944 it was estimated that there were still 175,000 Japanese left in the country.

In the air, Allied Air Forces (the R.A.F. and U.S.A.A.F. were almost equal in strength) lost 375 aircraft destroyed and 349 damaged. The Japanese lost 472 destroyed, 124 probably destroyed, and 401 damaged.

At sea the Allies lost forty-nine merchant ships, of a total tonnage of 308,000, one submarine, and one warship. The Japanese lost 177 merchant ships, totalling 90,000 tons, with another 33 (36,000 tons) probably sunk or damaged. They also lost a cruiser, an aircraft carrier, four submarines, and a mass of smaller craft. Two German U-Kreuzers, one U-boat, and two merchantmen (17,673 tons) were also sunk in Eastern waters.

15

THE THIRD ARAKAN CAMPAIGN

Offensive Operations in the Arakan—West Africans in Kaladan Valley—Landings Along Coast

BY the dawn of the New Year the 14th Army had begun to fan out across central Burma. The capture of Mandalay, though important, was merely a prelude to a general advance on Rangoon, 450 miles to the south. Because of the monsoon, which began in mid-May, speed was essential. If the 14th Army failed to reach Rangoon by the time the monsoon broke it would become bogged down in a 'no-man's land' and its supply would be most difficult. The speed at which the army could advance on Rangoon was conditioned by the stubbornness of the Japanese and the efficient maintenance of supply services.

While the army was in the area of Shwebo and Mandalay it could be supplied by air from Imphal. Once it had moved on south and had reached Meiktila or the Yenangyaung oilfields, Imphal would cease to be effective. It had already been found that 250 miles was the maximum range over which air supply was economic. Outside that distance it became too expensive when balancing time and petrol against the load.

Though there was a road from Imphal into central Burma and the Gangaw Valley, it could not carry anything like the tonnage required. Every mile added to the advance of the 14th Army reduced the load of the lorries and increased their consumption of petrol disproportionately—a situation similar to but on a much larger scale than in 1943 when once a week a team of mules left Milestone 109, on the Tiddim road, bound for the forward troops in the Bamboo Stockades.

Two-thirds of the mules' load was fodder for the animals and food for the muleteers.

The pre-requisite to the advance of the 14th Army towards Rangoon was the establishment of an alternative air supply base within the 250-mile orbit. The answer was Chittagong. It was 250 air miles from Meiktila and less from Gangaw and the oil-fields. As the 14th Army got nearer Rangoon so the air journey to and from Chittagong and Akyab, when captured, would decrease. The clearing of the Arakan therefore became a condition effecting the 14th Army's advance.

The Japanese were still in fair strength in the Arakan and maintained forward airstrips from which fighters and light bombers could harass Chittagong and its satellite airfields. While they remained in possession of Akyab, with its airfields, and maintained garrisons in the Kaladan and Kalapanzin Valleys, the Japanese always threatened Chittagong and Bengal's back door. They pinned down at least three Allied divisions in the area.

Preliminary operations, leading up to a general offensive in the Arakan, were begun in August 1944. Then the nearest Japanese to Chittagong were at Mowdok, in the Sangu Valley, and just outside the Indo-Burma border. Mowdok lay at the northern entrance to the Kaladan Valley, from which it was possible for the Japanese to raid the 15th Corps line of communications. The clearing of the Kaladan was the monsoon task of the 81st West African Division under Maj.-Gen. F. J. Loftus Tottenham.

From Taung Bazaar in the Kalapanzin Valley the division moved back to its firm base, Chiringa, whence it had begun its first expedition. It then began an advance towards the Kaladan Valley, which lies six valleys inland from the coastline, a distance of sixty miles as the crow flies but more than a hundred on foot when the path lay, with few tracks and passes, over successive ranges and across rivers.

The weather was at its worst and though the division was to be supplied by air it had to work out its field establishment on a basis of 'headloads'—how much one man could carry on his head. The only artillery it could take for the first part of the mission consisted of mortars. Mobility was the keyword and that meant travelling light.

The division consisted of two brigades, the 5th and 6th, since the 3rd had formed part of the Chindits.

The roads and tracks the Africans had previously made along this route were overgrown or washed away and engineers had to repeat their work. By the beginning of October, 5th Brigade had built up a concentration at Singpa, only eight miles from Mowdok, while other units had patrolled into the Kaladan Valley. By the end of October, despite the resistance at Mowdok, the Africans had established a line across the Sangu, Pi Chaung, and Kaladan Valleys and were advancing on Paletwa on the Kaladan river. The Japanese were retreating.

During a battle for Auklo, African casualties had to be carried back by the Divisional Auxiliary Group to the nearest airstrip, since the country round Satwei–Auklo did not permit a light strip to be built. The Africans found a hole on the Japanese Satwei–Paletwa line, moved through it early in December, and took Kyringi and Tinma, thus blocking the last route connecting the Kaladan and Kalapanzin Valleys whereby the Japanese might threaten the remainder of the 15th Corps.

The 81st Division had therefore completed the first part of these preliminary operations. By December they were in geographical line with the remainder of 15th Corps and ready to take part in the first stage of the offensive.

There was plenty of evidence, not only in the Arakan but all over Burma, that the Japanese were prepared for a widespread, though sometimes slow, withdrawal. In the north they were retreating down the railway corridor and, except for a determined stand at Bhamo, the whole of N.C.A.C. was loosely held. On the central front they were retreating in face of the 14th Army. The ease with which the West Africans had cleared the Kaladan provided evidence of the same in the south.

The Japanese had two advantages for their retreat. They were withdrawing along interior lines. The routes taken were the same as those along which the Allies had to advance. Those routes being few, far between, and generally narrow, it did not require much force to block them. The Japanese adopted the method of solidifying across the path of the advance long enough to give their main forces time to escape.

Their rearguards had the habit of fighting most sternly and holding up the Allies for just as long as they pleased, and then disappearing in the night. This uncanny knack of slipping away became more and more evident as the retreat continued.

At this time (December 1944), dispositions of the rest of the 15th Corps were: Maj.-Gen. G. Wood's 25th Indian Division around Maungdaw, which it had been building up as a firm base throughout the monsoon; Maj.-Gen. G. McI. S. Bruce's 82nd West African Division between Maungdaw and Buthidaung, with one brigade at Taung Bazaar; and Maj.-Gen. C. E. N. Lomax's 26th Indian Division and the 3rd Commando Brigade in reserve. Christison thus had four divisions, a commando brigade, and air support from the Earl of Bandon's 224 Group.

In opposition to this the Japanese had the 28th Army consisting of the 54th and 55th Divisions. The forward troops were mainly the 55th Division. Facing the 81st West Africans in the Kaladan were a battalion of the 111th Regiment of 55th Division, the 55th Divisional cavalry, and the 54th Field Artillery. On Akyab Island it was thought there was a Japanese regiment. The balance of the 55th

Division stretched forward as far as Buthidaung. Behind and down the Arakan coast was the 54th Japanese Division.

The immediate 15th Corps plan was for the 25th Division to clear the Mayu range to Foul Point, while the 82nd West Africans operating on the flank of the 25th Division captured Buthidaung. The 82nd Africans were then to link up with the 81st West Africans, coming down the Kaladan Valley, at Myohaung.

The 82nd West African Division (1st, 2nd, 4th Brigades), of which two brigades had fought in Abyssinia, was a new division in the theatre. It had arrived in India in the summer of 1944 and by October a brigade had taken over from the 26th Indian at Taung Bazaar and in the area of the Goppe Pass in the Kalapanzin Valley. The rest of the division had moved into the 25th Division's area at Maungdaw.

On 14 December, the 2nd West African Brigade and the 74th Brigade of the 25th Indian Division advanced through the Tunnels to Buthidaung while the 4th West African Brigade moved down the Kalapanzin Valley. Buthidaung fell the same day. The West Africans then crossed the Kalapanzin river while the 25th Division cleaned up the Mayu peninsula, reaching Foul Point by Christmas Day.

The clearing of the Mayu peninsula and most of the Kaladan Valley lifted any threat to the 15th Corps lines of communication, Chittagong and its airfields. Succeeding operations in the Arakan were designed with further objects. More airfields for the fighter and bomber aircraft were required to keep pace with the 14th Army's drive south. The Japanese army in the Arakan had to be contained, and, if possible, annihilated so that it could not reinforce those in central Burma. Maintaining four Allied divisions in the Arakan was considered expensive. One of the divisions had already been earmarked for the seaborne assault on Rangoon and others were required for the invasion of Malaya later in the year. The Arakan had to be cleared completely before any could be released.

The first step was the capture of Akyab. As the island was supposed to be held by a regiment of Japanese it was considered necessary to mount an amphibious force consisting of the 3rd Commando Brigade and the 25th Indian Division.

Christison's naval force was under the command of Rear-Admiral B. C. S. Martin. Known as 'Force W', it consisted of an odd assortment of crafts from cruisers to L.C.M.s, coastal skiffs, and river boats. The Akyab expedition was mounted in the Mayu estuary and on 3 January the Commandos landed and bicycled across the island. Not a Japanese remained to welcome them. The 25th Division carried out its part of the landing as a training exercise, watched through telescopes and binoculars by senior commanders sitting in deck chairs at Foul Point.

Good practice though the 25th Division's Akyab landing may have been, it had the more serious effect of delaying all the succeeding landings by several days. It was not known that two of the Japanese battalions had joined forces with those on the mainland some time previously, while the third battalion had evacuated the island on the night of 31 December–1 January, just over two days before the Akyab landings were due to take place.

Six more landings were made in the Arakan. Most of them were designed to cut the single coast road which was the main Japanese line of communication. Some of the landings were violently opposed, some certainly caught the Japanese by surprise. The claim that only one battalion escaped to reach central Burma was an exaggeration. By no means all the Japanese were killed, wounded, or captured. Many were driven into the Arakan Yomas (a range of hills), from which they emerged some months later when the last Burma battle was fought on the fringe of the Pegu Yomas. Had the landings at Myebon, Kangaw, and the several

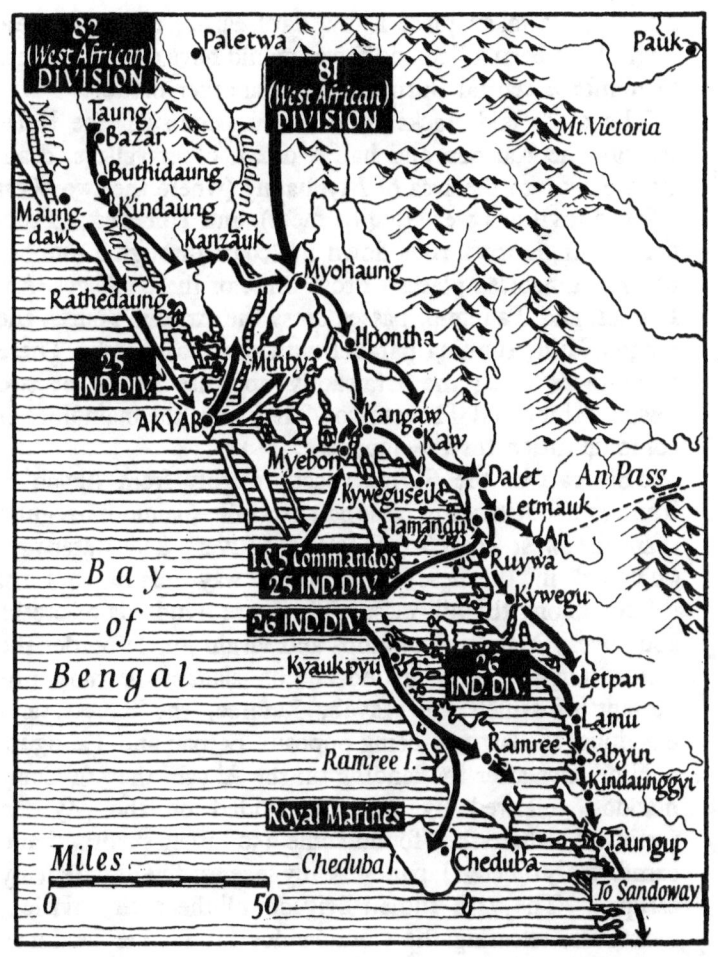

THE LAST ARAKAN CAMPAIGN

other places taken place a few days earlier more Japanese might have been killed and fewer would have escaped, either to reinforce central Burma or fight another battle.

The roads and tracks from Mayu peninsula, the Kalapanzin, the Kaladan and half a dozen other valleys, drain eventually into the area of Myohaung (where the two West African divisions were due to meet), and Hpontha. From there a single track runs down the coast through a number of small inhabited places. From three of these villages, An, Letpan, and Taungup, passes cross the Arakan Yomas, the range of hills running parallel with the coast track. These pass tracks reach the Irrawaddy opposite Prome at two towns, Minbu and Thayetmyo. They were the main lines of communication for the Japanese.

This part of the Burma coast, roughly from Akyab to Taungup, a distance of less than 150 miles, is more irregular than the west coast of Scotland. Rivers and waterways ('chaung' in Burmese) wind their way inland to form valleys among the hill mass. There are hundreds of creeks and coves. Mangrove swamps and virgin jungle border the water. Off the coast are dozens of islands, the most important of which are Akyab, Ramree, the largest, and Cheduba, the last two being opposite Letpan and Taungup.

Nine days after the landing on the Akyab, the 5th Commandos, followed by the 1st, landed on the Myebon peninsula, where they found some 350 rather surprised and comfortably billeted Japanese. Only seventy-five of the enemy escaped. The 74th Indian Brigade, of the 25th Division, took over, releasing the Commandos for further landings.

The Kangaw landing which followed almost immediately was the toughest of all. No longer were the Japanese unready, and Kangaw itself, a little way inland and up river from Myebon, was on their first direct escape route. It had to be, and was, defended desperately.

According to Lieut.-Col. G. Brinley Eyre, Staff Officer

Grade One of the S.E.A.C. Combined Operations branch, whose experience of landings ranged from Europe to the South-West Pacific, where he did three as a private soldier, the Kangaw landing was the most difficult he had ever experienced apart from Dieppe.

The 1st Commandos, men from eighty-four different regiments, many of whom had made similar landings in Norway, France, and North Africa, were crash-landed on to the muddy swampy mangrove banks of Kangaw at midday. They had to wade through mud up to their waists under shellfire, which continued for eight days. Assisted by an air strike, they reached a small hill.

The leading troops got into some Japanese diggings and throughout the first night there was fierce hand-to-hand fighting, the Japanese employing their usual jitter tactics. When morning came one wounded Commando found a Japanese officer lying dead on the edge of his hole; three more Japanese were lying only a few yards away.

The bridgehead the Commandos had won was only seventy-five yards wide. Reinforcements, casualties, and supplies all had to pass through this narrow gap. As the Japanese shelling increased so the R.A.F. increased their strikes, reaching a pitch of 130 sorties a day. When the bridgehead had enlarged to 300 by 900 yards the Japanese poured 800 shells into it in one day, using their biggest gun, the 150 mm.

One private soldier was wounded in the wrist when attacked by five Japanese. He seized the nearest one, held him with his injured arm, and pummelled him with his good one while a comrade shot the others. A sergeant-major was hit by a bullet from a couple of yards' range. The bullet deflected off his forehead down his nose. He was only slightly wounded.

In the first five days one medical dressing station dealt with nearly 700 surgical cases, under continuous fire and receiving four direct hits. Indian bearers evacuated the wounded to the beach. Fourteen of one party of sixteen bearers were killed or wounded.

After a week a brigade of the 25th Division (Punjabis, Baluch, and Hyderabads) landed and passed through the bridgehead. Tanks of the 19th Lancers assisted the Commandos. There was a lull for a few days before the Japanese renewed their violent attacks. On 31 January, twenty-four suicidal Japanese armed with dynamite poles charged the tanks. One Japanese threw himself under a Sherman, committing suicide in blowing it up. On the same night the 1st Commandos were relieved by the 5th.

The Japanese 55th Division suffered some 2,000 casualties in the Myebon–Kangaw area battles. In one fight they had lost 370 killed to the Commandos. The Indians claimed 750 others. Since Akyab, over 1,300 Japanese bodies had been picked up and 18 anti-tank and 7.75-mm. guns captured.

While the Kangaw fighting was going on, the two West African divisions merged then separated again at Myohaung. The 81st Division had cleared the Thandada area by New Year's Day after enemy guns had been pattern-bombed by Mitchells and Thunderbolts. In recent fighting the Africans had suffered nearly 300 casualties, which were flown out from a rapidly constructed Dakota strip. Other units of the division had made a successful detour march to Kyauktaw, at the junction of the Pi Chaung and Kaladan rivers.

The enemy, whose strength was then assessed at over three battalions, failed to appreciate that the Africans would not move south through the open paddy fields of the valley but through the hills where their inferiority in artillery would be less important and their troops less visible.

The 82nd Division, commanded during these operations by Maj.-Gen. Stockwell, formerly of 29th Brigade of the 36th Division, had been assisted across the Kalapanzin river by 400 small boats brought by lorry over the Mayu range and through the Tunnels. Parts of the division crossed the hills into the Kaladan and others the Lemro river to the east of Myohaung. On the way the division was given an air drop of mail. The mail-bag contained nothing but copies of the Army pamphlet, *Movement by Road and Rail*, an ironic comment on a part of the country containing no railways or roads but only rivers, a few tracks, mountains, and jungle.

By a series of enveloping moves through the hills, necessitating small battles for Myohaung's outpost positions, the three brigades of 81st Division and two of the 82nd gradually converged on the village. Resistance came, in most places, from small isolated groups of Japanese. On 25 January the 4th Brigade of the 82nd Division passed into the town. Once more the bulk of the Japanese, sensing the significance of the West Africans' moves had slipped away. This was the end of the story of the 81st West African Division. Their tour in South-East Asia was finished and they moved back to Chiringa to prepare for home.

The 82nd Division carried on. The 1st Brigade advanced towards Dalet, at the northern entrance of the road leading to the An Pass. Its capture would not block the pass but would preclude any possibility of a Japanese move against the flank of the other units of 15th Corps leap-frogging down the coast. The 4th Brigade moved as rapidly as possible to Kyweguseik to block the escape path of the Japanese in Kangaw. They were held, however, at Kyaukpandu long enough to give the Japanese a chance to escape. The small Japanese garrison at Kyaukpandu made eight counter-attacks in one night. The 2nd Brigade and 22nd Anti-tank Regiment came under command of the 25th Division, at that time doing the main fighting at Kangaw.

Simultaneous with these attempts to cut off the Japanese along the Arakan coast, a landing was made on Ramree Island, opposite Taungup, by the 26th Indian Division in conjunction with Advanced Naval Force 'W' under Captain Eric Bush, R.N. Naval forces included the battleship *Queen Elizabeth*, the cruiser *Phœbe*, the destroyers *Napier*, *Pathfinder*, and *Rapid*, the R.I.N. sloops *Kistna* and *Flamingo*, and the fleet carrier *Ameir*.

This was General Lomax's 26th Division's biggest operation. An original member of the 15th Corps in the critical days of 1942, when it and the 14th Division held Bengal and the Arakan, the division had played an unspectacular role un succeeding Arakan engagements. Composed of the 4th, 36th, and 71st Brigades, it included two British battalions, the Lincolns and Green Howards.

Ramree is a large, hilly, swampy, jungle-covered, and crocodile-infested island. It was occupied by about a thousand Japanese. Though penned in the swamps and facing the alternatives of death in battle or death by drowning, only twenty Japanese surrendered. The rest went on fighting for a month, and Ramree was not officially cleared until 22 February.

The fighting, however, did not hold up the development of Ramree's airfields, as advanced bases for the future landings on Rangoon. As a subsidiary to the Ramree expedition, marines landed on and occupied its neighbouring island, Cheduba.

The extended fighting in the Kangaw area and the holding up of the Africans on the road to Kyweguseik convinced Christison that too many Japanese were escaping from the Arakan. The coast road to Letpan and Taungup was still open and free to the Japanese. Further landings along the coast were necessary.

In mid-February, units of the 25th Division landed at Ru-y-wa, followed up by the 2nd Brigade Group of the 82nd West African Division, whose headquarters by then was established in the old, flat-bottomed river steamer, the *Jumna*.

Unsatisfactory though Ru-y-wa was as a landing-place, it provided the nearest disembarking point for An. Fortunately the landings achieved surprise and were unopposed, since the moorings for the craft were mangrove trees among the swamps and shallow coves.

The water line of communication for Captain Duncan Hill's Naval Force 64 was fifty miles long through uncharted areas. He succeeded in putting ashore nearly 20,000 men, 15,000 tons of stores, over 500 mules, and 400 vehicles, a remarkable feat of naval improvisation. The beach-head, such as it was, resembled a chaotic regatta.

The 25th Division crossed from Ru-y-wa to Tamandu, an old ferry steamer station, where the Japanese hurled mines attached to grenades into the Gurkhas' positions and, for a day and a night, offered stiff resistance. That, for a time, was the conclusion of the 25th Indian Division's operations. They had been fighting for a year without rest.

The last of the bigger landings took place at Letpan, a few miles north of Taungup. It was a final attempt at blocking the third and most southern of the Japanese escape routes to the Irrawaddy Valley. It was made by 4th Indian Brigade of the 26th Division on 13 March. Related to the landings were the moves of the 82nd West Africans and the 22nd East African Brigade, who came under the West Africans, after passing through the Ru-y-wa bridgehead.

Not until the end of March did the East or West Africans approach Taungup, which remained uncaptured until the end of April. Then some units of the Africans advanced over the Taungup Pass and others south down the coast. For the preceding weeks all had been held up, sometimes even boxed in, for a short time in the area of Dalet, An, Letmauk, and Tamandu. The Japanese made their final stands in the Arakan at the entrance to the Taungup Pass and around the junction of the Dalet–An and Tamandu–An roads, using artillery and tanks.

At that time the troops opposing 15th Corps were the 54th Japanese Division, a fairly fresh outfit with little previous fighting in this theatre. They proved as good as most other Japanese divisions. They achieved their object in delaying 15th Corps at salient points, despite the latter's attempts to get behind them, and permitted their 55th Division to escape across the Arakan Yomas and, in some instances, into the Irrawaddy Valley. They were assisted by the geography of the terrain, which suited defence. Even with 150 men they often had little difficulty in hindering a divisional advance.

Sometimes, as the West Africans found, the Japanese turned a defensive rearguard action into an enveloping or infiltrating attack. Though the 28th Japanese Army was disintegrating against a numerically superior force, it postponed its execution for some months. Moreover, it kept a division and a half occupied in the area up to, and after, the occupation of Rangoon.

The Arakan campaign of 1945, which began at Akyab and ended, except for the mounting of the Rangoon expedition, at Taungup, succeeded in providing the necessary forward airfields for the attack on lower Burma and the supply and support of the 14th Army. It also permitted the gradual release of 15th Corps divisions, starting with the 81st West African, then the 25th, and finally the 26th Indian Division and the Commandos.

It did not, as hoped, contain and annihilate the Japanese 28th Army, who were not long in doubt as to the reasons for the various moves (they must have known of their retreat in central Burma too). Had not time been wasted at Akyab or had fewer landings been made—a major one at, say, Letpan—fewer Japanese might have escaped. As it was, the whole affair resembled a policeman chasing a burglar up a ladder with the burglar's hob-nailed boot kicking him hard on the head every now and again. The triumph was really the navy's which, with little help, managed to land all those forces at so many different places, a feat calling for imagination as well as ingenuity.

16

THE CLEARANCE OF NORTH BURMA

Opening of Ledo Road—Completion of Operations in N. Burma

ON 31 January 1945, a ceremony was held on the Burma-China border at Wanting. On one side was a token convoy which had left Ledo, in north Assam, eleven days previously, on the other was the Chinese Sixth Route Army. The Ledo road to China was officially open and the convoy trundled over the Tali mountains to Kunming and eventually to Chungking, a journey of just under 2,000 miles. It was the first of many great convoys.

Since the road came within his command, Mountbatten signalled to the Combined Chiefs of Staff, the Prime Minister, and the President of the United States: 'The first part of the orders I received at Quebec has been carried out. The land route to China is open.'

Begun two years previously, the Ledo road had followed the course of battle through the Huwkawng and Mogaung Valleys and on to Myitkyina, which had fallen to Stilwell's Chinese and Americans in mid-1944. As the Japanese 18th Division had withdrawn, the road had been carried on to Bhamo. Parallel with it the Americans built a pipe-line which had, as its source, Calcutta, 1,200 miles away.

The Japanese had solidified at Bhamo just as they had at Myitkyina. Their 114th Regiment of 18th Division and elements of the 56th Division, which was responsible for the defence of north-east Burma, had held off attacks from three Chinese divisions for some weeks until Colonel Rothwell Brown's Chinese-manned tanks had stormed the town. The Japanese had fled as the tanks began their crushing entry.

THE CLEARANCE OF NORTH BURMA

General Sultan had been disturbed by the slowness of the Chinese round Bhamo and also by the inaccuracy of their intelligence. He ordered an inquiry to be made, while a correspondent of the American forces magazine *Yank*, Dave Richardson, conducted an inquiry of his own.

One of Stilwell's sons, also named Joe, was the Sultan's Chief Intelligence Officer. He told Sultan that, when summed up, the Chinese reports indicated that the division on the west of Bhamo was five miles to the east, the division on the north five miles to the south, and that the town was occupied by minus 500 Japanese. Richardson walked round Bhamo, often exposing himself to fire, so that he could mark up Japanese positions on a map. He found they had remained static for several weeks.

Once Bhamo was clear, the road which joined the old British road to Namkam took little rebuilding. The Japanese had used it and it only required widening and building up in places. The pipe-line and telephone lines connecting India, Burma, and China followed.

For the American engineers, two years' labour without leave or rest was finished, and the verse of Sergt. Smith Dawlish, of the American Engineers, is a moving and colourful commentary on life as they saw it and the spirit in which they worked.

> Is the Gateway to India at Bombay
> Really as beautiful as they say?
>> Don't rightly know, Ma'am. Did my part
>> Breaking point in the jungle's heart;
>> Blasted the boulders, felled the trees
>> With red muck oozin' around our knees,
>> Carved the guts out of Patkai's side,
>> Dozed our trace, made it clean and wide,
>> Metalled and graded, dug and filled:
>> We had the Ledo road to build.

Well surely you saw a burning ghat
Fakirs, rope-tricks and all that?
    Reckon I didn't. But way up ahead
    I tended the wounded, buried the dead.
    For I was a Medic, and little we knew
    But the smell of sickness all day through,
    Mosquitoes, leeches, and thick dark mud
    Where the Chinese spilled their blood·
    After the enemy guns were stilled:
    We had the Ledo road to build.

Of course you found the Taj Mahal
The loveliest building of them all?
    Can't really say, lady. I was stuck
    Far beyond Shing with a QM truck.
    Monsoon was ruggéd there, hot and wet,
    Nothing to do but work and sweat.
    And dry was the dust upon my mouth
    As steadily big 'cats' roared on south,
    Over the ground where the Japs lay killed:
    We had the Ledo road to build.

You've been gone two years this spring,
Didn't you see a single thing?
    Never saw much but the moonshine on
    A Burmese temple around Maingkwan,
    And silver transports high in the sky,
    Thursday river and the swift Tanai,
    And Huwkawng Valley coming all green,
    Those are the only sights I've seen,
    Did our job, though, like God willed:
    We had the Ledo road to build.

Since the dissolution of Merrill's Marauders, a new American combat force had arrived and was taking part in the Northern Combat Area Command operations. Known as 'Mars Task Force', it consisted of the 475th American

Infantry Regiment, the 124th dismounted Cavalry Regiment, and a Chinese Regiment commanded by Brig.-Gen. John P. Willey.

As the British 36th Division moved down the railway corridor, Mars Task Force took the more difficult route to the east of the Irrawaddy. The two groups shook hands across the Irrawaddy at Katha and parted again.

Mars Force steered south-east towards Lashio and, in the Hosi Valley, Lieut. Jack Knight of the 124th Cavalry earned undying fame when he was killed leading his troop against a Japanese-held hill. The hill was named 'Knight's Hill'. Without vehicles and transporting their supplies by pack mules, some of the Task Force marched over 300 miles in one month.

Scattered throughout north Burma were little nests of American Kachin Rangers, the counterpart of the British Kachin Levies, who had so long operated from Fort Hertz and Sumprabum. The Rangers had been the forerunners of the American-led push into north Burma. Since 1942, when the first few bands had begun operations in the Huwkawng Valley, the Rangers, the British Levies, Wingate's two expeditions, and then Stilwell's Chinese, had made north Burma the most difficult and dangerous part of the country for the Japanese to hold. During their two and a half years occupation they had employed two divisions, two independent brigades, and parts of third division.

The Rangers were among the highest fire-powered group of guerrillas in the East. They were equipped with Enfield and Springfield rifles, Bren guns, tommy-guns, bazookas, carbines, and mortars on a luxurious establishment. They moved from place to place on foot and by plane or were dropped by parachute. Some who parachuted had never previously been in an aircraft.

By the end of 1944 there were nearly 7,000 Kachin Rangers, officered by over 400 Americans. The officers averaged six months in the jungle, though some did a two-year tour before taking leave. In thirty months the Rangers claimed to have killed 3,000 Japanese, taken 35 prisoners, and saved the lives of over 200 Allied airmen.

As north Burma was cleared the Rangers began to disband, returning to their villages. The Americans desired to give them some reward—they had been paid a rupee a day—and signalled their headquarters in Kandy, Ceylon, for suggestions. A reply was received and the garbled transcription read something like 'Medal CMA'. The Americans concluded they should give a medal and call it 'Citation for Military Assistance'. They had one cut in Calcutta. Actually the signal had read: 'Money cma weapons cma other gifts.'

The Americans permitted many of the Kachins to retain their weapons. Though the great majority of Kachins are a loyal and orderly people, there were those, trained and experienced in war, whose sense of responsibility and social character was weak. They created a problem for the British administration. To some it appeared that the Americans were taking an unnecessarily irresponsible view towards the peaceful administration of Burma.

North Burma was the first testing-ground for the British Civil Affairs Administration which travelled with the army. As will be seen later, this body was not always as efficient as intended.

For north Burma, with its headquarters at Myitkyina, Civil Affairs possessed one truck and four jeeps, an establishment of vehicles hardly sufficient to cover an area the size of Wales. Rice, the principal requirement of the local people, was not forthcoming in anything like a sufficient quantity. Excuses were made for every failure, for every shortage. Had the army made such excuses it would still have been dawdling on the edge of the Chindwin river, frightened of falling in and getting its feet wet.

THE CLEARANCE OF NORTH BURMA

Many of the Civil Affairs field workers were men who had been in the country before the war in the British-run trading concerns. They were not, one felt, always in sympathy with the native people, but more often interested in their own personal business. Nor were the Americans, in this their area, sympathetic to the British. They chose their own British chief Civil Affairs officer and he found himself serving two masters, one at hand and the other chairborne in far-away Simla.

With the opening of the Ledo road Sultan's prime task was completed; his secondary task of clearing north Burma almost complete. His command, separated into column groups, turned southwards and began to comb north Burma, the Shan States, and the area of the old Burma road, closing with the capture of Lashio.

As these operations began, a threatening Japanese advance was taking place in western China. For a short time the Japanese occupied Kweiyang. It appeared as if they would advance on Kunming and cut the road from Kunming to Chungking. Had this happened, the Ledo road would have become useless and, worse, the series of American air bases in the Kunming area would have been untenable. The 14th U.S.A.A.F. readied themselves to move. Kunming was also the main American military base in China where there were training-grounds and facilities for the Chinese under American control. 'Y' Force was trained there.

Wedermeyer, commander of the China theatre, asked Mountbatten to release two Chinese divisions from north Burma and three squadrons of transport aircraft. Mountbatten did so at the possible expense, it was thought, of his chances of reaching Rangoon before the monsoon, for the number of troops relying on air supply was daily increasing. As more and more divisions were being poured into central Burma so the required daily tonnage increased from 2,000 to nearer 3,000.

The Kweiyang threat dissolved and the loss of the transport aircraft was partly compensated by the opening of the sea route along the Arakan coast. At the same time General Browning in London secured promises of more transport planes, which were rapidly forthcoming. On none of the three fronts in Burma was the time-table put behind schedule.

One Chinese column advanced down the old Burma road towards Lashio, meeting the rearguard of the 56th Japanese Division, which included light cavalry units. Other Chinese columns east of the Irrawaddy moved through the hill country of the Shan States to emerge eventually on the old Burma road below Lashio—between Lashio and Mandalay. With them went Mars Task Force. The town was isolated.

The 36th British Division temporarily split into two brigade groups. The 29th took a course west of the Irrawaddy. It crossed the great river at Tigyiang, some fifty miles to the south of Indaw railway junction. The 72nd Brigade, under the former English Rugby international, Brigadier A. R. Aslett, crossed the Irrawaddy at Katha—the Royal Sussex were first across—and moved through the flat teak forest country into the Shan Hills in the loop of the Shweli river. Opposition was for a time light, for the Japanese were retreating fast and leaving behind only small and not always too determined rearguards.

After crossing the Irrawaddy, 29th Brigade met elements of the 60th Regiment of 15th Japanese Division, stragglers from the Manipur expedition, and the 72nd Brigade were opposed to the rearguards of part of the 18th Division which had moved southwards through the hills in face of the Chinese advance.

It is not surprising that the two prongs of the 36th Division made a rapid advance. It was in fact so fast that despite several days' rain which immobolized the whole division for nearly a week—even amphibious vehicles became bogged down—the division made a rate of five miles a day during January 1945.

The leading infantry outstripped the signallers, who already had laid hundreds of miles of line, and the only communication the division had with the outer world was by wireless. Divisional signals were encoding and decoding at the rate of 30,000 to 40,000 words a day. Sometimes, when Japanese were reported in a village, the air strike called for had to be cancelled while in the air. By the time it arrived, a couple of hours at the longest, the division's own infantry would be in possession and the Japanese some miles farther on.

The 26th Indian Brigade joined the division and had its baptism of fire near the village of Mabein, where a company accounted for thirty Japanese after their own British company commander had been killed. The brigadier, noticing that most British troops in the division were wearing gay-coloured silk scarves cut out from the supply dropped parachutes, issued the following order:

'In order to preserve for as long as possible the outward signs of military force, I direct that coloured neckwear shall be worn only under the following conditions:

'(a) Only men who have actually killed or captured a Japanese may wear one.

'(b) Platoon commanders, sergeants, and section commanders on the same level as men. Company commanders may wear one when their companies have bagged fifty Japanese. No rules for battalion commanders and their seconds-in-command. The brigade commander and his staff may wear one only when the brigade has accounted for 250,000 Japanese or on Armistice Day, whichever is the latter.'

As a rider the brigadier ordained 'only picked-up birds to count'.

The main Japanese stand came at Myitson on the

fast-flowing Shweli river. The Indians, first to cross, were caught in a cross fire. Some were sunk in midstream, some forced to turn back, while a few managed to reach the far bank, where they were contained in a very small bridgehead. They lost several hundred men. Days of bitter fighting followed before finally the 72nd Brigade, crossing farther up-river, managed to turn the Japanese flank. The Japanese lost 500 in the battle for the Myitson crossing, but it was their last effort at stopping the division's drive towards the Burma road. Mongmit and Mogok, centre of the ruby mine district, lay ahead.

Meanwhile the 29th Brigade, having crossed the Irrawaddy at Tigyiang and moved south down the east bank, had been held by elements of the 15th Japanese Division at Twinnge, in a bend of the Irrawaddy. Between the 29th Brigade and the rest of the division there was no land communications. A shuttle service of light aircraft was the only link, though the two groups were only fifty miles apart.

The Japanese opposition of Twinggye melted and in March the 29th Brigade rejoined the division at Mogok where, for the first time since August 1944, they found a metalled road.

Emerging from the Shan Hills on to the Burma road south of Lashio, the division separated from Northern Combat Area Command and joined the 14th Army. After a brief pause, it entered the fighting around Meiktila and in the Federated Shan States around Kalaw.

From the time it had crossed the Irrawaddy at Katha all the way down to Meiktila, the division met elements of the 18th Japanese Division. In this respect the 18th Division was as remarkable as the 33rd Japanese for its persistence and fighting quality. It was one of the great fighting divisions of Burma.

In space and time, the 18th travelled as far as the 36th British Division without any of the luxuries of air supply, casualty evacuation, good food, and air support. And when it had decided to make a rearguard stand such as at Myitson, it did so with typical Japanese tactical cleverness and bravery.

The two purposes for which the 36th Division had joined Stilwell's and then Sultan's N.C.A.C. were successful. By his personality and the quality of his troops, Festing had restored American confidence in the British.

In the military field, as distinct from Exercise Propaganda, the advance of the division was as long in space and time as any made by an Allied division during the Burma campaign. It is impossible to compute the miles marched by the individual infantryman, but since reaching north Burma in August 1944 most must have covered at least a thousand miles on foot in ten months through swamp and jungle, hills and plain, and over two large rivers, the Irrawaddy and the Shweli. They had, moreover, suffered extremes of climate from burning heat and damp mugginess to the cold of the Shan Hills.

The division had fought against parts of two Japanese divisions and two independent motor brigades. Their rate of advance, varying from two to five miles a day, had been conditioned by the weather, the enemy, and the country. Yet a total average of two miles a day for nearly a year must be considered good in any theatre of war. In 1944 alone they killed 1,800 Japanese and themselves suffered 1,000 casualties.

On its way down the railway corridor the division had rebuilt parts of the 250 miles of railway and run, as an alternative supply line, a service of jeep trains, using the wheels and axles off derelict coaches on jeeps or showing even greater ingenuity by putting lorry engines in old guards' vans. One of these improvised engines was reputed to travel at 50 m.p.h. if a driver with the necessary daring could be found. It was called the Windsor Castle.

With the division travelled an American airfield construction unit which, assisted by the divisional sappers, made some fifty dropping zones, almost the same number of light plane strips, and half a dozen major airfields capable of landing Dakotas or C47s. Once the division had seven different dropping zones operating at the same time. Another time, eighty-one planes landed on an airfield during the first twenty-four hours after its completion. The air supply planes made 1,250 sorties a month in all weathers.

When work on an airstrip at Twinggye was held up for a spare part for a bulldozer, a wireless message was sent back to Myitkyina, 400 miles away. The spare part arrived in the matter of a few hours. The ordnance services required 50,000 separate items covering clothing and transport spares. They alone required fifty sorties a month. All casualties of a more serious nature were flown out in Dakotas or light planes.

This air supply service, as well as the air support and tactical bombing, was provided by the 10th U.S.A.A.F. based, after its capture, at Myitkyina. Its commander, Maj.-Gen. Howard C. Davidson, had a British soldier as his batman.

There could not have been a better ambassador of America to British troops than this air force. In the field there were few of the antagonisms found in such places as Calcutta, where the difference in pay between American and British troops led to much bitterness on the British side. Often the monthly case of beer each American soldier received was shared on some lonely airfield with a few British comrades. Alternatively, the very few luxuries a British soldier ever received were shared with an American. What strains and stresses there were between British and Americans rarely touched the ordinary man in the field. Mostly they appeared and festered in the higher formation headquarters.

The 10th Air Force grew out of a handful of planes which had arrived in India in late 1942 to a large force equipped with Lightnings, Kittyhawks, Thunderbolts, and Mustangs, Mitchell and Liberator bombers, Dakota and C47 transport planes, and the ubiquitous light plane. They had assisted in the early defence and supply of Imphal and had bombed as far south as the Arakan and Rangoon and east into China. At one time they converted some Liberators into air tankers and in 1944 flew two million gallons of petrol over the 'Hump' to China.

North Burma was, however, the 10th's home pitch. They ferried the American negro engineer battalions into the Huwkawng Valley. They flew in the two Chinese divisions from Ramgarh, 1,000 miles away, in two weeks. When Myitkyina airstrip fell, their planes landed while there was still fighting on the perimeter, and within a few days a plane was landing or taking off every eighty seconds. Into Myitkyina they flew over 150 artillery guns and engineer equipment, cut by acetylene torch in India, to fit the planes and welded together again in Burma. They supplied not only Stilwell's and Sultan's Chinese and Americans but the Chindits, 36th Division, and the Kachin groups.

Their fighter group was known as the Burma Banshees. At the height of fighting it was performing a mission every six minutes and giving close support along a forty-yard bomb-line, which meant forty yards in front of the nearest Allied soldiers.

In one aerial fight a Mustang, chased by a Japanese Zero, flew straight at a pagoda, lifting at the very last moment. The Japanese plane hit the pagoda. Possibly some of the most amusing aerial combats were those between the L5s and Japanese Zeros. The light planes were so slow and manoeuvrable that the Japanese fighters could never catch them, and there was not a single instance of an L5 being shot down. There was a 'Sky Ambush' squadron which, like the Pied Piper of Hamelin, once led a force of Japanese planes into a mass of forested hills. One of the American planes returned with part of a tree lodged in its wing; the Japanese, following their leader, crashed.

In picturesque language, Stilwell sent a parting message to Davidson. He said: 'From a fledgling force of a few fighters you have developed into a wallop-packing outfit which severely hampered Japanese communications and supply in Burma. You have supported tactically and logistically the advance of the Allied troops.'

With the capture of Lashio by the Chinese in March—as the Chinese converged from three sides the Japanese withdrew south towards Loilem, one of their few escape routes from Burma—and the parting of 36th Division, the combat role of Sultan's N.C.A.C. was concluded. It assumed the more peaceful task of organizing the passage of the convoys to China, which were soon rolling through at the rate of one every two weeks. All vehicles and their contents remained in China, the convoys' drivers and crews flying back to Ledo or Myitkyina to pick up the next convoy.

During 1944, the year the fighting in north Burma reached its peak, the ground forces of N.C.A.C. lost just over 20,000 men killed, wounded, and missing. The majority were Chinese, of whom 5,000 were killed or missing. The assessment of casualties inflicted on the Japanese was made difficult by the inaccurate claims of the Chinese who, it was proved, had once overstated to the tune of 10,000. A fair estimate was 10,000 Japanese killed.

Despite British and American criticism of the Chinese, their dilatoriness and disinclination to attack, their exaggerated claims of Japanese killed and ground captured, they made a signal contribution to the reconquest of Burma. Hundreds, sometimes thousands of miles from their homes and families, they fought in the worst parts of Burma. Two of their divisions took part in the retreat and were back in Burma at the end. Though once part of China, north Burma was to the Chinese soldier a foreign country ruled by a Western power.

The Chinese were brought into the Burma war by circumstances over which Britain had little control. The Japanese invasion was so swift and relentless that the loss of Burma looked certain unless some part could be saved by the acceptance of Chinese assistance. Britain unwillingly accepted the Generalissimo's offer of Chinese divisions.

From the Burma retreat emerged a great man in Stilwell who, as a Sinophile, played a large part in building up, training, and leading Chinese armies back into Burma. But for Stilwell it is doubtful whether Britain would ever have accepted Chinese troops in India or as part of a force for the reconquest of an Imperial possession. It is doubtful also whether the Generalissimo would have given the help he did, though it was important for him to regain a land link with the Allies.

Stilwell and his Chinese became inextricably woven into the Burma war. In many respects they, and the needs of China, dictated the whole strategy of the campaign, for as time went on and the British made only half-hearted attempts at offence in central and south Burma, Allied policy towards Burma became bound up with Stilwell, the Ledo road, and the Chinese troops. North Burma became the focal point in the Allied attack. Stilwell's Chinese were first back into Burma and first to recapture any notable landmark.

No doubt the Generalissimo had political reasons for permitting the divisions to fight in Burma. There was the opportunity of having Chinese divisions trained and equipped by the Americans and fed and paid by the British. They would later provide an *élite* corps for the Chinese army in China.

A Chinese army under American command in a British theatre of war was, to the Generalissimo, of considerable propaganda value. The Americans were certain to give it wide publicity which might, in part, offset criticism of the conduct of the war in China. The Generalissimo had little to lose, five divisions at the most, and a lot to gain by permitting the Chinese to fight in Burma. He knew it, the Americans knew it, and so did the British. The British, however, were not always too happy about it.

The personality of Stilwell illuminated the whole campaign in north Burma. To Americans it was an American campaign, whether fought by the Chinese under overall British command or not. What then was the American contribution to the reconquest of Burma? During the war Mountbatten refused to permit the publication of the facts in order to avoid unreasoned criticism from the British and Indian troops.

America put two combat teams into Burma. Both were not more than 2,500 strong and neither fought for more than six months or were in action simultaneously. In Assam and Burma, American operational strength, including the negro engineer battalions and the Ledo road supply and maintenance troops, was just over 30,000.

In April 1944, the U.S.A.A.F. operational strength totalled 30,000. A year later it was 60,000, only 10,000 less than the R.A.F. For most of the war the U.S.A.A.F. and R.A.F. were nearly equal in strength.

West of the Brahmaputra, within the orbit of India Command, there were over 130,000 American troops, including airmen, engineers, railway and docks operating companies, airfield construction engineers, and those solely engaged on Lease-Lend to China.

America made three great material contributions to the Burma war: in the air, in the field of engineering (e.g. the building of the Ledo road), and in training and inspiring the Chinese to fight and win back most of north Burma. Without any one of these Burma would not have been recovered when it was and the task would have fallen much more heavily on the shoulders of Britain.

17

FROM THE CHINDWIN TO THE IRRAWADDY

14th Army Advance in Central Burma—Preparation for Capture of Mandalay—Administrative Background—Criticism of Civil Affairs

OPERATIONS in north Burma and the Arakan have been taken forward to their virtual conclusion. After April, fighting in neither sector had much bearing on the knock-out blow delivered on the Japanese Burma armies by the 14th Army in the central sector. Between January and April, N.C.A.C. completed the road to China and cleared all but a few pockets of Japanese from north Burma. As the British and Chinese advanced through the north they drove the Japanese before them into the central sector. The landings in the Arakan opened the way for the new supply route for the 14th Army and drove the remnants of the Japanese 28th Army also into the centre. The seaborne expedition for Rangoon was prepared in comparative peace on Ramree Island.

During these same months the most important battles were fought by the 14th Army in the open country adjoining the Irrawaddy. They represented the largest clash of arms of the whole of the Burma campaign. The 14th Army was at its strongest and was opposed to the biggest concentration of Japanese left in Burma. These operations were the decisive blows of the campaign and, admitting a weakened enemy, they were boldly executed by General Slim who, for the first time, had time, space, and opportunity for manœuvre.

The 14th Army, probably the largest single British army in the world by January 1945, consisted of two army corps.

One was Stopford's 33rd Corps and the other was 4th Corps under Lieut.-Gen. Frank Messervy, who had taken over from Scoones.

At the start of the operations, 33rd Corps was composed of the 2nd British, the 19th and 20th Indian Divisions, and the 254th Tank Brigade. The 4th Corps comprised the 7th and 17th Indian Divisions, the latter with a third brigade, the 99th Indian, the 255th Tank Brigade, the 28th East African Brigade, the Lushai Brigade, and a Chin Hills battalion. Later the 36th British and 5th Indian Divisions entered the battle while, to suit the tactical position, divisions were switched from one corps to another. At one time or another, Slim had seven complete divisions, two tank brigades, and a host of other formations including, for the first time in history, an all-Indian independent brigade, the 268th. This brigade, an experimental formation, was composed of men from the non-martial races of India.

By January 1945 the estimated overall strength of the Japanese in Burma was 175,000, only half the maximum force they had ever deployed in the country. Two armies, the 15th and 33rd, were in the centre but neither was anywhere near at full strength owing to the losses suffered during the Manipur expedition. In the Mandalay and Meiktila areas were elements of seven divisions.

As the battle developed it was found that elements of the 2nd, 15th, 18th, 31st, 33rd, 49th, 53rd Japanese Divisions and the motor brigades had been drawn into the area. Some had withdrawn from the north in face of the N.C.A.C. advance. To the east of Mandalay was the 56th Division. The force, as a whole, was piecemeal and lacked cohesion and direction. For its power it relied on the fighting quality of individual units.

The general Allied plan was to draw as much Japanese strength as possible into the centre and, with the 14th Army, cut its line of retreat south and deliver a mortal blow.

Slim's plan was to strike at Mandalay across the Irrawaddy with 33rd Corps and, eighty miles to the south, use 4th Corps in one rapid sweep across the same river and capture Meiktila which lay on the main railway and road line from Mandalay to Rangoon. It was hoped that as the Mandalay battle developed so more Japanese would be drawn into the area, leaving Meiktila loosely held. Having captured Mandalay and Meiktila and broken up the Japanese forces, the 14th Army would advance south as fast as possible to Rangoon.

Slim's chief tactical difficulties were to deploy such a large force as two corps along a single axis of advance, the Imphal–Tamu–Kabaw Valley road, and disguise his intention to move against Meiktila. The various moves required accurate timing and a deception plan.

There was no deception in the preparations for the attack on Mandalay. Indeed, the Japanese would have been most surprised if the obvious had not happened. It was accepted that the Japanese knew the 14th Army consisted of two corps and would expect to see them in action along the Irrawaddy.

The 19th Division, which had crossed the Chindwin at the end of 1944 and had advanced across north Burma, was, for this part of the operation, under 4th Corps. The 7th Indian Division of the same corps had concentrated on the Chindwin for a similar crossing. The 2nd British Division spearheaded the 33rd Corps into the Shwebo plain, crossing the Chindwin at Kalewa, and was followed in December by the 20th Indian Division. These preliminary moves implied a two-corps drive on Mandalay from the north and south-west.

To clear the Gangaw Valley and feint at the Chauk and Yenangyaung oil-fields, Slim sent a force composed of the Lushai and 28th East African Brigades and the Chin Battalion. It was hoped that the Japanese would interpret this move as a separate and independent expedition aiming at the recapture of the oil-fields.

When these moves had developed and the Japanese saw which way the attacks were coming, Slim switched the 7th and the 17th Divisions of 4th Corps from the north to the south, building them up on the Irrawaddy at Pakokku opposite, and on the direct line of advance to, Meiktila some sixty miles away. The security of this switch called for an elaborate deception plan, much of which was organized by Lieut.-Col. Peter Fleming. Dummy parachutists were dropped at selected points across the Irrawaddy and in the oil-field area. The movement of large convoys was simulated by jeeps trailing brushwood which threw up clouds of dust. Feint attacks using Chinese crackers were laid on. Bombing raids were diverted to places where the Japanese might anticipate attacks. In some of these raids, tins of the infamous soya link sausage—the most unpopular form of Lease-Lend food America ever provided—were dropped with real bombs. There was, within 4th Corps, a wireless silence.

The Japanese fell into the trap. They made little attempt to oppose the original Chindwin crossings and offered virtually no resistance in the Shwebo plain. There they left forlorn rearguards as they attempted to build up to defend Mandalay, the prestige value of which was greater than its stretegic importance. Their main defence line was along the Irrawaddy, opposite Mandalay.

The initial 14th Army moves were those of the 19th Division. After capturing Wuntho in December and making contact with the 36th Division, they took over the central Burma extension of the railway corridor while the 36th Division crossed the Irrawaddy and advanced into the Shan Hills.

The 19th Division was, at the time, composed of the 62nd Brigade (Welch Regiment, 3rd Rajputana Rifles, 4/4th

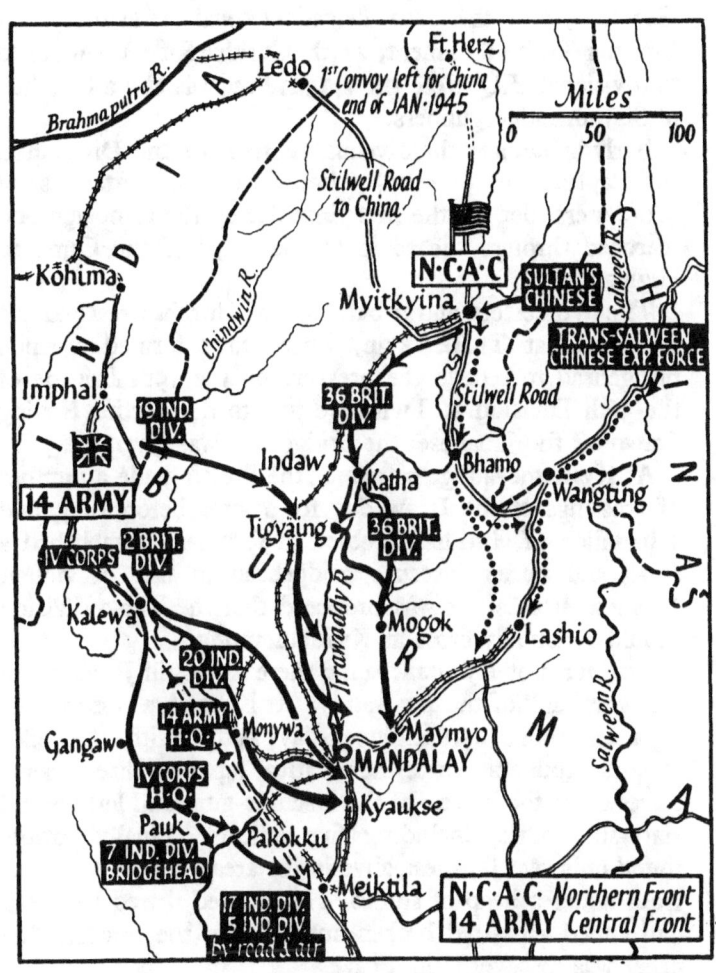

REINVASION OF BURMA AND ATTACK ON MANDALAY—JANUARY–APRIL 1945

Gurkhas); the 64th Brigade (Worcesters, 5th Baluch, 1/6th Gurkhas); and the 98th Brigade (Royal Berkshires, 2nd Frontier Force Regiment, 4/4th Gurkha Rifles). Attached to divisional H.Q. were the 1/15th Punjabis and a battalion of Sikh machine-gunners.

Early in January the division assisted the 2nd Division in the capture of Shwebo, where the two battalions of Worcesters met for the first time during the campaign and marched through the town to the pipes of the Cameron Highlanders.

The Worcesters and a battalion of Gurkhas reached the Irrawaddy at Thabeikkyin, where they formed a small bridgehead to relieve the pressure on the 29th Brigade of the 36th Division at Twinggye just to the north. Having drawn off the Japanese, the bridgehead was given up.

At Kyaukmeyaung, patrols of the Welch made a number of crossings of the Irrawaddy for a week before they, and a battalion of Gurkhas, crossed in force and established a small and rather insecure bridgehead in face of violent Japanese attacks. It was proposed that the whole division should eventually cross at Kyaukmeyaung.

Just north of Kyaukmeyaung there were still Japanese on the west bank of the Irrawaddy. At Kabwet, a company of Japanese fought an eighteen-day battle with the Sikh machine-gunners. Once the fanatical Japanese threw themselves on to the barrels of the machine-guns and left behind sixty-six bodies, including five officers. Finally patrols found only two Japanese alive in the area. One crawled out from under a heap of stones. He growled, bared his teeth and aimed a twisted broken automatic at the troops. The other was discovered in a cave.

Having taken over from the East Africans at Kalewa, the 2nd British Division was given the Kabo weir as their first objective. The weir irrigated the Shwebo plain and it was thought the Japanese might demolish it as they retreated.

FROM THE CHINDWIN TO THE IRRAWADDY 241

A flying column of the Royal Welch Fusiliers secured the weir intact on New Year's eve, advancing 112 miles in ten days, despite meeting opposition on the first part of their journey.

The Dorsets captured Ye-U a couple of days later at the point of the bayonet, but the airfields were attacked by Japanese Oscars before the transport planes could land safely. The division had already outrun its supplies and was subsisting on half rations.

There was a sharp scrap on the Mu river when the Dorsets and Camerons took prisoners before the Worcesters captured Shwebo on 9 January, by which time the 19th Indian Division had arrived on the scene and were blocking the Japanese escape route to Onbauk and the south.

In the bend of the Irrawaddy, just below Mandalay, lies the town of Sagaing among a sudden small mass of hills which run down to the west bank of the river. Anticipating attack, the Japanese reinforced their garrison there. The 2nd Division Reconnaissance Battalion made several feint attacks on Sagaing while other units cleared up small Japanese garrisons in surrounding villages.

The Royal Scots, aided by air strikes and using flame-throwers, killed sixty of a body of a hundred Japanese at Ywathitgye. The other Japanese got across the river. The Lancashire Fusiliers with tanks, artillery, flame-throwers, and air strikes killed over a hundred Japanese at Kyaukse (one of several villages of that name) and the Royal Norfolks had a small fight south of Saye.

Meantime, preparations were made for the division to cross the Irrawaddy at Nzagun.

It was during these operations that the officers of one of the British battalions asked to be relieved of their commanding officer. This was granted and the battalion was taken over in action by the young second-in-command.

This is mentioned chiefly because it was the third occasion

during the division's tour in the East on which a C.O. had been relieved after a *démarche* had been made to higher authority by his junior, and usually emergency, officers. Twice it had happened in action. It is, perhaps, an interesting reflection on the twentieth-century army that its younger officers could, if they considered their C.O. unfit to command in action or inefficient, ask for his removal. That their appeal was accepted by higher authority shows that the claims of an efficient fighting battalion were put before those of the army list and seniority.

Next into the picture came the 20th Indian Division, still under Maj.-Gen. Douglas Gracey. The division's brigades were the 32nd (Northamptons, 9/14th Punjabis, 3/8th Gurkhas); the 100th (Border Regiment, 14/13th Frontier Force Rifles, 4/10th Gurkhas), and the 80th (Devons, 9/12th Frontier Force Regiment, 3/1st Gurkhas).

In five days, using only local boats and rafts, the 32nd Brigade ferried across the Irrawaddy at Mawleik 5,000 men, 1,200 mules, and guns and vehicles. It made contact with the 2nd Division sixty miles south-east of Kalewa and joined in a battle, accounting for seventy Japanese. Its task was to clear the country between the axes of advance of the 2nd and 20th Divisions and to capture Budalin, which fell to the Northamptons. The brigade covered nearly 300 miles in the first month.

The main part of the 20th Division followed the 2nd over the Chindwin at Kalewa. Meeting the 32nd Brigade at Budalin, the division split into brigade columns, the 32nd Brigade capturing Monywa, the 100th taking Myinmu, on the Irrawaddy, and the 80th clearing the country around the confluence of the Chindwin and Irrawaddy. The division then prepared to cross the Irrawaddy at Myinmu.

At Letkapin, Gurkhas shot up five boatloads of Japanese trying to cross the river and killed or drowned 150. On the Allied side of the river twenty-four Japanese remained alive, and they, preferring suicide to a fight, marched in close column into the river and were drowned, as the legendary Prussians marched on orders of their officers over a cliff.

It was during these operations that the most famous of all Japanese-Burmese spies in Burma was apprehended after a hunt that had begun at the end of 1942.

Unandiya, aged thirty-three when caught, was educated by a Burmese priest and worked with the Bombay-Burma Trading Corporation before entering the 'church', in which he became a Buddhist monk and a most respected man in his village. Just before the war, however, Unandiya, like a number of the semi-educated intellectual Burmese priesthood, became a member of the Thakins, an extreme nationalist group.

In 1942 Unandiya discarded his robes and became Japan's chief spy in the upper Chindwin area. He dressed in Japanese uniform, carried a sword and revolver, and was known to have murdered at least a dozen Burmese, some by beheading.

On the evening of 31 January, the chief Civil Affairs officer with the 20th Division reported that Unandiya and eight followers had been seen in a village. A Field Security officer and a party of Gurkhas crossed the Chindwin in country craft, paddling with shovels. They got within a few yards of the suspected house, when two men rushed out and were taken. Inside were two women. None claimed to know the whereabouts of Unandiya. The British officer called for the village headman and, using firm language, ascertained that the elusive spy, his wife, sister, and two children, and five others had crossed the river and gone to another house. As the Gurkha party recrossed the river they saw two boats with a small party of people. One was Unandiya, who gave himself up without a fight. His fate is a secret now hidden in the Red Fort at Delhi.

By the beginning of February there were three divisions along the west bank of the Irrawaddy opposite Mandalay.

Parts of the 19th were already across at Singu, the 2nd was concentrating at Nzagun, and the 20th at Myinmu. In the north the 36th Division was crossing the Shweli at Myitson with the intention of going on to Mongmit and Mogok. Approaching the city from the north it represented a fourth threat to Mandalay.

As the Lushai and East African Brigades and the Chin Battalion swept the Gangaw Valley, so the leading elements of 4th Corps began to arrive and build up at Pakokku. The 7th Indian Division was the first. It split into columns on a pack basis and advanced into the Gangaw Valley.

The road, such as it was, was in a bad condition. The Japanese had demolished bridges and broken up parts of the road. Bridges had to be rebuilt with local material. What vehicles the division possessed often had to be winched over steep and rugged parts of the track. Even so, the 7th Division arrived at Pakokku at the beginning of February, having covered 350 miles in a month and with a tail extending back over 100 miles. Behind it came 4th Corps H.Q., which was later established at Pauk.

The 7th Division was commanded by Maj.-Gen. Evans, who had taken over from Lieut.-Gen. Messervy. The division consisted of the 14th Brigade (South Lancashire Regiment, 4/5th Royal Gurkha Rifles, 4/14th Punjabis); the 33rd Brigade (4/15th Punjabis, 1st Burma Regiment, 4/1st Gurkhas), and the 89th Brigade (K.O.S.B.s, 1/11th Sikhs, 4/8th Gurkhas).

So that these preparatory moves of 4th Corps should not be hampered in any way, the 17th Indian Division did not come under Messervy's command until the beginning of February. It was made responsible for its own move from Imphal to the Pauk area. Two brigades of the division were mechanized and were accompanied by the 255th Tank Brigade. The third brigade was airborne and remained behind at its airhead, Palel, in the Imphal plain.

Maj.-Gen. Cowan still commanded the 17th Division, as he had done since taking over from General J. G. Smyth after the Sittang bridge battle during the first Burma retreat. The divisional line-up was: 48th Brigade (9/13th Frontier Force Rifles, 1/7th Gurkha Rifles, West Yorks); 63rd Brigade (7th Baluch, 1/10th Gurkhas, Borders), and 99th Brigade (1/3rd Gurkhas, 6/15th Punjabis, 1st Sikh Light Infantry). The divisional reconnaissance battalion was the 6/9th Jats, the defence battalion the 6/7th Rajputs, and the machine-gunners the 9th Frontier Force Regiment.

By the beginning of February there was, on the Irrawaddy below its confluence with the Chindwin, the 7th Indian Division and behind it the 17th. To the south, holding the flank against any possible Japanese counter-threat, was the mixed force. 4th Corps objective was Meiktila, the capture of which would cut Burma in two.

When, on 9 February, Tactical H.Q. of the 14th Army opened at Monywa, the largest offensive force ever collected together in Burma was poised for its 'D' Day. Five divisions lined the Irrawaddy for a hundred miles.

Operations in the Arakan were, by this time, advanced enough for the safe use of the Chittagong and Akyab as air-supply bases. Already 4th Corps at Pauk was being supplied from Chittagong, though 33rd Corps was still reliant on Imphal.

The creation by Allied Land Forces of a lines of communication command under Maj.-Gen. G. W. Symes had taken a considerable load off Slim's shoulders. This new command was responsible for land, water, and air routes and rear echelon supply within Assam and liberated Burma, as well as base and reinforcement camps, hospitals, and training centres. By the time Rangoon had been taken, in May, the command trucks had covered 130,000,000 miles. The drivers were mainly men from the Royal Indian Army Service Corps. The strength of the command exceeded 200,000.

For the purposes of air supply there were two complementary organizations, the Army Air Transport Organization under Brigadier Dawson, responsible for the ground work, and the Combat Cargo Task Force under the American, Brig.-Gen. F. W. Evans. From January to March these organizations lifted 92,000 tons of stores and 98,000 men, an air-lift without precedent. Combat Cargo Task Force had 350 aircraft available for these operations, but even so each had to average twelve flying hours a day, with a time limit of fifteen minutes on the ground to unload, turn round, and take off.

Out of the already considerable experience of air supply to the army had grown two field organizations known as R.A.M.O. (Rear Airfield Maintenance Organization) and F.A.M.O. (Forward Airfield Maintenance Organization). These organizations were responsible for the dispatching and delivering of all supplies. As they grew they assumed even larger liabilities.

At Sinthe, main airfield for 4th Corps, there was one of the largest F.A.M.O.s in Burma. It was a complete air town. Its supply responsibilities included petrol, oil, and lubricants, ordnance stores, ammunition, canteen supplies, and medical supplies. It had complete medical centres including operating theatres, under canvas or below ground, blood transfusion refrigerators, a dental unit, a casualty clearing station, a malaria forward treatment unit, and an ophthalmic and a psychiatrical centre.

Its personnel had been drawn from the old beach groups which had been formed in India for the anticipated landings on the Burma coast. Its own airfield construction unit, assisted by engineers, pioneers, and local labour, carved out airstrips from jungle and converted them into concrete airfields with incoming and outgoing aircraft runways as well as bays for unloading.

It took only ten days to complete the Sinthe airfield, with

its twelve miles of road and circuits, unloading bays, water-points, dumps, control towers, and airstrip irrigation channels to keep down the dust. But from the very first day, when bulldozers had flattened part of the countryside, transport aircraft had been able to land.

The unloading routine was worked out to a fine art. As an aircraft landed it was flagged to its bay. A lorry drove up to the plane's open doorway (many transport planes flew without doors) and a British checker and eight Indian engineers unloaded the stores and took them to the requisite dump. The operation took only thirteen minutes for a four and a half ton load. Corps H.Q. had been then informed of the consignment which, by a coding system, was marked for a particular unit.

The men worked from six o'clock in the morning to eleven o'clock at night, for in January–February weather it was possible to fly at night. The Indians handled ten tons a day as an average. On one day forty British soldiers and seven trucks unloaded over one hundred aircraft. The transport aircraft were C46s carrying a four and a half ton load, or C47s holding two and a quarter tons.

Within a few days of the opening of the Sinthe F.A.M.O., 500 tons of stores were being received daily. Within a week the number of planes per day had reached nearly 200. Many were for casualty evacuation and on one day 250 men were flown out. This was by no means the maximum achieved, for there were 500 casualties, mostly sickness cases, passing through the F.A.M.O. medical centres every day. F.A.M.O. had beds for 200, excluding the Malaria Forward Treatment Unit, which was expanded to deal with 800 at any one time.

Operations were performed on the spot. It is a fact that a man shot in the head in the battle that was going on down the road to Pakoku—small skirmishing battles—was back in Comilla, former 14th Army H.Q. in Assam, within two hours, including time taken for an operation at F.A.M.O. One surgeon was, even in the early stages of the battle, performing up to twenty operations a day. Though Sinthe was at first under gunfire, nursing sisters were there from the start.

This 4th Corps F.A.M.O. must not be regarded as an exception but as an example, for others were already operating and more would follow. It has been singled out in order to quote factual instances of what one F.A.M.O. could do. As it was responsible for only one corps, the very large task of organizing the supply of more than two corps and of army groups on the move can be appreciated. The R.A.M.O.s were complementary to the F.A.M.O.s and merely repeated at the base what happened at the front, except that they had the added job of packing the supplies, whereas F.A.M.O. was a primarily distributive organization.

18

THE CAPTURE OF MANDALAY

Reaction of Japanese—Allied casualty Figures—14th Army cross Irrawaddy—Battle for Meiktila

THE 14th Army reached the Irrawaddy about the same time as the first convoy drove from Ledo into China and the 26th Indian Division were fighting on Ramree Island. A fairly large, though certainly not the most populated, area of Burma had been liberated and could look forward to a return to peaceful conditions and administration. The Myitkyina and Bhamo districts in the north and the Shwebo plain in the centre were the most important areas. What was the reaction of the local Burmese?

The 14th Army had found few Burmese remaining in their villages as they passed through the Kabaw Valley and upper Chindwin areas. The people had either fled from the ebb and flow of battle, which had been going on since 1942, or were intensely frightened after the Japanese reprisals following the Wingate expeditions.

The Shwebo area had, however, seen little fighting even in recent months, when the 14th Army advanced across it in pursuit of the retreating Japanese. Wingate had not crossed their country and the Japanese had interfered little with the everyday life of the people. But the Japanese occupation had caused a considerable deterioration in the standard of living; there was inflation and dacoity and a great shortage of consumer goods.

For these things the Burmese blamed the Japanese. Under such circumstances they were pleased to see the British and Allied troops, who possessed plenty of articles which they could barter for eggs, vegetables, fruits, and other local produce. But this did not mean they were pro-British. They were definitely anti-Japanese and, though their welcome to the British was warm, they made no bones about their own nationalistic aspirations. In fact they wanted neither British nor Japanese but, if they had to have one of them, they preferred the British.

It was therefore important that the British Civil Affairs staffs responsible for the rehabilitation of the freed parts of the country should be completely equipped to raise the standard of living of the people to at least a pre-war level, and should be capable of inducing a friendly atmosphere among the people, so that once Burma achieved self-government the Burmese would remain in some form of partnership with the British. The second condition was dependent on the fulfilment of the first.

By the middle of January not one consignment of consumer goods, even such small items as needles and thread or matches, had arrived in central Burma. The Shwebo bazaar, main marketing centre for the area, was closed with no prospect of reopening. Native doctors who had stayed at their posts in the local hospitals and dispensaries throughout the war were still subsisting on hardly any medical supplies. Surely an army of hundreds of thousands of men arrayed across the countryside with all the modern paraphernalia of war, including the finest medical science could produce, could have spared something for what Ian Morrison, of *The Times*, described as 'pathetic little hospitals and dispensaries'? As the army swept past, the poor Burmese peasants picked up the empty food tins, treasuring them as gold. An army blanket would buy the best woman in the village. Yet army blankets were produced by the million in Australia, America, India, and Britain.

The H.Q. of Civil Affairs was in Simla. They claimed, among other things, that there were not enough trucks to carry the supplies for the Burmese into the country because of military requirements. Morrison wrote: 'No sort of propaganda or information work is being done among the people. Material problems are paramount, *ad hoc* problems of welfare and living. The way in which these things are being tackled does not inspire much confidence in the later solutions of the much more complicated political problems. The lack of foresight and intelligent planning is matched only by the lack of vigour that is being displayed now.'

Morrison continued his appraisal of the unhappy situation at some length. On such dispatches all censorship had been lifted, military security being the only censorship stop. His dispatch should have been passed to the high-speed transmitter and sent to London without delay. It was, however, read by Public Relations officers who, fearful to let it through because of its criticism, passed it to higher authority. The outcome was that the dispatch was held up for some time, Morrison being requested to withdraw it. He refused. Its appearance in *The Times* leader was followed by changes in the personnel of the Civil Affairs branch.

Only occasionally did the Japanese air forces appear over the Irrawaddy area as the 14th Army were preparing to cross. By then what air forces they still possessed in South-East Asia had moved back to Siam, Malaya, and China. Persistent and increasing calls from the Pacific and China theatres steadily drained the theatre of aircraft, and the size of the Allied air forces, over one hundred squadrons by 1945, made it uneconomical for the Japanese to risk a fight. Hit and run in small numbers was their only tactic.

With their position at sea just as bad, the Japanese in Burma were fighting a lone battle for which they could expect neither support nor reinforcements. Their main chance of survival was to escape overland into Siam or Malaya. This could only be achieved by keeping the 14th Army and the N.C.A.C. troops away from the eastern routes to the Salween, which ran through the Shan Hills at Loilem and Loikaw, and from the southern routes across the Sittang via Pegu.

There is little doubt that the Japanese foresaw their eventual eclipse in Burma. They could only delay it as long as they held Mandalay. Once it fell the 14th Army, a powerful and mobile force, would have the freedom of the good terrain in central and south Burma.

Burma was Japan's most far-flung conquest. It jutted out from their ring of conquests in South-East Asia against the north-eastern mass of India. It was vulnerable from the land, air, and sea. Once the Japanese had failed to carry its boundary into Assam, once they had proved themselves incapable of a land or seaborne assault against India, it was merely a matter of time before the Allies began a counter-offensive starting in Burma. After Burma the Allies would go for Malaya. There was no secrecy about the proposed invasion of Malaya, except the time and place. The Japanese were prepared to forfeit Burma in their own time.

The evidence pointed to the Japanese making their final stands in the theatre at Singapore, in the Dutch East Indies, and in the Solomon and Bismarck Islands. During the last few months of 1944 and the early part of 1945 they increased the size of their garrisons in these stations by nearly fifty per cent. There was little hope, by then, of their moving on to Burma. It can only be presumed that the Japanese decided that somehow the Allied forces in South-East Asia must not link up with those in the Pacific. Singapore was the cross-roads of the war in the East.

It was the 14th Army's task not only to capture Mandalay and, if possible, Rangoon, but also to prevent the Japanese from escaping across the Salween and the Sittang. It was not easy. The Irrawaddy was an obstacle, Mandalay would take time to capture, and the routes to the Salween were few and lay through mountainous country which was easily

THE CAPTURE OF MANDALAY 253

defended by a small force. The Japanese in the south had plenty of time to cross the Sittang, which formed yet another barrier to the 14th Army. The time available, from February to May, did not permit of the sending of independent expeditions on encircling movements into the Shan Hills. The weight of the 14th Army had to be directed at Mandalay and Meiktila, which presented the best chance of splitting up and disorganizing the Japanese army, and then Rangoon. The odds were on a great many Japanese escaping.

The 14th Army lost time at Mandalay and Meiktila and never reached Rangoon. Though the actual plans of the capture of Mandalay did not go entirely according to detail, the disorganization of the Japanese armies was more complete than hoped for. In the final analysis less than half the force which opposed the 14th Army at the start of 1945 was alive a few months later. The rest was scattered throughout the length and breadth of eastern Burma.

The crossing of the Irrawaddy by the 19th Division on 14 January at Singu—a bridgehead which was gradually built up—had drawn opposition in men and artillery from the Japanese. By the end of January they had brought up some fifty guns and were beating a day and night drum fire on the narrow bridgehead. Gurkhas trying to penetrate farther inland were cut up. Men of the Welch Regiment trying to break out southwards along the river bank, were contained on Pear Hill and their supply line back to the actual bridgehead was cut. One half of the hill was occupied by the Japanese, the other by the Welch. Neither side could see the other, and from the air the Welch could be seen walking about and hanging out their washing, although only a few yards from the Japanese.

In the bridgehead everyone lived below ground. There was no room for manœuvre, and the small bodies of troops ferried across the river had to move in snaky single file columns. Life was hazardous.

The climax in the battle for the Singu bridgehead came at the beginning of February, when it was decided that only tanks could break the Japanese ring. Six tanks of the York and Lancs were ordered to cross at night. Counter-attractions, demonstrations, and deceptions were laid on to cover the actual crossings. Low-flying aircraft flew up and down the moonlit waters of the Irrawaddy on a 'noise' patrol. A large tree-trunk floated down the silent brown waters of the great river, twisting and turning as if a derelict cut loose from a raft of logs. In reality it was paddled by troops who, a mile or two from the tank-crossing point, let off Chinese crackers and other weird noises. Men of Mountbatten's private army, the Seabees, swam underwater across the river as they had been doing for a week or more and diverted the attention of the Japanese. These Seabees (underwater swimmers) were a small and specially picked British force trained in California.

A single shaded light on the east bank of the Irrawaddy was the only guide for the tanks. The first tank rumbled through the trees down to the mud-banked crossing-point. For those on the west bank the noise of its approach and preparatory moves seemed a thunder the Japanese were bound to hear. All the time the Japanese artillery kept up a persistent, if inaccurate, artillery barrage.

The first tank manœuvred on to its raft, which slid away into the gloom. It was across by eleven o'clock. The raft returned for the second, the third, and then the others. By half-past two—in three and a half hours—the last tank had crossed. And a Japanese shell exploding on the water-line killed an Indian soldier on the raft. There were no other casualties.

For more than a week the tanks, infantry, and guns attempted to break the lock on the Japanese door. The bridgehead was enlarged, and more troops, vehicles, and guns were ferried across.

South of Mandalay the 20th Indian Division crossed the

Irrawaddy on 11 February at Myinmyu. Their crossing was opposed as violently as any in the whole course of the Burma war. Having obtained a foothold on the east bank of the Irrawaddy, the 20th Division were contained in a small semicircle for two weeks, during which the Japanese attempted to push it back into the river. Some of the craft used to ferry the division across had been borrowed from the 19th and 2nd Divisions, for there were not enough 'dukws' and other landing-craft in Burma to go round. The 'dukws', being most valuable, had to be nursed with great care and imposed restrictions both on the time which could be taken on the crossings and on the size of the force employed. Secrecy was also essential.

The 20th Division actually killed some 1,500 Japanese while consolidating their bridgehead, and the fierceness of the fighting may be gauged by the awarding of one V.C. to a Jemadar of the Frontier Force Rifles. His company, reduced to a quarter strength, held off three times their strength in Japanese.

The 2nd British Division was next to cross. The leading troops of the Worcesters had their boats sunk beneath them. The Japanese had anticipated the crossing at Nzagun. Under fire the Camerons tried to cross, and the fast-flowing river swung their boats downstream. Eventually they reached the east bank some distance below the place intended. Royal Welch Fusiliers and men of the Manchester Regiment secured a foothold.

In seventy-two hours, despite losses in craft—more important perhaps, than men at this stage—General Nicholson got 6,000 men and 200 vehicles across the river. They represented the bulk of two brigades, the 5th and the 6th. The divisional R.E.s and R.A.S.C. worked continuously under fire to get the troops across.

South of the confluence of the Irrawaddy and Chindwin the 7th Indian Division of 4th Corps crossed the Irrawaddy on 14 February. They did not achieve the surprise for which they had hoped, and for several days there was bitter fighting in which the leading elements of the division were supported by tanks of the 116th R.A.C. (Gordon Highlanders). It was not until a week after the initial crossing that the 63rd Brigade of 17th Division plus two regiments of tanks (Probyn's Horse and the Royal Deccan Horse) were able to get fully across and advance on Meiktila, and then they were held temporarily at Oyin.

By the end of February there were five divisions across the Irrawaddy, three of them attacking around Mandalay with the prospect of assistance from a fourth (the 36th).

None of these river crossings was easy either in preparation or execution. The shortage of 'dukws' has already been mentioned and there were far too few of them even to carry one division, let alone five. Mainly the 14th Army had to cross the Irrawaddy, which was anything from a thousand yards to a mile wide, in country craft, rafts, Ranger dinghies, and a few motor-propelled craft carried by the sappers or dropped in pieces from the air. It was a very hazardous operation from the outset, calling for courage, ingenuity, and improvisation. In military history it will stand comparison with Montgomery's crossing of the Rhine. It had none of the equipment possessed by the British armies in Europe. On the Irrawaddy there was not one single armoured amphibious craft. Many of the boats were leaky, cracked by age and the sun. As an achievement it probably equals anything in Europe.

The 4th Corps crossing south of Pakokku produced immediate reactions from the Japanese, who saw the threat to Meiktila and their main line of communication. They began diverting troops southwards from the Mandalay area. This weakened the 19th Indian Division's front but temporarily strengthened the forces opposing the 2nd British and 20th Indian Divisions to the south of Mandalay.

THE CAPTURE OF MANDALAY 257

The 19th Division were the first to break loose, and they thrust towards Mandalay from two directions while diverting a brigade group to Maymu, headquarters of the Japanese 15th Army.

The main 19th Division drive was held up at Madaya, but a second advance by a smaller mobile force moving down the west bank of the Irrawaddy cut into Mandalay at the end of the first week in March. Mandalay Hill fell to Gurkhas and men of the Royal Berkshires, though snipers remained hidden among the shrines and pagodas, which unfortunately necessitated the machine-gunning and bombing of holy places. General Rees, always prominent because of a red scarf round his neck, came riding into Mandalay with the tanks. He was always well to the fore and his orderly was shot at his side.

The capture of Mandalay Hill gave the division a dominant position for the capture of Fort Dufferin. In the fort were Japanese as well as British and Indian prisoners of war. The walls were breached with artillery fire (reminiscent of Wellington's breaching the walls of Ahmednagra's Fort before breakfast a hundred and fifty years previously), and a Burmese emerged from the dust and rubble carrying a white flag. The Japanese, he reported, had fled.

It took ten more days to clear up Mandalay, by which time the 2nd and 20th Divisions had fought their way into the city. On 20 March it was officially captured. There was little left of the legendary beauty of this City of the Kings. The brewery, one of the main objectives of encouragement for the British troops, was partially derelict, and the Japanese (or Burmese) had removed some of the plant's vital parts. Though it had been promised that the brewery would be open for the troops as soon as possible, administrative blocks and official procrastination never permitted it.

The 2nd Division had been slower than intended after crossing the Irrawaddy. There were several reasons.

Firstly, the shock of the disaster of their initial crossing was considerable. Secondly, the movement of the Japanese from Mandalay south to Meiktila added weight to the forces opposing the division. Thirdly, the division had lost the aggressiveness which had been so evident at Kohima and which, it was hoped, would carry it through to Mandalay. The original plan had detailed the capture of Mandalay to this British division because of the British soldier's traditional association with the city and because of the propaganda value to the British all over the world. As it was, the prize went to an Indian division which, considering the part played by the Indian soldier in the Burma war, was deserved.

The plan for the capture of Meiktila entailed a rapid move to the town and its group of airfields by two brigades of the 17th Division and the tank brigade, followed by the fly-in of the 99th Indian Brigade by the numbers One and Two Air Commandos. The whole operation should have been completed before the beginning of March, but Japanese opposition was so stiff that the schedule was not kept. The fly-in of the 99th Brigade was postponed several times. The airfields changed hands almost daily.

For a week the Meiktila battle hung in the balance. The tide turned following a concerted attack by 63rd Brigade from the north, 48th Brigade from the north-east, and the 255th Tank Brigade from the east.

On 1 March—400 Japanese were killed on that day—the 17th Division had secured enough of Meiktila to permit the 99th Brigade to fly-in, though the Air Commandos had to land under fire. By 3 March it was officially considered that Meiktila itself was cleared, though large-scale skirmishings continued for several more weeks. The 9th Brigade of the 5th Indian Division had to be flown in to assist.

Meantime the 28th East African Brigade, fighting in the area of the Chauk oil-fields, had been heavily counter-attacked and suffered severe losses. It was relieved by a

THE CAPTURE OF MANDALAY 259

brigade of the 7th Division, another brigade of which fought a stiff action at Myingyan, which it cleared by 22 March, two days after the capture of Mandalay. Fighting throughout this area continued for several weeks, for the Japanese, determined to keep clear an escape route eastwards, left rearguards who fought with characteristic intensity, although greatly outnumbered. Though the Japanese forces were piecemeal by then, identifications proved that troops of the redoubtable 18th and 33rd Divisions had been concerned in the defence of Meiktila. By the beginning of April much of what had remained of the Japanese forces had melted into the Shan Hills and others were trying to get south across the Sittang River. As for the 14th Army, it faced south and drove on towards Rangoon.

The deterioration of the 2nd British Division served to emphasize the growing fatigue and decreasing morale of most of the veteran British troops in Burma. The cause was the repatriation plan and the excessive amount of publicity it received in South-East Asia.

For some weeks the Forces' newspaper, *SEAC*, admirably produced and distributed to all troops throughout the theatre, had given considerable prominence to the lowering of the repatriation period to three years eight months. This new time limit meant that the 2nd British Division, the 36th, and many British battalions were nearing the end of their tour in the East. Having left Britain in March 1942, the 2nd Division would be due to leave S.E.A.C. in about August 1945. So, when they crossed the Irrawaddy in February, all ranks concerned knew they had only six months to go.

Had the facts been left at that, had every soldier been told he would be on the way home by August or September and then the story dropped, all might have been well. Though repatriation would undoubtedly have been at the back of every soldier's mind, he would not have been faced with it every day of his life. He could not have been aggravated by incorrect statements by generals and politicians and the continual impact of twisted facts, counter-facts, and counter-orders to be read daily in the pages and letter columns of *SEAC*.

Officers were affected no less than the troops and those responsible for the maintenance of morale and efficiency within battalions or divisions, commanding officers, brigadiers, and major-generals, were up against a wave of demoralization almost as great as that which swept through the army in Italy. The result was that when a British battalion crossed the Irrawaddy, as many did, the junior officers and the men who sat in the boats, manfully though they tried, did not look east towards the Japanese but west, back over their shoulders. As the western bank receded in the early morning mist each man felt he was moving one more mile, perhaps an eternity of miles, from the journey back home.

These facts may be hard to accept, but they were to be found in the monthly intelligence reports submitted by units. Every month saw the same references to the growing depression among the British troops. No attempt was made at the highest level to halt the process.

The troops' reaction was natural and to be expected. For over three years, in some cases, the British soldier had sweated in the East, fighting a war he did not fully understand, for honour and glory he could not visualize, against an enemy he knew very little about. He became cynical and bitter and wondered whether he was fighting in the Burma jungles so that the country could once more be delivered to the great British trading corporations. Was he really trying to kill Japanese so that the Burmese could have their land? Why could not they or someone else do it, anyhow? And every mile he trudged nearer Burma's heart his own longing to get home increased.

19

THE RECAPTURE OF RANGOON

Aung San changes sides—Race for Rangoon—An Assault from the Sea—Formation of 12th Army—The General Election at Home—Last Battles in Burma

THE Allied success in central Burma was the signal for the disaffected Burmese groups to attempt to change the colour of their clothing. Leaders of the Burmese National Army, known also as the Burma Traitor Army, approached the British with offers of assistance against the Japanese. They were accepted on a purely military basis.

Such a metamorphosis may appear strange and requires explanation.

Before the war there were several political groups in Burma, notably the Communist, the Thakin, and the People's Revolutionary Parties. All of them had been outlawed by the British and their leaders gaoled on account of their nationalistic aspirations.

The coming of the Japanese was preceded by a spate of Tokyo propaganda offering independence to the Burmese. In 1940 a number of young nationalist-minded Burmese went to Japanese Hainan for military training. Others, including the late Maj.-Gen. Aung San, later commander of the Burma National Army, attended courses in Japan.

The Japanese invasion of Burma, the breakdown of the civil power, and the defeat of the British-Indian forces gave these illegal Burmese parties the opportunity to come out into the open. Japanese-trained Burmese *agent provocateurs* inspired and hastily recruited a Burmese Independence Army which operated against the British, the Indians, and even their own kith and kin during the retreat in 1942.

The traitor groups received considerable publicity during the retreat, possibly because of the high emotional pitch reached by the beaten Allied soldiers and the sensationalism of the press. General Slim has since computed the numbers of the population actively engaged against the Allies as five per cent.

Soon after the Japanese had taken over Burma, public opinion caused them to suppress the hooligan elements of the Independence Army, who were using the war as a good excuse to pay off personal scores and acquire other people's worldly goods.

The Independence Army was renamed the Burma Defence Army under the government of Burma's Premier and chief war traitor, Dr. Ba Maw. As a fighting force against the Allies it was given about as much latitude as the Indian National Army of Subhas Chandra Bose, the Indian traitor. The Japanese were extremely sceptical of the military efficiency of either, a judgment which appeared justified on the few occasions when the Allies met them in action.

Unrest within the ranks of the Independence Army at not being allowed to fight against the Allies and disillusionment within the ranks of all the national groups at the realization that early promises of independence by the Japanese were not being granted led to the growth of underground organizations.

The most important and largest of these was the Anti-Fascist Organization, an amalgamation of a number of political and quasi-political groups, which boasted 200,000 adherents. Its armed section was the Burma National Army under Aung San.

When the 14th Army advanced into central Burma and the Japanese were plainly in retreat, the A.F.O. and B.N.A. considered the moment ripe to change sides. Such a move had been under consideration for some time and the Allies were not exactly unprepared for it. The B.N.A. offered to fight with the Allies and their offer was accepted. It proved a well-trained and well-disciplined force whose chief value lay in mopping up isolated groups of Japanese and in intelligence work. Aung San was permitted to retain his rank of major-general. He must be the only commander of the war to hold high rank on both sides.

There remained the question of renaming the Burmese force. The B.N.A. was redolent of traitordom. 'Patriotic Burmese Forces' was suggested, but this *nom de guerre* was rejected by Mountbatten's H.Q. as it was thought that British troops would use the initials P.B.F. to call the Burmese 'poor bloody fools'. It was, therefore, renamed the Burma Patriotic Front, 'B.P.F.'

Mountbatten had to fight hard to keep Aung San as the B.P.F. leader, for he was opposed at home by the political leaders who considered that Aung San and the others should, if captured, be tried for treason. That Mountbatten won the battle behind the battle proved him to be an able and persuasive diplomat, and there is no question that the course he chose was correct.

It had its amusing aftermath when, some time after Rangoon had fallen, Mountbatten and Aung San sat next to each other at an official dinner. The Supreme Commander turned to the Burmese general and said: 'Do you know I ought to hang you? If you don't behave I still might.' The remark was meant as a jest and was accepted as such by Aung San.

Unquestionably the open uprising of the Burmese assisted the 14th Army in its advance to Rangoon. But it had a more far-reaching effect, perhaps, on Japanese plans. While the Japanese, anticipating an assault on Rangoon, had no desire to get caught in an Allied pincer movement, they were no less desirous of facing a hostile population. No doubt they precipitated their plans for the evacuation of south Burma.

Except for some severe fighting in the Chauk and Yenanyaung oil-field areas, the advance on Rangoon was fairly smooth, the only hazards being administrative and climatic. To reach Rangoon by 15 May at the latest—the date the monsoon officially began—called for rapid movement, with few risks, on half rations. Supply, apart from air-drop, depended on the building of airfields. During most of the 14th Army's previous advance this had been possible, but in the advance on Rangoon the army moved so rapidly that time could not be wasted on airfield construction, though those captured from the Japanese could be used. It is a fact that while previously over 200 Dakota strips had been built within the battle zones of Assam and Burma, very few indeed were constructed during this final drive.

Slim switched over his two army corps. He moved Messervy's 4th Corps from the right to the left, since it was more mobile than Stopford's 33rd Corps. It was then on the road to Rangoon via Pegu, which was the easier path from the viewpoint of terrain and possible Japanese resistance. Stopford's corps had to move from left to right to get on to the Prome route to Rangoon. This switch has been criticized, for it was said that it wasted two weeks when time had already been lost in the battles for Mandalay and Meiktila. Slim had made plans for the switch beforehand and he did not feel justified in altering them. He was also uncertain whether the Prome road was suitable for a mobile force such as 4th Corps.

There was also a redeployment of troops, and Messervy's corps consisted then of the 5th Indian Division, which was flown in to join him, the 17th and 19th Divisions, and the 255th Tank Brigade. Stopford's corps comprised the 7th Indian Division, the 20th, the 2nd British, the 254th Tank Brigade, the Lushai and Chin units, and the 28th East Africans. Not all these units completed the run to Rangoon. Some were dropped off on the way, others remained as

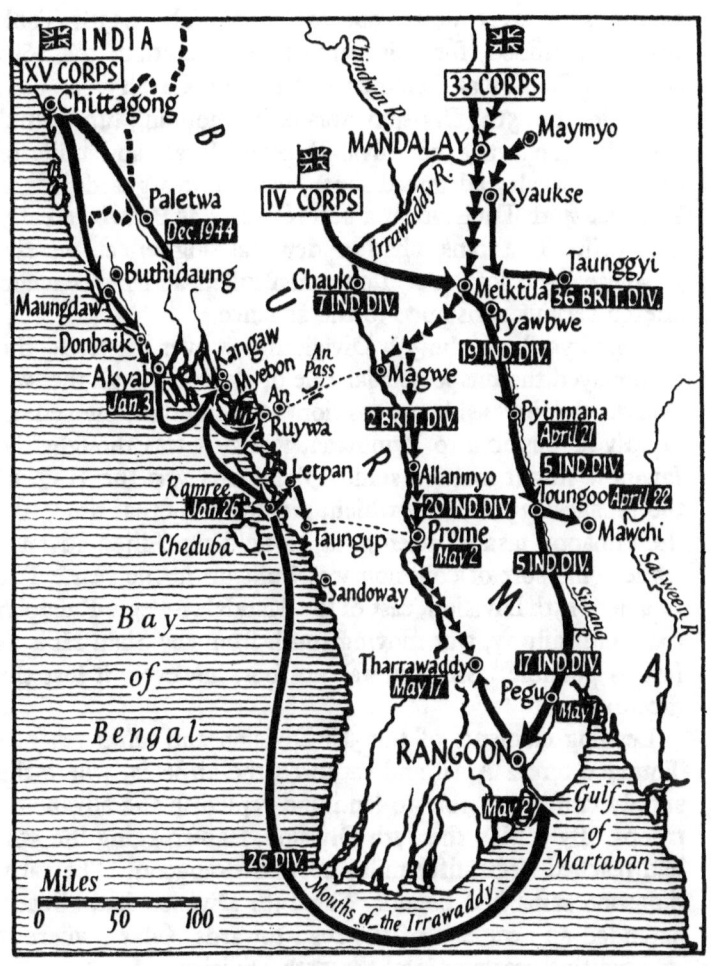

THE RETURN TO BURMA—DECEMBER 1944–MAY 1945

14th Army advance down central Burma, 15 corps landings on Arakan Coast, The Race for Rangoon

garrisons or were flown out to India. The 255th Tank Brigade included, for this part of the operation, the 16th and 11th Cavalry and elements of the 7th Cavalry.

While the 5th Division was still mopping up round Meiktila, the 17th, the Royal Deccan Horse, and units of the 16th Cavalry advanced south, meeting rearguards of the Japanese 49th Division in a severe battle at Pyawbwe early in April. The tanks had a demoralizing effect on the Japanese, who lost over 1,000 men killed and never again offered serious resistance to the advance.

After Pyawbwe, the 5th Division took over the lead—the 19th played the unspectacular role of clearing up all the way —and, clearing aside opposition at Yamethin, moved as rapidly as possible to Pyinmana, where it was thought the Japanese might make a stand. Pyinmana was the H.Q. of the Japanese 33rd Army which, piecemeal by that time, had the unhappy task of attempting to hold the Allied advance while some sort of cohesion was built up in the rear. The Japanese 15th Division, east of the Mandalay-Pegu-Rangoon road and railway, was moving south from the Shan Hills as fast as possible. Since it was on foot, however, it lost the race to Pegu.

Leading elements of the 5th Division and tanks reached Toungoo on 22 April and captured the airfields, where the supply craft were able to land and replenish the advancing troops. By 1 May the 17th Division, leap-frogging the 5th, had reached Pegu, fifty miles north of Rangoon. The early monsoon rains had begun. The 19th Division had already extended an arm east of the road towards Kalaw, where it was fighting rearguards of the 15th Division.

The main part of the 33rd Corps operations was to clear the area of Chauk-Yenanyang-Magwe. The capture of Taungdwingyi on 14 April by the 20th Division caused the Japanese to cross the Irrawaddy from east to west as their retreat line east of the river was barred. The 20th Division moved on towards Prome, which it reached by 2 May, while other groups of the corps cleared the oil-fields and surrounding towns and villages. Nowhere was opposition severe, although the pre-monsoon heat, around 105 degrees in the shade, made life uncomfortable for the troops.

The capture of Prome sealed the main escape route of the Japanese 28th Army in the Arakan via the An and Taungup Passes. Many thousands of Japanese did get away from 15th Corps in the Arakan by forsaking the main tracks and roads and making a gruelling forced march through the hills. They escaped battle until July, when they attempted to break out of the Pegu Yomas across the Pegu road and join their fellows across the Sittang river.

While these operations were in progress, plans for the assault from the sea on Rangoon and later the invasion of Malaya were being put into operation. Ever since he had assumed command of South-East Asia, Mountbatten had been in favour of seaborne expeditions either against Burma or, when he considered it better to by-pass Burma altogether, against Sumatra, the Andamans, Malaya, and Java. That he had been previously unable to carry them out, apart from the Arakan, Akyab, and Ramree landings, was because of shortage of equipment.

In March the decision had to be taken as to whether the 14th Army could capture Rangoon before the monsoon or whether it would be late and become bogged in the central plains of Burma during the wet season. The decision was of importance for future operations. Rangoon was necessary as a port from which to mount the invasion of Malaya in September, the approximate time laid down by the Combined Chiefs of Staff.

Slim considered his chances of reaching Rangoon were good. His appreciation was that the Japanese, having been mauled in the Arakan and defeated in central Burma, would retreat as fast as possible across the Sittang to Moulmein, where they would stand to permit their armies to reorganize and escape to Siam or Malaya. He reckoned that the Japanese, knowing the increased weight of the land forces opposing them and the complete air and sea domination held by the Allies, would be prepared to evacuate Burma. Events proved him correct. Stilwell had always maintained similar views, although his main interest had always been focused on the operations designed to free north Burma and create a land link with China. He had maintained that once this had been achieved the Japanese would have little further use for Burma.

Mountbatten and Leese were not prepared to risk the 14th Army failing to reach Rangoon in time. Moreover, both wanted something more publicly spectacular to complete this phase of the war in South-East Asia. Both wanted to make a dramatic climax to what for so long had been a criticized, partially unknown, and to a great extent defensive war against the Japanese. To sail into Rangoon (or within sight of it) with the British flag flying, a fine fleet at sea, and another in the air, would greatly impress the Burmese with Britain's long-awaited might. It was the traditional British way of doing things in the East, and was something the Americans did not perhaps fully appreciate, although they are masters of the spectacular.

There was never much question of possible sea or air interference with the invasion fleet. Admiral Power's East Indies Fleet had, for some months, been sailing the Indian Ocean with freedom. Japan's biggest naval units in South-East Asia, the cruisers *Haguro* and *Takao*, were in Singapore waters. The main Japanese battle fleets were being engaged by the Americans in the Pacific. In January the East Indies Fleet with the aircraft carriers *Illustrious*, *Indefatigable*, *Indomitable*, and *Victorious* had shelled and destroyed most of the oil refineries at Palembang in Sumatra without hindrance.

In the air the position was similar. The 221st Group was supporting the 14th Army as it advanced down Burma. In one month it flew nearly 8,000 sorties. With 15th Corps in the Arakan operated 224th Group, which claimed to have destroyed nearly 700 enemy vessels in Arakan waters. Liberators and Beaufighters of the Strategic Air Force ranged from Siam to Malaya on their bombing missions. They concentrated on smashing the bridges along the Bangkok–Moulmein railway, built by imperial prisoners of war, and succeeded in keeping down the traffic to 100 tons a day. During the first four months of 1945 the combined air forces lost 177 aircraft, against 184 Japanese destroyed, and the navy lost one submarine (H.M.S. *Porpoise*) and a Liberty ship, with seven small ships or submarines damaged. From this it will be realized that, though the scale of air support and supply was huge, the opposition to combat aircraft was not great and sea operations were on a very small scale.

The Rangoon assault force consisted of Maj.-Gen. H. N. Chambers's 26th Indian Division, which had previously landed on Ramree Island, Commandos, and a Gurkha parachute battalion. It was mounted from Ramree Island, Rear-Admiral Martin being in charge of the landing and Vice-Admiral H. T. C. Walker commanding the fleet covering the landings.

A few days before the operation was set in motion, 14th Army Intelligence was informed that the Japanese were rapidly evacuating Rangoon. A signal was sent to H.Q. Allied Land Forces, but was either mislaid or disregarded. The expedition sailed to Rangoon.

Gurkha parachutists were dropped by the Combat Cargo Task Force, covered by Mustangs of the 2nd Air Commando, on Elephant Point on D minus one (1 May). Their object was to neutralize any Japanese coastal guns in the area. They found fewer than forty Japanese. On the following day troops of the 26th Division landed and were met by two R.A.F. officers who had force-landed near Rangoon. These officers reported that all the Japanese had moved out. As aircraft flew over Rangoon's gaol they saw written in white letters on the roof: 'JAPS GONE EXDIGITATE', the last word being a piece of R.A.F. slang signifying that the message was no ruse, and partly ridiculing such elaborate operations on a virtually empty city.

On 7 May the assault forces linked with the 14th Army north of Rangoon. With the 14th Army was an R.A.S.C. unit which had originally set out from Delhi in April 1942. It had been in all campaigns on the central front and still retained three of its original trucks. Each had done 60,000 miles.

A great deal of the purpose of the assault on Rangoon had gone with the Japanese who, with 500 Allied prisoners, moved towards Pegu for the Moulmein road. They were caught and the prisoners liberated. But Mountbatten showed the flag with a naval review at which he flew an admiral's flag from his craft. Only admirals in active sea command are permitted to do this, and it was a breach of etiquette which did not escape Admiral Power.

The capture of Rangoon necessitated much reorganization. Already divisions from 15th Corps had been released and removed to India to form, with divisions from the 14th Army similarly released, a new force for the assault on Malaya, 15th Corps was to retain its title under General Christison. A new corps, the 34th, was formed under Lieut.-Gen. O. L. Roberts, formerly commander of the 23rd Indian Division.

There came the question of whether the invading force should be the 14th Army or a new one. Some considered that the 14th Army, having so long been associated with Burma, should remain to fight the last battles there and finally garrison the country. Others contended that, since it had provided Britain's principal land contribution to the Japanese war, it should be allowed to win new honours. The latter view was accepted. It was decided to form a 12th Army for Burma in addition to the 14th for Malaya. Slim and Stopford were to be the two commanders.

Among the rank and file of the whole theatre there was never any doubt but that General Slim would continue to command the 14th Army. This indicated no depreciation of General Stopford, but was obviously founded on the troops' affection for Slim and his long association with the 14th Army. Leese decided that Slim should command the 12th Army. Slim declined. As the only general in the theatre (apart from Maj.-Gen. D. T. Cowan, still commanding the 17th Division) who had fought both in the retreat and in the advance; as the only general of his rank for whom the Americans had any regard; and as the best-known, best-loved of all generals, Slim had a strong claim to retain his command. Moreover, the power of removing him from his command did not lie with anyone in South-East Asia. Army commanders cannot be removed except by the Prime Minister or the C.I.G.S., although such a course can be recommended by their seniors within the theatre.

The outcome of this unfortunate incident was that Stopford was given the 12th Army, Lieut.-Gen. Sir Miles Dempsey, commander of Britain's 2nd Army in Europe, the 14th, and Slim became Commander-in-Chief Allied Land Forces in South-East Asia in place of Leese.

The 12th Army made its headquarters in Rangoon, parts of which had been badly damaged by Allied bombing. Its main operational role was the capture of Moulmein. But it still had to account for the Arakan Japanese, who lay in the hills west of the Prome road, and to fight its way into the Shan Hills where the Japanese were escaping via the Loilem and Loikaw tracks across the Salween into Siam. There was a general movement of the Japanese who had fought in the north and centre from Loilem southwards to Loikaw, which commanded the road leading down to a suitable place for crossing the Salween.

The 12th Army, over 300,000 strong, disposed its main forces along the Rangoon–Pegu–Toungoo road. Columns fought eastwards into the hills towards Kalaw and Mawchi. The Japanese rearguards were as determined and stubborn as ever. The main 12th Army concentration was in the bend of the Sittang river, east of Pegu. It was the only land route to Moulmein and the Japanese held the line of the river.

With the monsoon in full spate, conditions of fighting were extremely bad. Units became isolated by water. In one instance a commanding officer awoke one morning to find his hut isolated from his mess by an overnight lake. A raft had to ferry him a matter of a few yards. One brigade in the bend had three battalions out on three different supply lines consisting of a rutted, muddy track, a single-line jeep railway on an embankment, and a river in spate. There was no room for deployment. Units were spread forward like fingers of a hand.

Maps became useless since the water blotted out the natural geography. Men went out on patrol by boat or swam from island to island, floating their personal effects and cigarettes before them in their bush hats. Non-swimmers were helped with bamboo poles. Supplies became short. One unit was reduced to wearing Japanese army boots and smoking captured Japanese cigarettes, while doctors were forced to use Japanese syringes for inoculations. There was little sleep at night, for every man did his tour of guard. It was a pity, perhaps, that after three parts of Burma had been liberated, the troops had to be exposed to such conditions. They were the same troops as had been fighting for two, in some cases for over three, years.

Rangoon had to be prepared as a reception centre and

embarkation point for thousands of troops returning to India and the United Kingdom on leave and repatriation. Its port had to be improved to accommodate the expeditionary force for Malaya. It is to the great credit of the administrative branches of the 12th Army and the Women's Auxiliary Services, including the Wasbees (Women's Auxiliary Service of Burma), that the welfare arrangements in Rangoon expanded at a greater rate than in any other part of India or South-East Asia. Besides the Army Welfare branch, there were nine separate voluntary and charitable welfare organizations working in Rangoon within a few days of the landing. The clubs were reopened for other ranks as well as officers. In cities such as Bombay and Calcutta they had been exclusively for officers.

A report on the welfare arrangements was called for by the Home Government. It was prepared after an unconducted, unannounced tour, and it reported accurately that matters were considered satisfactory by the troops in Rangoon. Outside the city, in the battle areas, welfare was almost non-existent. In most cases it was impossible, for even cigarettes had to be dropped in waterproof packets to outlying troops by low-flying aircraft.

It was during these last battles in Burma, fought with the knowledge that Germany had surrendered and that substantial help would soon be on the way, that the General Election was being contested in Britain. Because of the difficulties of communication and the shortage of reliable news from home, troops viewed the election with considerable apathy and not a little bewilderment. They could not understand why so soon after the European war a political team which had worked successfully should split up. They wondered whether a new government would provide all the help they knew was needed out East.

Viewed from a jungle hut, a muddy patch, or a bomb-shattered town, the stunts, mud-slinging and carpet-bagging of politicians at home had a bewildering effect on the British soldier. Rain, mud, and war were hardly suitable cultures for breeding political fervour. Election slips arrived in fair quantities, but many were too late. In his heart the British soldier was Labour. He had been so for a long time. The war out East, bound up irrevocably in his mind with colonies and imperialism, and added to what he had seen of the British civilians in India, tended to turn him more firmly Socialist.

But, quite naturally, the soldier thought of the election in terms of how it might help him. The veterans were concerned with getting home, the young soldiers with having as short a tour out East as possible. More immediately, they wanted beer, comfort, cinemas, and increased welfare and leave facilities. For the future, they wanted a job, a home, and social security. To them the social security scheme of Sir William Beveridge, though few knew much about it, was the soldier's dream.

Realizing the veterans' feelings on repatriation, the Conservatives made one final bid to capture their vote by reducing repatriation from three years eight months to three years four months on the eve of the election. That it failed shows how deep-rooted had become suspicion of the Tory party. That it robbed Mountbatten of eighty thousand British troops for the proposed assault on Malaya was a much more serious effect. Mountbatten, one believes, was not informed beforehand of the alteration in repatriation time and had already planned the composition of the 14th Army for Malaya. The first news he received came in a B.B.C. news bulletin.

The last major battle in Burma was fought at the end of July. It was the 'Battle of the Breakthrough'. Over ten thousand Japanese from the Arakan and west of the Prome road had collected under General Koba in the Pegu Youmas, a mass of hills between the Irrawaddy and the

Pegu-Toungoo road. General Koba was reputed to be leading his men mounted on a white horse.

With the very considerable remnants of the Japanese Arakan army, General Koba had achieved a remarkable trek through the Arakan Hills, over the Irrawaddy in face of the Allies, and across the Pegu Youmas. Though they had no ammunition, the Japanese manhandled their artillery guns all the way. They had little food or medical supplies and their morale was low. Yet they plodded on, finally lying up in the foothills of the Pegu Youmas just a few miles from the Pegu-Toungoo road along which were lined the Allied divisions. The Japanese intention was to cross the road and the Sittang and reach their compatriots.

Had they attempted to do so in small packets they would probably have succeeded, for there were not enough Allied troops to watch every mile of the road. But they decided to make one grand breakthrough, which began on 20 July. Their plans, discovered later, were elaborately made, but failed to take into consideration either the presence or the quantity of the Allied forces.

The climax to this battle came on 26 July, by which time 3,500 had been killed, over 500 had been taken prisoner, and 1,200 had managed to cross the Sittang. Over seventy per cent of those taken prisoner were convinced Japan had lost the war, though they had had no news from the outside world for some time. Their morale was very low.

Finally, in the 'Battle of the Breakthrough' and in other battles along the 12th Army axis, over 10,000 Japanese were killed during July alone. Over 1,000 were taken prisoner, the largest bag in the history of the Burma war. Even so, it was thought that within Burma there were still 75,000 Japanese.

Japanese casualties in killed then exceeded 100,000 since the beginning of 1944, while their wounded up to 1 May were computed at 143,000. After that date attempts at assessing the wounded ceased. Total British, Indian, Gurkha, and African casualties for the first six months of 1945 were just over 20,000, of whom 5,000 were killed. During that same six months every man in the 14th Army had been given a new pair of boots. It was an army which reckoned that a pair of boots lasted 1,000 miles!

At sea, as on land, these last months in South-East Asia were successful. In May the Japanese 15,000-ton cruiser *Haguro* was challenged and sunk in the Malacca Straits by five British destroyers, H.M.S. *Saumarez, Venus, Verulam, Virago,* and *Vigilant*. In July a British midget submarine, with Lieut. Ian Fraser, R.N.R., and Leading Seaman James Magennis aboard, penetrated the defences of the Johore Straits and sank with fixed charges the Japanese cruiser *Takao*. Both officer and rating were awarded the V.C.

20

SURRENDER AND CONCLUSION

15 August 1945: Japanese Surrender—Operation 'Zipper'—Relief of P.o.W.'s and Internees—Strife throughout South-East Asia—Landing at Singapore and Local Surrender Ceremony—The Campaign in Retrospect—The Atom Bomb

ON 5 August 1945, Japan surrendered after the atom-bombing of Hiroshima and Nagasaki. For some time the Japanese High Command had been weighing the alternatives of surrender or continued war. The surrender scale had been growing heavier and heavier.

Nearly three months previously Germany had surrendered, leaving Japan and her few satellites, lukewarm and ineffective in the case of Siam, to fight the world. Throughout much of her new empire in the countries of South-East Asia there was a growing resentment against the Japanese occupation.

In the Pacific the Americans were preparing for the invasion of Japan itself. It was inevitable, and the Japanese knew it. They had no way of stopping it.

In Manchuria there were one million Japanese troops facing the possibility of a declaration of war by Russia, now released from all but occupational commitments in Europe.

The actual loss of Burma may have been relatively unimportant to Japan except that it exposed the red light of defeat to the other millions of subject people in the adjoining countries.

Japan still had 600,000 men in South-East Asia cut off from their homeland by the American control of the sea. What fleet Britain maintained in S.E.A.C. had little to take its attention off preparations for the landings on Malaya.

The Japanese knew the British would land either in Sumatra or Malaya, or both, within six months. Though they might hold Malaya and Singapore for a little longer, eventually they would be starved into defeat, if not driven into the sea.

Japan's sea and air power was crippled. They had only their army still virtually intact. Of the millions of men they had scattered throughout the East only a few had actually fought. Their armies were hardly scratched, either by the British in Burma or the Americans in the Pacific, for casualties had been at the rate of hundreds and thousands, and not thousands and millions, as in Germany and Russia.

Japan had to balance a decentralized and scattered but unbeaten and formidable army against all the other factors, including the venomous snorts of Winston Churchill, determined that Britain should be in at the kill, and the hard fact of the American battering-ram poised at the castle gate.

At the Potsdam Conference Mountbatten asked Stalin whether he would come in against Japan. Stalin said 'Yes'; and when asked whether he thought Japan would surrender, he replied, 'Yes, very quickly'. Certainly Churchill and Truman thought Japan would give in, for they possessed the secret of the atom bomb. With the dropping of the atom bomb the scale came down on the side of surrender.

In Burma, fighting did not immediately cease, for many outlying Japanese garrisons were either unaware of or unwilling to accept their country's defection. Many were still trying to cross the Sittang, others were fighting rearguard actions in the Shan Hills covering the retreat across the Salween into Siam. Loudspeakers, the radio, and leaflet-dropping were employed by the Allies to stop the Japanese retreating and fighting. Slowly and tentatively the Japanese began to give in.

In Rangoon, India, and Ceylon, 'Operation Zipper' was in the last stages of preparation. 'Zipper' was the landing

SURRENDER AND CONCLUSION

on Malaya destined for 9 September, only a month ahead, by the 14th Army under command of General Dempsey.

The invasion force, seven divisions and a brigade of tanks comprising the 15th and 34th Corps under Generals Christison and Roberts, was to land at Port Swettenham, 200 miles north of Singapore in the Malacca Straits. After the landings the columns were to spread out north, east, and south across the country. Simultaneously a brigade of parachutists, including an Australian parachute battalion, was to be dropped on Singapore. The city was to be captured by 30 September, when the columns from the north would link up with the parachute brigade whose primary task was to protect the P.o.W.s and internees from Japanese anger and possible massacre.

The whole invasion force was 100,000 men strong. Against it Allied Intelligence computed that there was one Japanese division and 52,000 troops in Malaya. The operation had the virtue of surprise since it was considered unlikely that the Japanese would guess the point of landing because of the physical hazards and handicaps in the area of Port Swettenham.

This assumption proved correct, for the Japanese expected a landing on Sumatra and another around Penang, and their preparations for defence lacked co-ordination. Moreover there was no liaison on plans between the 7th Japanese Army H.Q. in Singapore and the 29th in Taiping, Malaya. Both had different sets of ideas and plans.

The Allied numerical estimate of Japan's Malaya garrison was incorrect and when, later, the 5th Indian Division landed on Singapore Island they found 84,000 Japanese. Whether the majority were army troops or not made little difference since already one had learnt that all Japanese fought well. There were also twelve generals on the island.

The Japanese surrender did not stop preparations for 'Zipper'. If anything it complicated them considerably, for the Combined Chiefs of Staff suddenly extended the area of Mountbatten's command to half a million square miles. Whereas previously S.E.A.C. had covered Burma, Siam, Malaya, Sumatra, and Java, it was now increased to include French Indo-China south of the 16th parallel (to the north it became a Chinese sphere) and all the islands in the East Indies as far east as Timor. It took a convoy a month to sail from one end of Mountbatten's command to the other. Its sea-line was over 6,000 miles long. MacArthur was relieved of all his occupational burdens except the Phillippines and Japan.

The main problems facing Mountbatten and his staff were the occupation of the many Japanese-held islands and countries, the disarming of over half a million militant Japanese, and the protection and relief of the Allied prisoners of war and internees, who were designated collectively as A.P.W.I.

MacArthur, who had become Supreme Commander in the East, ordered Mountbatten not to occupy any Japanese-held territory until after the Tokyo surrender. Mountbatten was, however, permitted to send small parties of medicals into the various countries and islands to attend sick P.o.W.s and internees. In the meantime, most Allied prisoners and internees had to languish in their camps for at least another month.

When Mountbatten protested to MacArthur that he wanted to move immediately the American general replied in a signal, 'Keep your pants on'. Mountbatten signalled back, 'I will keep mine on if you take Hirohito's off'.

MacArthur's chief reason for this delay in occupation was the unknown temper of the Japanese armies, which might not accept the surrender until it was ratified and signed by the Emperor and the High Command in Japan. Once the Emperor had openly accepted surrender it was felt all Japanese would do likewise. It was galling, however, both for the troops under Mountbatten—his command had been increased to 1,300,000—and the prisoners and internees to have to wait.

The number of prisoners and internees in the area of S.E.A.C. was not known with any accuracy. The estimated figure was 227,000 but this later proved short by 60,000. Java was the largest reservoir with 144,000 A.P.W.I., including 6,000 British and 2,000 Australians. There were 36,000 in Singapore. The rest were scattered in large numbers in countries like Siam and Sumatra and in small numbers on the lonely islands of the East Indies. Many are still unaccounted for. Groups of armed parachutists were secretly dropped near most of the known P.o.W. camps throughout South-East Asia to come out into the open and protect them in the event of a possible Japanese attempt at massacre. Immediately after the surrender they assisted in the evacuation of the prisoners and in Siam and Indo-China the flying-out of prisoners began directly it was known the Japanese would not resist.

The increased pressure of work on Mountbatten's H.Q. in Kandy, Ceylon, may be judged by the daily number of signals reaching it. During the combatant period of the war 450 signals arrived daily. It increased to over 700 after the surrender.

One of the immediate tasks was the handing over by the Japanese of their armies in Burma. For this purpose the two chiefs of Staff, Lieut.-Gen. Browning and Lieut.-Gen. Numata, met in Rangoon. Numata described himself as 'honest but stupid'.

Mountbatten's opposite number in South-East Asia was sixty-seven-year-old Field-Marshal Count Terauchi, benevolent and much loved by his officers and men. He was sick at the time and could only move with the aid of a stick. Although among the five most senior officers in the Japanese Army, it is doubtful whether he had much idea of what was happening in his command. It appeared later that Numata was not much clearer.

A few days after the surrender General Kimura, Japanese commander in Burma, had signalled Mountbatten. He said, 'I beg to inform your Excellency I have ordered the cease fire in Burma except for scattered bodies. If your Excellency would inform me where they are I will endeavour to get orders to them.'

Thus, when General Browning and his staff met the Japanese in Rangoon, the Allies knew more about the Japanese battle order in Burma than either Kimura or Numata. The Japanese claimed they had 150,000 men still in Burma. The Allies' estimate was nearer 60,000, which proved correct, for it was found that only 33,000 men remained of the ten divisions (the 2nd, 15th, 18th, 31st, 33rd, 49th, 53rd, 54th, 55th, 56th) and two brigades which Japan had put into Burma. There were 29,000 other troops. The total casualties were estimated at 300,000, of which nearly 150,000 had been killed, a very high figure indeed.

After the Tokyo surrender, the 5th Indian Division was diverted from 'Operation Zipper' to take over Singapore; the 20th Indian began landing by air in Saigon, French Indo-China; and the 7th Indian in Bangkok, Siam. Smaller formations were sent to Java, Sumatra, and the islands.

For the British, Singapore was the focal point in the whole war in South-East Asia. It was the obvious choice for the final scene in the drama, the surrender of all Japanese forces within the theatre.

At the end of August the cruiser, H.M.S. *Sussex*, flying the flag of Rear-Admiral Holland, sailed from Trincomalee, Ceylon, to take over Singapore from the Japanese prior to the landing of the 5th Indian Division. Already the Eastern Fleet had put to sea and, demonstrating off Penang and the north tip of Sumatra, had received words of defiance from the Japanese.

General Itagaki, second senior officer to Field-Marshal Terauchi in South-East Asia, announced from his Singapore H.Q. that any ships attempting to land troops or bombarding the mainland would be fired upon by shore batteries. Itagaki was ordered to cease defiance by the Field-Marshal and to hand over Singapore to Admiral Holland.

On 4 September, the *Sussex* lay in Singapore Roads, a channel down the Malacca Straits having been swept by minesweepers. A small Japanese naval craft drew alongside. In it were General Itagaki, Admiral Fukudome, and a British officer who had been sent as a guide. As he reached the top of the gangway Itagaki stood for a moment, looked at the Union Jack flying from the cruiser's mast, and then saluted the naval guard and officers. He was dressed in an open-neck white shirt and the drab khaki-green Japanese military uniform. He wore only one medal, the Star of Japan, but carried his sword.

Admiral Holland's cabin was converted into a conference room with arc lights in the corners pointing downwards on to the central table. The Admiral said: 'I can raise a Rear-Admiral, myself, and a Lieut.-General (Christison), and we'll make this show as impressive as possible.' Itagaki and Fukudome were allotted a small cabin and given tea, Grade 3 salmon, and rice to eat.

The conference lasted for hours. Though he knew he must finally accept the Allied terms of handing over Singapore, Itagaki wriggled. Finally his inscrutability broke down, and with tears running down his face he signed over the city that three and a half years previously had been Japan's greatest conquest in the East and Britain's most ignominious defeat of the war. At eleven o'clock the following day the King's Harbourmaster and a small party landed, followed by troops of the 5th Indian Division.

There were no flags out on the arrival of the British and Indians. Doors were shut and few people were in the streets.

At street crossings white-sleeved Japanese policemen stood on point duty. There were signposts in Japanese and English and arrows directing the 'invaders' to the various parts of the town and the Japanese headquarters. There was not a single incident and both Indian and Japanese soldiers behaved with cold detachment and decorum.

After a few hours doors and windows began to open. Allied flags began to appear—they had been stored or made by the Chinese—and the streets became increasingly full of people. The Chinese, who make up the largest majority of Singapore's population, were the most open in their welcome. The military precision of the 'invasion' and the apparent lack of gaiety on the part of the invading troops at first damped the pent-up feelings of Singapore's inhabitants. The Chinese would have preferred a British division. Not for thirty-six hours did Singapore blossom out into a real show of liberation.

On landing a few British officers made straight for Changi P.o.W. camp and the Syme Road civilian internment camp. At the latter in the women's section—men and women were rigidly segregated—Lady Shenton Thomas, wife of the Governor of Singapore, was found clad only in tattered underclothes, without stockings or shoes, and kneeling down by a little flickering fire brewing grass soup in an old bully beef tin.

For the most part the internees failed to grasp the significance of the moment. They had waited so long, so many years and then weeks after the surrender, for the British to come that they hardly dared believe they had really arrived. As one kilted British officer walked into the camp, the inhabitants stared at him speechless until one man slowly and tentatively moved out of a group and handed him a broken silver-knobbed regimental cane belonging to the Highlanders regiment. It had been found while digging a grave for a dead internee.

Count Terauchi was too sick to attend the final surrender in Singapore on 12 September 1945. Mountbatten had sent his own personal doctor to the Field-Marshal to report on his condition. The doctor said he could limp to the ceremony but Mountbatten decided that such action would be unjust and that he would accept the Field-Marshal's sword in surrender at a later date. Terauchi deputed Itagaki to sign.

The day before the ceremony, held in the Singapore Municipal Buildings, Itagaki signalled his Field-Marshal asking to be spared 'this last indignity'. He received no answer. On 12 September, Itagaki, commander of all Japanese armies in Malaya, Sumatra, and Java, Kimura of Burma, Nakimura of Siam, Numata, and Admiral Fukudome, filed into the Council Chamber, bareheaded and swordless. They sat at a single bare table facing Mountbatten and his chiefs of sea, air, and land, at another table. General Browning carried the surrender papers to Itagaki. He signed, this time with no outward show of emotion.

Outside on the Maidan, Singapore's cricket ground, a flag-mast had been erected. As Mountbatten, his commanders, and the guard saluted, a kilted soldier ran up the Union Jack. It was the same Union Jack that had been used at the surrender of Singapore to the Japanese in 1942. During the years it had lain hidden in Changi Gaol. When the Japanese had asked for it in 1942, Major Wild, its custodian, told them he had burned it from the ramparts of Fort Canning.

The flag waving, the cavalcade of troops and ships and aircraft at Singapore; the docile, almost servile, march into captivity of thousands of Japanese soldiers, undefeated on the field of battle; the journey home of thousands of Allied prisoners and internees: those were the outward and visible signs that the war against Japan had ended.

It is not part of this narrative to describe in detail the

aftermath of the war in South-East Asia, the occupations that had already begun or were continuing and the conditions and unhappy lives of the prisoners and internees. Although the flying out of all American A.P.W.I. by the Americans within forty-eight hours of the landing at Singapore caused some misgivings among the British and Empire personnel, it was soon realized that Britain, India, and Australia had a gigantic task in S.E.A.C. compared with America whose A.P.W.I. numbered only a few hundred.

The whole story of the lost years of those who were captured by the Japanese has been wonderfully told by the Australian, Rohan Rivett, in *Behind Bamboo*. It is a poignant and heartbreaking documentary of capture in Java and final release in Siam; of the building of the notorious Siam–Burma railway through some of the world's worst country from Ban Pong, on the Singapore–Bangkok line, to Thanbyuzayat, on the Moulmein–Ye railroad in Burma. Along those 260 miles of jungle railroad lie not only the graves of thousands of British and Australians, some killed by Allied bombing, but of many thousands of native labourers whose conditions were if anything worse.

To the unimaginative Westerner who has neither seen nor experienced the East, the jungle, starvation, and disease, the tale of misery and horror appears unreal, sometimes exaggerated and often boring. It is a pity, for nothing will ever erase the grim years from the minds of those who were captive. They require the sympathy of those who stayed at home and do not see.

Fortunately not all prisoner camps were as awful as those along the railway. Changi was, for instance, quite reasonable when judged by Japanese standards. One remark made by an Australian on liberation from Changi tells a whole story. He was relating how in the camp concerts men made themselves up as female chorus and cabaret girls with considerable ingenuity and likeness. 'But,' he said, 'there was never a case of homosexuality. We were all too weak to bother about sex.' If that could happen in a good camp what were the depths of weakness and human deterioration in the bad ones?

Throughout South-East Asia new problems arose which added to those of evacuating A.P.W.I., returning the liberated countries to normal, and disarming the Japanese. Siam was still, theoretically, at war with Britain. There were clashes in Bangkok between the Siamese and the Chinese minority. The Annamite National Movement (the Vietnam) in Indo-China and the Indonesian National Movement in Java and Sumatra, both of pre-war origin had, during the war, been encouraged and fostered by the Japanese who were determined to leave a legacy of trouble for the Allies which would take time and blood to clear up.

Throughout the world there was a great deal of emotional sympathy with the Annamite and Indonesian movements which were directed against the return of the ruling powers, France and Holland. Much of this sympathy came from countries which had decided that United Nations policy must be the return to pre-war *status quo* of constitutions prevailing in colonial states. All other constitutions were to be considered illegal.

It was Britain's difficult task to restore Indo-China and Indonesia to French and Dutch rule. It meant the shedding of more Allied blood. Often British, Indian, Gurkha, and Japanese soldiers found themselves fighting side by side against armed and hostile elements (mostly extremist) of these two movements. For months the sores festered and world criticism, which rose to a peak, fell again as other things claimed its transient and capricious attention. Despite his youth Mountbatten proved a most capable, tactful, and diplomatic leader, though some of his generals found the problems of peace more confusing and complexing than those of war.

Just over a year after the Singapore surrender, South-East Asia Command came to an end. Two of the great captains, Mountbatten and Slim, had already returned home to continue their service careers in different spheres. A third, Stilwell, had died in retirement in his native America. His successor, Sultan, died also. Auchinleck remained as Commander-in-Chief India, probably the best-loved and greatest commander India has yet had. Wavell, from his high office as Viceroy, began to hand over the destiny of nearly five hundred million mostly illiterate Indians from the guardianship and safe-keeping of Britain (yes, India was kept safe during the war) to their own politically intellectual few.

The normal evolutionary trend of India and its aspirations of self-government had been speeded up by half a century in a few years of war. India began to emerge as one of the sole winners in World War two, richer in skill, money, industry, manpower, and hope. Few other countries could say the same. The inscription on the Kohima War Memorial to the dead of the 2nd British Division might well have been written for India. It reads: 'For your to-morrow they gave their to-day.'

Hundreds of thousands of British, Indian, and American servicemen returned to their lands and villages and homes hoping to reach that horizon which, even in the darkest and thickest parts of the Burma jungle, had never seemed very far away. Many of them found that bamboo and swamp, mangrove and scrub, may be the physical components of a jungle but that other and different jungles had grown up in their own countries; jungles of dispute, intolerance, and intransigence such as were never found even in the grimmest moments of the Burma war.

For most of these returned warriors, wrestling with their personal problems of peace, the memory of war in the East is becoming, if it has not already become, obscured by that human reaction of forgetting the worst things in life and remembering only the more pleasant. Any thought given to the war will rarely dwell on the reasons why it was fought, what was achieved and who won. It will, perhaps, focus on the more colourful sides of life. It may be the strange fascination of the Burma jungle or the friendships made in foxhole and battle; the few moments of real hospitality in an inhospitable India; the women and drink in a land where one was rare and the other mostly bad; the picturesque but smelly bazaars and the bargaining with extortionate bazaar-wallahs (vendors); the beauty of the Himalayan snows; or the humorous side of the jungle struggle. But few will ever attempt to analyse or bring the Burma war into focus. How does it fit into the general picture of the Second World War?

21

BURMA IN FOCUS

BURMA was Britain's principal shop window in the war against Japan. Though the shop was, from 1943 onwards, fairly well stocked, the display was not always inspiring. The situation compared with America's Park Avenue or Bond Street frontage in the Pacific was Greenwich Village or Bloomsbury. The policy of salesmanship was often in dispute and the administration creaked a bit until some new directors were appointed at the end of 1943. Even then it took time to brighten the window display in its drab, back-street surroundings. The American public hardly knew the whereabouts of this shop; the British public were more concerned with the glittering lights of Regent Street or Oxford Street—the war in Europe.

This is not a cynical analogy of the war in Burma in relation to the war in the rest of the world, for the facts are well known to anyone whose job it was to inform the British or American people about the Burma war. As the outcome of the battle for Burma was hardly likely to bring about the rapid defeat of Japan, American attention was riveted on a theatre, MacArthur's theatre, where it could happen. As France and Germany were so much nearer the British people than India and Burma, the war in Europe held a much higher and more personal place in their estimation. Even when the war against Germany was over and the rejoicings had ended, the British people, apart from those whose relatives were drafted out East, could hardly be expected to accept the war against Japan as their war. They were understandably tired of war and Burma and Japan were a very long way away. And despite the publicists' 'green hells' it was impossible to project on to the average Western imagination what life and war out East were really like.

Obviously Burma had a place in the pattern of World War II, otherwise Britain would not have expended such a considerable amount of effort in building up a very large force out there. Obviously, unless it was important, no country would chose such a battle-ground as the Assam-Burma border which consisted of hundreds of miles of jungled mountains. To Japan that tangled border was important because it brought their armies within sight of India. To Britain it was important that the Japanese should not step into India. To America it was important that the only possible air or land route to China lay from India through Burma. To the Allies, in terms of global strategy, Burma meant only one thing—India. To Britain, China, and America, in terms of the Japanese war as distinct from the global war, Burma meant the last possible land-air link with a flagging China.

India was the key locking the door between war in the East and war in the West; between the possible linking up of the Japanese and German armies. The fall of India would have altered the whole course of the World War in ways which even now can hardly be visualized. It would certainly have split the Allies into two distinct halves—America, Britain, and Russia in Europe and, thousands of miles away, America, Australia and what Britain could get to the Pacific. China would have been completely isolated and, no doubt, eventually submerged. There would have been no link between the Allied war effort in East and West except via America and the Pacific Ocean. Britain would have had no great reservoir of manpower and war materials for her part in the battle against Japan. She would not even have possessed a base from which to start fighting in South-East Asia. Therefore the defence of India and, for a similar set of reasons, the defence of Australia, became the Allies' first tasks. India was traditionally a British responsibility. Because of geography and her great resources, America assumed responsibility for Australia.

To start with there was, perhaps, little difference in the importance and urgency of the two tasks. A lot depended on the actions of the Japanese and they left India in comparative peace until the end of 1943. By that time the Americans and Australians had ensured the safety of Australia and were well ahead with their offensive against Japan itself. During those months Burma became a 'forgotten front', or what the Americans were pleased to call 'a do-nothing front'. The focus of the war against Japan was definitely on the Pacific. One could hardly expect otherwise since the Americans brought an urgency and vitality into the Pacific theatre which was lacking in Burma. Britain seemed preoccupied with keeping order within India, training a larger Indian army, and gearing up that slow-moving country for a war which was already on its doorstep. Apart from Wingate's first expedition, Britain's war against Japan appeared rather half-hearted, limited in scope and action.

Britain's attitude towards the Japanese war was not however, unrealistic. Because Britain could not afford either the men, the materials, or the possible casualties, to fight a vigorous war in Burma, the policy of holding was reasonable providing the defence was dynamic and not passive.

The problem of securing India was much greater than many people, including the Americans, realized. In the early part of the war India was a boiling-pot of political hate and intransigence, a most suitable medium for Japanese fifth-column activity and, in fact, for the reception of the Japanese Army if it chose to invade. It took time and effort for Britain to keep India internally peaceful and the process pinned down a large number of troops who otherwise might have gone to the Middle East or the Indo-Burma border, or who could at least have been training for those roles. Moreover the administration of this vast sub-continent was, due to the impact of war, in a near-chaotic state. Time, patience, and vision were needed in the process of building up before anything like a major offensive could be launched in Burma.

There were, however, two outside stimuli which jerked into life what otherwise was fast becoming a stagnant front. The first was America and the second Japan.

America's interest in any war that might be fought along the Burma border lay, apart from her obvious desire to see Britain whole-heartedly joining in the battle against Japan, in the building of a road from India to China over which supplies might be carried to that harassed country. America's interest in China was very real, inspired by a genuine desire to help, by the responsibility America had assumed for keeping China in the war, and by the effect it might have on her influence in post-war China. America therefore minded little what happened in South-East Asia providing the Japanese were thrown out of that part of Burma through which they wanted to build their Ledo road. For this purpose she was prepared to send troops and air forces as well as engineers and supplies. She was also prepared to train and equip guerrillas inside north Burma, and did so with success.

Britain's apparent procrastination and caution did not please the Americans, whose sense of urgency was upset by the lack of action against the Japanese and the lack of support for a combined offensive by the British-Indian forces on the border in conjunction with Stilwell in the north. It was then the Japanese stepped in and the Burma front flared up, taking, momentarily, the spotlight away from the Pacific.

Burma became the centre of interest not because of any British success but because of a distinct possibility of a

British failure. For if the Japanese lost their gamble in the Arakan early in 1944, they set foot in Assam and stayed there for some months while the battle ebbed and flowed. It was a spotlight of gloom and criticism, of Britain's feeble effort against the Japanese, of her lack of support for the Americans who were doing their utmost to drive this Ledo road through to China.

For six months the Japanese remained on Indian soil before they were hurled back and broken. As the British-Indian forces prepared to chase the invader from Burma, the Americans and Chinese recovered Myitkyina in the north—the first great landmark inside the country. That was the first tangible success within Burma. It was not achieved by the British, though some British forces were there. What had the British done all these years anyway? Why did Britain allow the Japanese to strike at India after two years of war against Japan? Britain's effort, admittedly limited, was torn to shreds in criticism and controversy. The policy, open to argument, of caution, preparation, and conservation, was ridiculed. Britain, America maintained, was making a pretence at fighting the Japanese.

The Ledo road journeyed on into China, and the Burma war returned to what it had been a year previously—a sideshow compared with the main battle, against Japan. With India safe and the road to China open once more, what went on within the area of South-East Asia became a matter of prime concern to the British Commonwealth and, to a lesser degree, the French and Dutch Colonial Empires. Success for British-Indian arms in Malaya, Siam, French Indo-China, and the Dutch East Indies could not seriously affect the greater issue, the battle between America and Japan, for the Americans were hell-bent on Japan itself, the heart of the Empire, the Land of the Gods. There only could the war against Japan be won. The Russians might growl across the Manchurian border at the great Japanese armies; the Chinese might advance yard by yard towards the South China coast and Hong Kong; the Australians might invade Borneo and the British and Indians might retake Singapore, but none of these things, individually or in combination, would defeat Japan.

Let us look at the Burma war from the Japanese viewpoint. What was the importance of the country to Japan? The conquest of Burma carried the Japanese to within striking distance of India; it sealed off China from her Allies; it carried the outer limit of her new Empire a few more hundred miles away from Japan itself, and finally it was calculated to bottle up the British. It was pretty certain to ensure a straight fight between America and Japan, for Britain, with limited resources, would be bound to use everything she could spare to defend India and then, to regain 'face' and prestige throughout the East, be honour bound to attempt the liberation of her own possessions in South-East Asia. If things worked out well there was always the chance of invading India and there is no doubt that originally Japan intended to do so. But once American sea-power revived, as it did in mid-1942, Japan's chances of a successful adventure in India were very small indeed. She did not possess the navy to spare for any large-scale expeditions in South-East Asia, a theatre at the end of Japan's longest sea-line of communication.

The invasion of India, such as it was in 1944, was a brave attempt to extend the frontier of her defence, hinder the Allies in every way possible, and put back their timetable of events by months. It was not an attempt to conquer India, for with only half a million men, a few hundred aircraft, and few ships, Japan hardly had enough to defend and police her conquests in South-East Asia, let alone take on more. Nor by 1944 could Japan have seriously thought help would come from within India. It might have done two years previously, but not in 1944.

If any of those who fought in South-East Asia and, perhaps, spent years there, should consider this attempt at putting the Burma war in focus a belittling of their effort, let them take heart in their achievements which, in their own way, were very considerable.

The battle for Burma, which was eventually won, was the largest single action fought against the Japanese and more of the enemy were killed there than anywhere else. It atoned in part for the calamity of Singapore and opened the way for the liberation of people of the British Commonwealth and for the freeing of the Imperial prisoners of war and internees. It was the start of much greater operations which would have taken months, if not years, to complete and would have cost Britain and India more many lives. After a slow start followed by some exciting moments, it ensured the safety of India.

Burma was not fully liberated when the atom bombs were dropped. Had those bombs not brought about Japan's surrender the British and Indians would have required many months more effort to clear the country completely. But the significance of the atom bomb was that it was the most complete, the most powerful, and the most ruthless sign that America and Britain were directing one hundred per cent effort against Japan and would not stop or even hesitate until Japan itself lay in ashes. It was a sign the Japanese war lords could not misinterpret for against it they had no defence. It had not entered into any of their calculations against any emergency. It meant disaster from which there was no escape.

All other previous signs, and there were several, that Japan would lose the war were seen by the Japanese just as clearly as by the Allies. The success of the Allied landings on the European continent meant that such things could happen in face of the strongest opposition. If it could happen in Europe why not on Japan? The continually increasing power and deadliness of the American Pacific fleets meant that one day Japan would have no warships left and that her empire would become a series of occupied islands or lands without any inter-communication. The defeat of Germany meant that Japan had lost not only her only powerful ally but that the avalanche swamping Europe could be released over the East.

All those factors were obviously accounted for in Japan's long-term strategy. Even way back in 1942 when the Americans won the battle of Midway there were no doubt those high Japanese who foresaw their eventual defeat or, at the best, a stalemate. Those less pessimistic still hoped that Germany would tire the Allies so much that even if Germany were defeated the British and Americans would call it a draw in the East and Japan would be able to hold some of her many conquests. Then, perhaps, she might make another attempt at dominating the East after a few years' rest and rehabilitation while the Allies suffered the normal war reaction. But the atom bomb altered everything. It was sudden, unexpected, melodramatic, shockingly deadly and inescapable.

Had no atom bombs been dropped what might have happened in the Japanese war? How long would it have lasted? Though there may have been some intelligent Japanese who were prepared to parley with the Allies sooner or later, denoting a virtual surrender, there were undoubtedly others who were prepared to see the great Japanese gamble through to the end despite the fact that the Allies did not appear worn out by the European war.

Despite most intense preparations for the defence of Japan it is doubtful whether the Americans would have been halted in their march on to the island providing their weight was sufficient and, if early attempts were not too successful, the American public remained determined to back their troops and defeat Japan. Mountbatten, when asked, as he was frequently, how long Japan would last after Germany's defeat, would reservedly say eighteen months to two years. He and others knew well that the occupation of Japan would not mean the end of the war. Nothing except the surrender order, starvation, or lack of the mechanical power to fight could stop those thousands of Japanese soldiers scattered throughout the East from fighting to the last man. Every one would have to be sought out and killed whether he was the sole defender of some tiny island in the Celebes or one of the garrison defending Saigon. A mathematician might attempt to work out how long it would take to kill off several million Japanese if, during the three and a half years of war against Britain and American, less than 500,000 were actually killed in battle. How much shipping and aircraft would be required to move forces from island to island and land to land? How many men and guns and bullets? A million men were assembled to kill nearly 150,000 in South-East Asia. There is no doubt that many Japanese could have held out for several years. Would, when Britain had recovered Singapore and Malaya, her people have said 'enough'?

For the Japanese the known prospect was one of slow attrition unless such an imponderable as a change of temper by the Allies brought about a stalemate. The Japanese war lords, foreseeing the slicing off of their empire from Japan, knew well that their outlying garrisons would continue to fight. They knew the danger which loomed over Japan and were prepared to leave the Japanese people to their fate. Their last possible move was to Manchuria where there was still an untouched, unscarred Japanese army of a million, backed and bolstered by considerable industrial power and potential. In Manchuria the Japanese could cry defiance unless Russia came in on the side of the Allies as she did and diverted all her available resources to the Eastern front. They might even hold Russia until the Americans landed in the south. Japan possessed an armed potential of eight million men. From experience few of them were unwilling to fight.

Japan's declaration of war in the East was a gamble and, when it was made, there was every chance of success. There were too many factors against the Allies. Would Germany defeat them? Would Germany tire them? Would they be prepared for more war for years and years? Would the conquered Orientals welcome the Japanese more than the British and French and Dutch and remain peaceful and docile under their new rulers or even actively back them? At the best it seemed Japan could achieve victory in the East. At the worst it might be stalemate. As we know now the gamble did not come off because none of the things Japan hoped for came off. And since they did not happen Japan no longer knew how to win.

But, decisive though the atom bomb was in time of war, it left Japan with the largest undefeated army in the world —an army of soldiers prepared to die for their Emperor. It is worth pondering over this fact.

INDEX

ABDA (S.W. Pacific Theatre), 45, 46
'Aberdeen', 156, 164
'Admin. Box', 99, 179
Air Supply, 6, 59, 105 *et seq.*
Allied Air Forces:
  Air Commandos, 1st, 258
  Air Commandos, 2nd, 258, 269
  Airborne Forces Research Centre, 106
  Army Air Transport Command, 246
  A.V.G., 36, 42
  Eastern Air Command, 8, 74, 111
  R.A.F., 36, 42, 51, 89, 129
  R.A.F. Group 221, 64, 111, 269
  R.A.F. Group 224, 98, 208
  R.A.F. Squadron 31, 106
  R.A.F. Wing 170, 111
  R.I.A.F., 36
  Strategic Air Force, 111, 130
  Tactical Air Force, 3rd, 111, 148, 149
  Troop Carrier Squadron, 2nd, 106
  U.S.A.A.F., 10th, 64, 111, 169, 186, 230, 234
  U.S.A.A.F., 14th, 186, 225
Air Forces, Japanese, 28, 29, 251
Akyab Island, 2, 14, 55, 61, 62, 64, 68, 95, 96, 103, 206, 210, 212, 218, 245, 267
Alexander, Gen. Sir Harold, 40, 41
Alexander, Lt.-Col., 79
A.L.F.S.E.A., 193, 269
Ameir, Fleet Carrier, 216
A.P.W.I., 281, 286
Arakan, 25, 54, 56, 61, 95, 102, 103, 107, 124, 179, 226, 231, 235, 245, 267, 269, 275
Armies, Allied:
  Army Group, 11th, 90
  Army, Eastern, 54
  Army, 12th, 271, 272, 273, 275
  Army, 14th, 5, 7, 93, 128, 133, 152, 172, 179, 194, 206, 207, 228, 235 *et seq.*, 245, 249, 251 *et seq.*, 262 *et seq.*

Armies, Allied—*contd.*
  Chinese 5th, 42, 111
  Chinese 6th, 42, 111, 220
  Indian, 55, 58
Armies, Japanese:
  Arakan Task Force, 98, 101
  Arakan, 274
  7th, 279
  15th, 20, 110, 113, 173, 186, 236, 257
  28th, 173, 208, 218, 235, 267
  33rd, 173, 236, 266
Army, Burma Defence, 262
Army, Burma Independence, 261, 262
Army, Burma National, 261, 263
Arnold, General, 124, 152
Aslett, Brig. A. R., 226
Assam, 54, 56, 93, 125, 128, 163, 252
Atrocities, 86
Auchinleck, Gen. Sir Claude, 85, 86, 91, 110, 125, 188

Baldwin, Hanson, 112, 190
Bawli Bazaar, 95, 99
Bhamo, 89, 162, 167, 171, 221, 230, 249
'Blackpool', 161, 167
Bombay, 48, 55
Border Regt., 120, 242, 245
Bose, Subhas Chandra, 262
Bradshaw, Fl.-Lt., 50
Brahmaputra, 56, 178
  Valley, 126
Brigades:
  1st Indian, 54
  6th, 64 *et seq.*
  7th Armoured, 36, 38, 57
  14th, 156, 160, 162, 168
  16th, 161, 163
  22nd East African, 217
  23rd, 136, 142, 153, 174
  28th East African, 236 *et seq.* 258, 264
  29th, 228

Brigades—contd.
  49th Indian, 54
  50th Parachute, 122, 132
  72nd, 228
  77th, 154, 167, 168
  99th, 258
  111th, 155, 160, 161, 167, 168
  161st, 124
Broad, Lt.-Gen. Sir C., 54
'Broadway', 152, 154
Brodie, Brig., 153, 156
Bromhead, Maj. R. S. G., 79
Brown, Col. Rothwell, 164, 220
Browning, Lt.-Gen. F. A. M., 193, 226, 281, 282, 285
'Burma Banshees', 231
Burma Road, 1, 4, 7, 41, 43, 63
Burma–Siam Railway, 86, 269, 286
Bush, Capt. E. R. N., 216

Calcutta, 48, 54, 55, 64, 163, 220, 230
Calvert, Brig. J. M., 79, 80 *et seq.*, 153, 154
Cameronians, 34, 36, 155
Cameron Highlanders, 136, 139, 142, 255
Cavalry
  7th, 266
  11th, 266
  16th, 266
  116th (Gordon Highlanders), 256
  124th Dismounted, 223
  Hussars, 7th, 36
  Lancers, 19th, 214
  Probyn's Horse, 256
  Royal Deccan Horse, 266
Ceylon, 2, 4, 48 *et seq.*, 278
Changi Gaol, 284, 286
'Charing Cross', 120, 121
Chennault, Lt.-Gen. Claire, 35
Chiang Kai-shek, Generalissimo, 14, 40, 41, 78, 191
Chindits, 6, 8, 14, 18, 61, 77 *et seq.*, 90, 112, 128, 129, 151 *et seq.*, 160, 161, 167 *et seq.*, 231
Chindwin, River, 3, 43, 60, 61, 78, 89, 94, 113, 132, 161, 164, 166, 187, 198, 237, 249

Chittagong, 25, 48, 96, 98, 101, 206, 209, 245
'Chocolate Staircase', 94, 196, 197
'Chowringhee', 160, 162
Christison, Lt.-Gen. Sir A. P. F., 95, 102, 270, 279
Civil Administration, 224, 250
Cochran, Col. Phillip, 91, 152 *et seq.*
Colombo, 48, 50
Combat Cargo Task Force, 7, 246, 269
Commandos:
  1st, 212, 213
  2nd, 208
  3rd, 210
  5th, 212
Cook, C.S.M., 139
Cooke, Lt.-Col. S. A., 79
Cornwall, H.M.S., 49, 50
Corps, Allied:
  4th, 54, 58, 64, 78, 90, 93, 94, 111, 122, 126, 129, 134, 147, 166, 167, 236, 237, 256, 264,
  15th, 54, 90, 95, 98, 175, 207, 209, 218, 267, 269, 270, 279
  33rd, 126, 134, 179, 187, 236, 237, 264, 266
  34th, 270, 279
Cowan, Maj.-Gen. D. T., 115, 118, 245, 271

Davidson, Maj.-Gen. Howard C., 169, 193, 230, 232
Dempsey, Lt.-Gen. Sir Miles, 271, 279
Devons, 141, 142
De Witt, Netherland's Navy, 49
Dimapur, 54, 56, 108, 120, 124, 128, 132
Dinjan, 55, 166
Divisions:
  African, 11th East, 174, 195, 198, 201
  African, 81st West, 95, 102, 128, 129, 160, 175, 206 *et seq.*, 215
  African, 82nd West, 208, 209, 214, 215
  British, 2nd, 54, 57, 58, 60, 64, 90, 135 *et seq.*, 146, 149, 174, 198, 235 *et seq.*, 255 *et seq.* 288

Divisions—contd.
  British, 5th, 54, 57
  British, 18th, 36
  British, 36th, 90, 95, 101, 102, 175, 182 et seq., 199, 201, 223, 226, 228 et seq., 256, 259
  British 70th, 54
  Burma, 1st, 34, 36, 38
  Chinese, 14th, 186
  Chinese, 22nd, 52, 112, 164, 186
  Chinese, 30th, 186
  Chinese, 38th, 52, 90, 164, 186
  Chinese, 50th, 186
  Indian, 4th, 55
  Indian, 5th, 55, 90, 95 et seq., 124, 125, 134, 142, 175, 195, 196, 197, 236, 264, 266, 279, 282, 283
  Indian, 7th, 90, 95 et seq., 136, 175, 236 et seq., 255, 259, 264, 282
  Indian, 14th, 54, 64, et seq.,
  Indian, 17th, 18, 22, 34, 36, 37, 40, 55, 64, 111, 113, et seq., 125, 174, 236, 245, 258, 264, 271
  Indian, 19th, 198, 236, et seq., 253, 255, 256, 257, 264, 266,
  Indian, 20th, 90, 95, 111, 113, 119 et seq., 141, 147, 174, 198, 236 et seq., 254, 255, 257, 264, 266
  Indian, 23rd, 58 64, 111, 117, 121, 125, 142, 174, 270
  Indian, 25th, 95, 175, 208, 209, 210, 212, 214, 216, 217
  Indian, 26th, 54, 67, 90, 95, 101, 175, 208, 209, 215, 216, 249, 276
Divisions, Japanese:
  2nd, 173, 236, 282
  15th, 120, 133, 174, 187, 228, 236, 266, 282
  18th, 18, 172, 173, 179, 220, 226, 228, 236, 259, 282
  31st, 122, 124, 132, 174, 187, 236, 282
  33rd, 18, 22, 125, 142, 146, 187, 228, 236, 259, 282
  49th, 236, 266, 282
  53rd, 172, 186, 282

Divisions, Japanese—contd.
  54th, 98, 208, 282
  55th, 18, 98, 208, 218 282
  56th, 186, 220, 226, 236, 282
D.L.I., 138
Doi Force, 98, 100
Dorsets, 136, 139, 241
Dorsetshire, H.M.S., 49, 50
Dunlop, Maj. G., 79

East Lancs Regt., 200
Eldridge, Lt.-Col. Fred, 185
Emeny, Stuart, 156
Emmett, Maj. A., 79
Evans, Brig.-Gen. F. W., 193, 246
Eyre, Lt.-Col. Brinley, 212

Fergusson, Brig. B. E., 79 et seq., 112, 152, 153, 155
Festing, Maj.-Gen. F. W., 182 et seq., 229
Flamingo, Sloop, 216
Ford, Col. O'Neill, 53
Fort Dufferin, 257
Fort Hertz, 5, 53, 60, 70
Fort White, 94, 113, 114
Fraser, Admiral Sir Bruce, 190
Fraser, Lt. Ian, R.N.R., 276
Fukudome, Admiral, 285

Galahad Force, 90, 94
Gardner, F.O. Charles, 50
Giffard, Gen. Sir George, 90 et seq., 103, 122, 181, 192
Gloucesters 34
Goppe Pass, 95, 98, 99, 101
Gracey, Maj.-Gen. Douglas, 119, 242
Graybourn, Sir Vandelaur, 87
Green Howards, 216
Grover, Maj.-Gen. J. M. L., 58, 138, 147, 150

Haguro, Japanese cruiser, 268, 276
Hanaya, Lt.-Gen., 98, 101
Harman, L/Cpl. John, 135
Hawksley, Brig., 203
Hermes, H.M. Aircraft Carrier, 50, 51
Hill, Capt. Duncan, R.N., 217
Hill 1070, 102

INDEX

Hirohito, Emperor, 280
Holland, Rear-Admiral, 282, 283
Homalin, 161
Homma, Col., 19
Houston, U.S.S., 49
Hsaing, Lt.-Gen. Liano Yo, 199
Huwkawng Valley, 44, 90, 94, 112, 128, 165, 166, 220, 223, 231

Illustrious, H.M. Aircraft Carrier, 175, 268
Imphal, 52, 58, 78, 94, 107 *et seq.*, 133, 146 *et seq.*, 188, 205, 231, 245
    Front, 179
    Plain, 18, 22, 54, 108, 121
Indefatigable, H.M. Aircraft Carrier, 268
India Command, 55, 58, 75, 126
Indomitable, H.M. Aircraft Carrier, 268
Irrawaddy, River, 2, 3, 80, 81, 195, 223, 228, 237, 238, 241, 242, 249, 252 *et seq.*, 266
Irwin, Lt.-Gen. N. M. S., 54, 58, 61, 65
Itagaki, Gen., 283, 285

Java, Dutch destroyer, 49
Java Sea Battle, 29, 32, 48, 49
'Jungle Happiness', 11

Kabaw Valley, 28, 94, 95, 113, 119, 121, 174, 195, 249
Kaladan Valley, 96, 102, 103, 128, 149, 206, 212
Kalapanzin, River, 95, 100
    Valley, 99, 101, 103, 206, 209, 212
Kalewa, 43, 62, 90, 95, 237
Kamaing, 89, 151, 163, 166, 167, 168
Karachi, 56
Kawkereik, Pass, 37
Kennedy Peak, 94, 113
Kimura, Gen., 24, 177, 282, 285
King's (Liverpool), 77, 154, 155
King's Own, 155
Kinoshita, Gen., 28
Kistna, sloop, 216
Knight, Lt. Jack, 223

Koba, Gen., 274, 275
Kohima, 17, 54, 108, 122, 124 *et seq.*, 132, 135 *et seq.*, 146, 258
K.O.S.B.s, 96, 102, 244
K.O.Y.L.I., 34
Kubo Force, 98, 99
Kunming, 220, 225
Kyaukmyeyaung, 12, 240

Lancashire Fusiliers, 138, 154
Lashio, 41, 223, 225, 226, 232
Ledo, 52, 56, 60, 164, 220, 232, 233, 249
    Road, 61, 63, 68 *et seq.*, 82, 89, 112, 155, 174, 194, 220, 225, 293, 294
Leese, Lt.-Gen. Sir Oliver, 193, 268, 271
Leicesters, 155, 162
Lentaigne, Maj.-Gen. N. D., 153, 155, 160, 164
Lincolns, 216
Lindsell, Gen. Sir Walter, 91
Luang Pradit ('Ruth'), 32, 33
Lushington, Maj.-Gen. Wildman, R.M., 165

MacArthur, Gen., 177, 280
Madras, 51, 56
Magennis, Leading-Seaman James, 276
Malaya, 2, 252, 267, 273, 274, 278
Manchesters, 20, 255
Mandalay, 3, 23, 43, 194, 205, 237, 252 *et seq.*
Manipur, 20, 25, 94, 108, 161, *et seq.*, 174
    Invasion of, 100
    Maharajah of, 108
'March on Delhi', 25, 101, 176
Mars Task Force, 222, 223, 226
Martin, Rear-Admiral B. C. S., 210, 269
Masters, Lt.-Col. J. R., 160 *et seq.*
Maungdaw, 96, 99, 128
Mayu Peninsula, 64, 209, 212
    Valley, 95, 99, 102
Meiktila, 18, 205, 228, 236, 237, 245, 253, 256, 258, 259, 264, 266
Merrill, Brig.-Gen. Frank, 113, 164

Merrill's Marauders, 22, 94, 113, 164 et seq., 222
Messervy, Lt.-Gen. Frank, 99, 193, 236
Milestone, 22 114
Milestone 75, 188
Milestone 82, 116
Milestone 109, 116, 118, 205
Mogaung, 89, 94, 151, 161, 166 et seq., 220
'Morris Force', 162, 169
Morrison, Ian, 250, 251
Moulmein, 37, 60, 267, 271, 272
Mountbatten, Admiral Lord Louis, 5, 7, 15, 25, 30, 33, 84 et seq, 89, 91 et seq., 99, 103, 111, 120, 125, et seq., 158, 160, 165, 177, et seq., 190, 192, 220, 225, 234, 263, 267, 268, 270, 274, 278, 280 et seq., 298
Munster, Lord, 150, 151
Mutagachi, Lt.-Gen., 26, 110, 113, 126, 188
Myitson, 227, 228, 229, 244
Myitkyina, 18, 22, 53, 70, 89, 93, 94, 128, 144, 151, 162, 164 et seq., 192, 220, 224, 230, 231, 232, 249

Nakimura, Gen., 285
Napier, H.M.S., 216
New York Times, 112, 190
Ngakyedauk Pass, 95, 96, 98, 99, 100, 101
Northamptons, 242
Northern Combat Area Command, 222, 228, 232, 235, 251
Numata, Lt.-Gen., 281, 282, 285

O'Callaghan, Father, 137
Old, Brig.-Gen. William, 73, 91, 100, 193
Operation 'Axiom', 181
Operation 'Capital', 93, 94
Operation 'Thursday', 112, 151
Operation 'Zipper', 278, 279, 282
Owen, 2nd Lieut. Frank, 94

Pakokku, 238, 244, 256
Palembang, oil refineries, 268

Pathfinder, H.M.S., 216
Pearl Harbour, 31, 32
Pegu, 252, 264, 266, 270
Pegu Yomas, 26, 274, 275, 276
Peirse, Air Chief Marshal Sir Richard, 91, 193
Phoebe, Cruiser, 216
'Piccadilly', 152, 153
Pierce, Lt.-Gen. Sir Noel Beresford, 54, 58
Pinwe, 24, 164, 200
Potsdam Conference, 278
Power, Admiral Sir Arthur John, 190, 270
Pownall, Lt.-Gen. Sir Henry, 90, 171, 194
Prince of Wales, H.M.S., 33, 49
Prome, 264, 267, 271
'Propaganda', Exercise, 183

Quadrant Conference, 93
Quebec Conference, 151, 178, 189
Queen Elizabeth, H.M.S., 175, 216
Queen's Regiment, 138, 155

Ramree Island, 212, 215, 216, 249, 267, 269
Rangoon, 3, 7, 32, 33, 34, 37, 38, 89, 194, 205, 225, 231, 237, 245, 252, 253, 259, 263 et seq., 278, 281
Rapid, H.M.S. destroyer, 216
Razabil, 96, 102
Recce Regt., 139, 155
Rees, Maj.-Gen. T. W., 198, 257
Renown, H.M.S., 49, 175
Repulse, H.M.S., 33, 49
Resolution, H.M.S., 49
Revenge, H.M.S., 49
Richardson, Dave, 221
Richelieu, French battleship, 175
Roberts, Lt.-Gen. O. L., 121, 270, 279
Roosevelt, President, 41, 191
Rose, Lt.-Gen. Angus, 59
Royal Berkshire Regt., 137, 240, 257
Royal Deccan Horse Regt., 256
Royal Inniskilling Fusiliers, 34
Royal Norfolk Regt., 138, 241

INDEX 305

Royal Scots Fusiliers, 200, 201
Royal Scots Regt., 138, 139, 241
Royal Sussex Regt., 184, 226
Royal Tank Regt., 36
Royal Welch Fusiliers, 66, 138, 200, 241, 255
Royal West Kent Regt., 135, 197

Sakurai, Maj.-Gen., 98
Salween, River, 2, 3, 37, 252, 271, 272
San, Maj.-Gen. Aung, 261, 262, 263
Saratoga, U.S.S., 175
Saumarez, H.M.S., 276
Scoones, Lt.-Gen. Sir G. A. P., 58, 111, 112, 124, 126, 193
Scott, Maj.-Gen. Bruce, 34
Scott, Lt.-Col. Robert, 139
S.E.A.C., 84 *et seq.*, 89, 110, 177, 178, 181, 280, 286
SEAC, Newspaper, 259, 260
Sextant Conference, 93
Shan Hills, 228, 253, 259, 266, 271, 278
Shenam Saddle, 121, 140
Shinbwiyang, 5, 44, 94
Shwebo, 240, 241, 250
Shwebo Plain, 76, 237, 249
Shweli, River, 229, 244
Siam, 2, 4, 31, 32, 271, 277
Singapore, 2, 7, 18, 31, 32, 252, 278, 279, 281, 282, 283, 285
Singh, Lt.-Col. Balwant, 143
Sittang Battle, 38, 39
Sittang River, 2, 18, 252, 253, 259, 267, 272, 275, 278
Slim, General Sir William, 6, 22, 41, 92, 93, 95, 101, 103, 113, 122, 126, 134, 159, 160, 166, 181, 193, 235, 236, 237, 262, 264, 267, 268, 271
Smyth, Maj.-Gen. J. G., 34, 37, 38, 39
Snelling, Maj.-Gen. Alfred, 100
Somerville, Adm. Sir James, 49, 50, 90, 91, 190
South Lancashire Regt., 244
South Staffordshire Regt., 154
Stanley Camp, 87

Stilwell, General Joseph, 14, 41, 43, 47, 52, 60, 61, 63, 70, 72, 78, 90, 91, 92, 93, 94, 109, 112, 122, 128, 133, 151, 164 *et seq.*, 173, 177, 179, 181, 183, 189, 190, 191, 192, 199, 220, 231, 232, 233, 234, 268, 288, 293
Stilwell, Maj. Joe, Jnr., 221
Stockwell, Maj.-Gen. Hugh, 214
Stopford, Lt.-Gen. Sir Montague, 126, 134, 147, 193, 271
Stratermeyer, Lt.-Gen. George E., 74, 91, 193
Sultan, Lt.-Gen. Dan I., 192, 220, 225, 231, 288
Sumatra, 176, 267, 278, 279
Sussex, H.M.S., 282, 283
Syme Road Camp, 284
Symes, Maj.-Gen. G. W., 245

Takao, Japanese cruiser, 268, 276
Tamu, 44, 52, 94, 108, 120, 187
Tanabashi, Col., 66, 98, 100, 101, 102
Tank Brigade, 254th, 125, 142, 236, 264
Tank Brigade, 255th, 236, 244, 258, 264, 266
Tate, Colonel, 73
Taung Bazaar, 99, 100 103
Tenasserim, 3, 31, 33, 37
Terauchi, Field-Marshal Count, 25, 281, 283, 285
Thakins, 261
Tiddim, 54, 94, 95, 107, 119
Tiddim Road, 196
Tigyiang, 226, 228
Tojo, General, 51
Tottenham, Maj.-Gen. F. J. Loftus, 286
Trident Conference, 72
Trincomalee, 48, 50, 282
Troop Carrying Command, 96, 100

Valiant, H.M.S., 175, 176
Venus, H.M.S., 276
Verulam, H.M.S., 276
Victoria Point, 2, 33, 37
Victorious, H.M.S., 268

Vietnam Movement, 287
Vigilant, H.M.S., 276
Virago, H.M.S., 276

Walker, Vice-Admiral H. T. C., 269
Wallawbum, 165, 166
Walsh, Maj.-Gen. G. P., 193
Warspite, H.M.S., 49
Wasbees, 273
Wavell, Field-Marshall Sir Archibald, 39, 40, 45, 46, 49, 55, 57, 60, 62, 2, 70, 776, 78, 86, 158, 288
Wedermeyer, Maj.-Gen. Albert C., 90, 192, 225
Wei-Li-Huang, Gen., 174
Welch Regt., 238, 240, 253
West African Regt., 149
West Yorks Regt., 34, 116, 197, 245
Wheeler, Lt.-Col. L. G., 79
Wheeler, Lt.-Gen. Raymond C., 70, 91

'White City' airstrip, 160, 162, 167
Wilcox, Lt.-Gen. H. B. D., 58
Wild, Major, 285
Wilson, Major David, 59
Wilson, Gen. Maitland, 127, 130
Wingate, Maj.-Gen. Orde Charles 6, 61, 75 *et seq.*, 90, 92, 93, 110, 151 *et seq.*, 156, 157 *et seq.*, 164, 166, 171, 172, 178, 179, 249
Wingate's expedition, 223
Willey, Brig.-Gen. J. P., 223
Wills, Stanley, 156
'Windsor Castle', 228
Women's Auxiliary Services, 273
Worcester Regt., 137, 240, 241, 255

Yamagata, Field-Marshal, 23
Yamashita, Gen., 19
Yamethin, 266
Yenangyaung Oilfields, 42, 237, 264
'Y' Force, 113, 174, 225
Yunnan, 62, 63, 93

Printed by Jarrold & Sons, Ltd., The Empire Press, Norwich

For Product Safety Concerns and Information please contact our EU
representative GPSR@taylorandfrancis.com
Taylor & Francis Verlag GmbH, Kaufingerstraße 24, 80331 München, Germany

www.ingramcontent.com/pod-product-compliance
Lightning Source LLC
Chambersburg PA
CBHW071155300426
44113CB00009B/1213